S0-BYA-245

The Attractiveness of God

The Attractiveness of God

ESSAYS IN CHRISTIAN DOCTRINE

R. P. C. Hanson

JOHN KNOX PRESS
Richmond, Virginia

British edition published by
SPCK, London

American edition published by
John Knox Press, Richmond, Virginia

Library of Congress Cataloging in Publication Data

Hanson, Richard Patrick Crosland.
The attractiveness of God.
Includes bibliographical references. 1. Theology, Doctrinal. I. Title.
BT75.2.H37 1973 231 73-5345
ISBN 0-8042-0473-X

Printed in Great Britain

Contents

Acknowledgements

I have to thank a number of people for help with compiling the indexes of this book, my daughters Catherine and Monica, Miss Janet May, and especially Mrs May.

The following material is reproduced from journals by kind permission of their editors and publishers, page references to this book being given in parentheses:

Anglican Theological Review, Vol. XLIII, no. 2 (April 1961), pp. 145–52: The Inspiration of Holy Scripture (pp. 10–18).

Church Quarterly, Vol. 3, no. 1 (July 1970), pp. 7–17: Development and Reform in Christan doctrine (pp. 29–40); Vol. 2, no. 4 (April 1969): The Divinity of the Holy Spirit (pp. 116–27); Vol. 3, no. 4 (April 1971): The Position of the Holy Spirit in the Trinity (pp. 127–37).

Eastern Churches Review, Vol. II, no. 2 (1968), pp 127–37: The Age of the Fathers: its Significance and Limits (pp. 58–70).

New Divinity, Vol. 1, no. 3 (Summer 1971), pp. 1–7: The Last Things (pp. 190–6).

The author's thanks are also due to the Council of the University of Durham for permission to reproduce the text of his Inaugural Lecture as Lightfoot Professor of Divinity (March 1936): *The Bible as a Norm of Faith* (pp. 18–29).

R.P.C.H.

1 *The Attractiveness of God*

In Evelyn Waugh's famous novel, *Decline and Fall,* one of the characters is a Church of England clergyman who has abandoned the pastoral ministry and taken to schoolmastering because he cannot answer the question, Why did God want to make the world at all? He is not concerned about reconciling the book of Genesis with the theory of evolution nor the concept of God as creator with contemporary physics, but with the primal and to him unanswerable question, Why should God have wanted to create? Had this puzzled and peculiarly ineffective priest read the essays which follow in this book he might, in his dim and querulous way, have remarked that, though they discuss a wide variety of questions about Christian doctrine they never attempt to answer the basic and crucial question, Why should anyone want to believe in God at all? This introductory essay, written last but placed first, will attempt to answer this question.

First, it must be made clear what precisely is being attempted here. This is not an attempt to answer the theological question, Does God exist? nor the philosophical question, Can anyone know God? The question with which this essay is dealing is primarily a psychological question, Why should anyone desire to believe in God? Indeed, it is a more personal question even than that suggested by the form which this last question has taken. This essay will try to answer the question, Why should I, and why do I, the writer of this essay, want to believe in God? Perhaps in the course of this primarily psychological and personal discourse some theological and even conceivably philosophical issues will arise. But the reader can see that the question is primarily psychological.

If I am to put the answer to this question in a single sentence, that sentence would have to run in some such way as this: I want to believe in God and I do believe in God because I cannot resist the attraction which such belief holds for me. Over a long period, about thirty-five years, I have found that belief in God as he is understood in the Christian religion attracts me so deeply that I cannot stop believing unless I turn against the dearest inclination of my heart. The matter could be put in a very simple way, perhaps in too simple a way: I believe in God because I want to believe in God.

It will be at once obvious that I am here opening myself to the accusation that my belief in God is a mere wish-fulfilment, that I am using this belief as a mere pretext for satisfying my need for protection against cosmic loneliness or for allaying inherited guilt-feelings, or even for justifying unreasonable prejudices. The Afrikaans-speaking South African wants to believe that coloured people are inferior to whites; such a belief suits his interests. So he convinces himself that this is so. The Protestant in Belfast really wants to believe that all Roman Catholics are liars and instigators of violence. It soothes his sense of outrage and relieves him of the awkward necessity of making any irenic gestures towards Catholics, so he believes. At first sight, the statement that I believe because I want to believe seems dangerously vulnerable.

But this statement needs to be explained and qualified and it will then be found that there is more to be said for it. First, the fact that a person wants to believe something is no proof of the truth of that belief, but it is no disproof either. I want to believe that my wife loves me. This is no disproof of the proposition which I want to believe. Further, there is nothing discreditable in wanting to believe such a comfortable doctrine, nor in deriving pleasure in believing it. Because a belief gives somebody pleasure and comfort it does not follow that the belief must be untrue. Perhaps the development of psychology along with some other contemporary movements of thought has made people deeply suspicious of any beliefs which are hopeful or comforting or likely to make the believer happy. One gains the impression, for instance, from Iris Murdoch's novel *Bruno's Dream* that the authoress is obsessed with the idea of God but utterly refuses to believe in him because such a belief would be too good to be true. Popular intellectual taste today is dominated by the sceptic and the cynic. Perhaps the occurrence of two world wars within one generation have made such an attitude inevitable. But it is not necessarily logical. If God does exist, and if he is such a God as the Christian faith represents him to be, then it is not the least surprising that people should find belief in God attractive and should derive pleasure from it.

Too many people today in considering the subject of God submit to what might be called psychological intimidation. They give in easily when other people explain to them why they believe what they believe. Psychological intimidation has become a stock weapon in controversy. In the eighteenth century when you wished to annoy your opponent you accused him, not only of being weak in argument, but also of sexual immorality, and, if you could, of treason to the government. In the nineteenth century you accused him of being an 'infidel', and hinted darkly that because of this his character was not what it ought to be. In the twentieth century instead of using these methods you explain to your opponent the absurd or discreditable or deeply self-interested unavowed motives which cause him to use his weak arguments. It is a rather more sophisticated weapon, but just as illogical as the others. And, just as the derided opponent in former centuries was able to return abuse for abuse and innuendo for innuendo, so this contemporary psychological argument is double-edged. If I am accused of wanting to believe in God for motives which are not genuine, it is open to me to retort by questioning the motives of those who do not want to believe in God, or who want not to believe in God. They are unwilling to embarrass themselves with serious thought, or they find it disturbing to face the moral issues involved in belief, or they are afraid that they may have to abandon their immoral practices if they profess belief, or they are simply anxious to appear to be in the swim intellectually and unwilling to give the impression of being dated. None of these arguments is logical. They rank rather as refined forms of abuse than as serious argument. But they suffice to show that the weapon of psychological intimidation is a dangerous and in the long run a useless one. If I say that I believe in God because I want to believe, this is no necessary proof that my wish is simply father to my thought. We have to ask why I want to believe.

We should examine next what is meant by wanting to believe. A desire to believe can, of course, arise from circumstances quite unconnected with the truth of the thing believed in, and it is sometimes difficult to distinguish spurious belief from genuine belief. The inhabitants of Berlin at the very end of World War II believed firmly that the German armies were winning victories and successfully driving back the Americans and British on one side and the Russians on the other, and it was only when shells began dropping in the very middle of the city and the sound of artillery came nearer that they realized that their belief was completely unfounded. This was an example of belief based upon immediate self-interest yielding reluctantly to hard facts. The Duke of Wellington during the battle of Waterloo believed that Prussian reinforcements under Blücher would reach him in time to win the battle. His belief proved well founded. In either case, it is worth noting, those who held the belief very much wanted to believe. There are different levels of desire and different sorts of motive in belief. We may distinguish impulse from inclination, self-interest from self-satisfaction, an immediate appetite from a lasting state of mind. When I say that I want to believe in God I am referring to a lasting state of mind. This is an inclination of the heart, involving all that I can discover or take to be best in me, not reached without long heart-searching, careful consideration of my motives and a constant review of my reasons for believing. When anyone finds that his whole personality at its deepest level is possessed by a strong and lasting inclination towards one direction and that this inclination persists in spite of being constantly reviewed by the intellect, then it is absurd to speak of this inclination in terms of wish-fulfilment or escape mechanism. When a person's heart is engaged, then this inclination must be taken seriously.

Hitherto I have spoken in almost entirely subjective terms, concerning what it feels like to want to believe; I have attempted to convey the quality and depth of my wish. But I have said nothing about one important aspect of this business of belief. Belief in God holds an attraction for the believer; it presents itself, not as a pleasant whim or charming fancy, but as a proposition independent of him, attracting him from outside himself. It appears to offer him the best sort of satisfaction, satisfaction not only of his intellectual and moral needs but of his intellectual and moral demands. It does not merely fill a psychological hiatus; it satisfies something that he feels ought to be satisfied. It may indeed be said to exercise a moral attraction, even a moral constraint, upon him. Once again, a state of mind such as this cannot be classed with a mere piece of psychological self-deception or subterfuge, like someone indulging in hysteria in order to avoid making some difficult decision. On the contrary, the believer regards himself precisely as making a difficult decision and refusing to run away from reality. In short, for believers, belief in God exercises an attraction upon them which they finally conclude they ought not to resist.

But to talk in these terms of belief exercising attraction is a curious way of putting it, and I am only describing it in this way in order to answer in its own terms the question which I raised, Why should anyone *want* to believe in God? It would be much more sensible to say at this point that the believer becomes convinced that he has found God and that he has simultaneously found truth. The word 'truth' is used here in the sense of what one might call moral truth, that is to say a true clue to the significance of the universe, of man's purpose in it, a true understanding of values, a true understanding of oneself. This truth does not impress those who have found it as purely subjective, even though it is tested by criteria some of which are subjective, e.g. that it satisfies the psychological needs of the individual. But this truth is thought by the believer to be real, to be objectively true whether he were to believe in it or not. If the believer thought that he was deluding himself with fantasy, even though he enjoyed the sweet delusion, or that he was just opting for a set of values that he liked and that he chose to impose upon a morally neutral world, he would not be a believer in the sense intended here. The believer believes that he has found truth, not just abstract truth but God himself, the source of truth. He thinks that this truth is true because it satisfies the deepest needs of his personality and demands of his conscience. He does not know any better.

At this point we must face the most serious objection to conceiving of belief in God as truth, indeed to thinking of truth in this way at all. It can meet no test of universal verifiability or acceptability. It may bring forward arguments in favour of believing in the God of the Christians, but somebody else could produce the same sort of arguments as have been employed here to support a quite different belief, which he could claim as truth, say a devout Muslim or indeed a convinced atheist. While it would not be fair to say that my argument amounts simply to a statement that I believe because I choose to believe, at least the process whereby conviction is formed in my mind is apparently just the same as the process whereby utterly different convictions, indeed convictions contrary to mine, are formed in other people's minds. What sort of truth is this, which seems to differ radically according to who believes in it? Can it be called truth at all?

I have tried to show that it cannot justly be called idle fancy nor wayward idiosyncrasy nor self-interest bigotry. Part of the process of conviction consists of a careful and constant review of my belief according to the highest standards of critical examination that I know. This criterion will eliminate some potential rival candidates for the title of truth, such as the nonsense (however deeply held) which the Witnesses of Jehovah profess, and the convictions which the 'Free Presbyterians' in Northern Ireland parade so loudly. Neither of these groups is able or willing to face the test of critical examination of their beliefs by competent scholars.

Again, I could claim that my belief can pass one kind of rough-and-ready experimental test. It works as a creed to live by. It is satisfying as a means of meeting the vicissitudes and trials which life brings upon us, even when tested over a considerable span of years. It is part and parcel of a life of worship and prayer which enriches belief and is itself enriched by belief. The late D. R. Davies tells us in his autobiography that at one point in his career as a Congregationalist minister he came to the conclusion that he had no gospel to preach. The message of social betterment based on a thin Christian idealism which he had been preaching up till then appeared to him at that point to be inadequate. It was not a creed to live by. By way of contrast, I can recall a beautiful and moving article in *The Times* written by the mother of a Mongol child. She describes how she had come to accept and love her daughter, and related how prayer in the local church of her Devonshire parish had helped her to reach this state of mind. She began to realize that we are all part of God's family and that she had been given one of the weak ones of the family to love and care for. Here was a creed that passed the practical test. Perhaps I can therefore enhance the claim of truth for my belief in God by declaring that it has passed the practical test.

Further, because people with different beliefs hold them with the same sense of conviction as I do it does not necessarily follow that one or other of us must have found the truth and the others be deluded by sheer falsehood. What I have called 'moral truth' is a many-sided and rich reality which can be apprehended in part by many different people whose apprehensions of it appear to differ. To put the same statement in theistic terms, God is both resourceful and inexhaustible. Men can understand aspects of God without exhausting the whole of him, and there is no reason why we should deny to others the understanding of a part of the truth of which we too understand a part. This admission cannot be carried as far as to say that while we realize that two and two make four others have a grasp of the truth that two and two make five. But we can agree to echo the fine words of the pagan noble in Rome at the end of the fourth century when, in the face of the shrill bigotry of Church and Emperor, he said that access to so great a mystery is not available by one way only.

When all is said and done, however, we must cheerfully concede that what has here been called moral truth cannot be subjected to the same kind of tests as scientific or mathematical truth. This applies to all truth which affects us existentially, truth about our purpose in existence, the important decisions that we have to make, the values which we acknowledge, the way in which we behave, the assumptions by which we live. The late Hesketh Pearson, an agnostic, put this matter in an oversimplified but useful way when he remarked in his autobiography that science can tell us nothing worth knowing. Men cannot live without making decisions in this sphere of moral truth. It is not merely that they would become sub-human if they succeeded in living without regard to truth of this kind; it is that they cannot live apart from it any more than they can live apart from air. The reason why this truth cannot be assessed by scientific or mathematical standards is that it involves commitment, it entails not merely intellectual assent but moral decision. If truth of this sort were merely a matter of intellectual assent, of seeing how the sum comes out or how the theory fits, then it would not necessarily involve the will. But moral truth does involve the will. It calls for a movement of the whole personality, much more than any purely intellectual proposition could do. It is therefore unreasonable to expect uniformity and universal assent here. On the other hand, it is not only unreasonable to exclude the possibility that commitment to what I have called a moral truth may be a means of finding reality; in the end such a denial would be suicidal. It would mean in effect saying that man cannot achieve something which his whole nature demands that he shall achieve. It would be to envisage man as a creature doomed to eternal frustration and eternal failure incapable of becoming fully human, and mocked rather than enriched by his scientific and technical discoveries and achievements. I revert therefore to the view that in being attracted by God I am neither unreasonable nor unscientific nor fantastic.

It was Augustine who saw most clearly and described most satisfactorily how we are attracted by God. Augustine realized that the most significant part of us is not our intellect but our will, and he defined the will in terms which are not radically different from those which a psychologist might use today. We are not morally neutral individuals, surveying from some independent vantage-point the various choices open to us and then choosing one. We do not stand upon some psychological island past which the currents of motivation run, finally deciding to plunge into one or another. We are either controlled by good impulses and motives or bad; as Augustine put it, we are either enslaved by bad motives or under the influence of good motives and therefore free. We choose that which is good because it attracts us more than that which is bad. We choose God, not out of a stern sense of duty nor in a spirit of cool calculation of expediency, but because God makes himself sweet to us. We cannot resist the attraction of his goodness. What we all want in our heart of hearts is rest in happiness. This is what our desires, hidden or acknowledged, are ultimately driving at. Augustine agrees with modern psychology that what makes us ourselves is not our power of reasoning but our desires. We choose God when we see him as the most desirable thing of all, as the highest, greatest satisfaction of our deepest desire.

God moves us with the power of love. The motive-power in Christian belief is the attraction of God's love. This is not a new discovery of trendy modern theologians. Paul and Augustine knew it long ago, and so have millions of Christians, famous and obscure, ever since, whether they could express their knowledge or not. At the heart of the gospel is the paradoxical, extraordinary, love of God, declared and expressed in his Son Jesus Christ who chose to be born as a man among us, to live a life of unselfishness, and to die a voluntary death by crucifixion for us. This love, vindicated and fully revealed at the resurrection, is what keeps Christianity going. One could heap up epithets about it—undeserved, unexpected, gratuitous, generous. It discloses an endlessly resourceful and compassionate God, always one jump ahead of us, capable of producing a situation which reverses our values and overthrows our conventional religion and leaves us bankrupt before him, able to use evil for good purposes, never at a loss to retrieve the most apparently hopeless situation, nor allergic to acting in history, not so aloof as to be incapable of suffering, but above all continually master of the situation and because he is a loving God completely trustworthy. These are the ingredients of the attractiveness of God and this is why I, with many others, find belief in him an irresistibly attractive proposition.

This is also why it is valuable and indeed necessary to study Christian doctrine. God's movements cannot be left unexplored and unexplained. If belief in him is worth entertaining, then it is worth while following out this belief into its logical consequences. It is proper to pay God the compliment of assuming that his disclosure of his attractiveness can be worked into a body of consistent doctrine and related to contemporary secular thought. If we do not ask about the connection between God's love and the Holy Spirit and the Church, if we do not examine the relation of Christ's Person to the being of God, we are in effect assuming that the subject of God's love is not a serious one. We cannot label our religion, 'For Sunday Schools Only', nor put a notice before it, 'Intellectuals Keep Out'. Many sincere Christians are tempted to wrap their faith in a cosy cocoon of biblical language and enjoyable religious experience and to revel in it while they protect it from the cold blasts of the outer world. They want to enjoy their religion as if it were their own possession, sheltered from the unkind, searching questions of theologians, immune from criticism, in a comfortable state of arrested development. This is in fact to retreat silently from the claim that what they believe is truth; it is to sacrifice religion to piety. Religion protected by piety from critical investigation becomes fantasy. We must ask all the questions which flow from our acceptance of the love of God. We must examine the doctrine of the Trinity, the dogma of the incarnation, the meaning of the atonement, the nature of the Holy Spirit. We must try to determine the proper function and status of the Bible which is our documentation for God's love, and consider the relation to it of the Church, which is at once the object, the *locus* and the organ of God's love. We must involve ourselves in thinking about the Church's ministry and with it about the Church's authority. We must ask questions about God's relation to history and so find ourselves speaking about the development of doctrine and about the elusive but unavoidable subject of eschatology. We must, in short, do theology. We cannot withhold this homage of our minds to the attractiveness of God.

2 *The Bible*

I

What has often been called the Catholic doctrine of the inspiration of holy Scripture, that which has the best right to be called traditional and which has been accepted for a longer period in the history of the Church than any other, has a composite origin. The first ingredient in it is the rabbinic teaching about the inspiration of the Hebrew Scriptures prevalent in the first century A.D. This can scarcely be dignified by the name of a theory. It was a working assumption that all the Hebrew Scriptures were inerrant and accurate in every detail and that every phrase and every word in them, however obscure or irrational, had been ordained in its place by God. It was the task of the rabbinic commentators and interpreters, on this assumption, to make sense of the Scriptures. The Christian Church unreflectingly took over this teaching about the Old Testament as it took over so much else from Judaism. By the year 220 the Church had applied this doctrine of scriptural inerrancy to the New Testament also. There are plenty of signs that at first the New Testament was not put on a level with the Old and that acceptance of a book as canonical did not necessarily mean applying to it a doctrine of inspiration. But by the time of Irenaeus, parallel with the gradual acceptance of the Fourth Gospel as authoritative, the movement to regard the New Testament as holy Scripture on a level with the Old is well under way. Irenaeus first applies to the New Testament the allegorical method of exegesis whose use in interpreting the Old Testament was well established by his day. Everywhere Christian writers followed suit, and by the time that Origen wrote his first book the great majority of Christians must have regarded the New Testament as quite as inerrant and accurate and quite as much guaranteed against imperfection as they did the Old.

The second ingredient in the traditional doctrine of inspiration was imported by Origen, direct from Philo. Origen before he died had articulated and permanently impressed upon the mind of the Church an elaborate and carefully thought-out doctrine of inspiration, based almost entirely on the doctrine of the inspiration of the Pentateuch which he had learnt from the ingenious and speculative Hellenized Jew Philo, who lived at Alexandria from about 20 B.C. to about A.D. 50.[1] God himself was the author of holy Scripture and he dictated every word in it, though the writers did not actually lose consciousness as they were being inspired. The Bible therefore was inerrant, that is to say, accurate in every statement which it makes. Not only every word, but every letter was directly inspired by the Holy Spirit. To question this conviction was to undermine the veracity of the whole evidence of the truth of the Christian faith. Obscure or apparently irrational or shocking passages or passages apparently unworthy of God's authorship, and all inconsistencies, mistakes or imperfections, were deliberately inserted by the Holy Spirit in order to call attention to the fact that almost all parts of both Old and New Testaments were to be allegorized. Indeed the credit of the Christian faith was bound up with this kind of exegesis of the Bible. Any passage might be torn out of its context and allegorized uncritically. This was essentially an *oracular* view of the Bible. The ancient world into which Christianity was born had a fondness for oracles.

This 'oracular' doctrine of the inspiration of the Bible continued, unchanged in its essentials, to be the official doctrine of the Church until the nineteenth century. It underwent some elaboration and some modification at the hands of medieval theologians and sixteenth-century Reformers, but it experienced no significant setback until the advent of historical criticism as applied to the Bible. Then indeed it disappeared, totally and for ever. This doctrine of inspiration was indissolubly linked with a doctrine of the inerrancy and entire accuracy of the whole Bible. But the advance of historical criticism made it impossible to hold this doctrine without either grave intellectual dishonesty or sheer disregard of firmly established facts. Whatever other achievements of biblical criticism we may be doubtful of, this conclusion we cannot possibly refuse—that the Bible is not an inerrant oracle divinely guaranteed against the possibility of inaccuracy. We can today accept neither the rabbis of the first century, nor Philo interpreted by Origen, as satisfactory authorities on the subject of the nature and function of the Bible.

II

One of the worst blows which the development of historical criticism dealt the Church of the nineteenth century was to demolish its doctrine of the inspiration of the Bible. It is significant that the subject of one of the essays in that book which sparked off the controversy over biblical criticism in this country, *Essays and Reviews*, was on the inspiration of the Bible. It was some time before scholars who still wanted to retain dogmatic Christianity while accepting biblical criticism began to formulate a coherent alternative theory. By the turn of the century, however, such a theory had begun to find wide acceptance, and Sanday's book, *Inspiration*, which was published in 1894, was designed to express this theory in a sober, scholarly, and attractive way. Though Sanday advanced other reasons for believing in the inspiration of the Bible, his main argument can be summed up in the well-known phrase, 'The Bible is inspired because it is inspiring'. At first sight this is a hopeful theory. It points to the great part which the Bible has played all through the ages in nourishing Christian piety, in inspiring Christian work, in bracing Christians to meet adversity and even martyrdom, in sustaining the faith and feeding the life of the Church. It can bring in evidence the lofty passages of Deutero-Isaiah, the tremendous words of Amos, the profound poetry of Job, those sentences of the Psalms which touch the human heart with such a pathos and such an appeal, the simple but pregnant utterances of the Sermon on the Mount, the lyrical sweep of St Paul's paragraphs, the mysterious power of the images painted by the author of the Revelation. It can appeal to such testimonies as the words of Samuel Taylor Coleridge about the Bible:

> I have found words for my inmost thoughts, songs for my joy, utterances for my hidden griefs, and pleadings for my shame and my feebleness.

But though this theory long found wide acceptance and still is warmly favoured in some quarters, on examination it proves a most unsatisfactory one, even when all its claims have been granted. It is unsatisfactorily *eclectic*: parts of the Bible are inspiring, but parts are not. In what way could Leviticus, Judges, Esther, Ecclesiastes, Psalms 109 and 137, Jude, and 2 Peter be described as inspiring? Many parts of the Bible are obviously inspiring, but many parts are much less so than others, and some parts are not inspiring at all. The theory is unsatisfactorily *subjective*: I may find the book of Job inspiring, but somebody else may regard it as merely a farrago of bewildering obscurity. One man may find himself in sympathy with the writer of the book of Nehemiah; another may feel nothing but repulsion at his self-righteousness. The theory is unsatisfactorily *vague*: the Bible may be inspiring, but then many other books on religious themes are inspiring too. One may instance Aeschylus' *Oresteia*, Virgil's *Aeneid*, Dante's *Divina Commedia*, Bunyan's *Pilgrim's Progress*. There does not seem to be any good reason why these should, on this argument, be regarded as any less inspired than the Bible. This theory, in short, forfeits the Bible's uniqueness.

Alternative theories to these of the inspiration of the Bible are not easily found in the Church today and when found are not convincing. Dr Austin Farrer in *The Glass of Vision*, which he published in 1948, argued with his customary ingenuity and persuasiveness for a theory that the biblical writers were inspired in the images which they used, and that if we take this line of argument we can still with a clear conscience speak of the Bible as inspired. But, in the first place, this is a theory rather of the writers being inspired than of the book which they wrote deserving this epithet. In the second place, it is very difficult to confine this doctrine of inspiration to the Bible. In what way, for instance, are the images used by the writers of the Book of Daniel and the Revelation more inspired than the very similar images used by the writers of *I Enoch* and the *War of the Children of Light and the Children of Darkness* among the Dead Sea Scrolls? Or how are the images of 2 Peter more inspired than the many vivid and effective images used by Ignatius of Antioch in his seven letters, written probably earlier than 2 Peter? Contemporary Literalists (this seems a preferable word to the commoner Fundamentalists) and contemporary Roman Catholics are at one in their use of very similar arguments in their attempt to defend the traditional doctrine of the inerrancy of Scripture. A reading of, e.g., the Encyclicals *Divino Afflante Spiritu* (1943) and *Mystici Corporis* (1950) of Pope Pius XII will reveal how tortuous, how complicated and how implausible are the arguments to which those are reduced who accept, even in a modified way, the results of historical criticism and yet who seek to retain a belief in the Bible's inerrancy. This doctrine of inerrancy appears more nakedly as each generation goes by to be an arbitrary and superfluous theory imposed by force upon the recalcitrant material of the Bible. The Literalists who profess to accept biblical criticism, but who in fact do so only on condition that biblical criticism will always come to conservative conclusions, use almost identical, and just as unconvincing, arguments to support a belief in biblical inerrancy which, though placed in a different theological context, is for all practical purposes identical with that of the Roman Catholics.

III

It seems to me that it would be more satisfactory and more honest if theologians gave up altogether using the words 'inspired' and 'inspiration' in connection with the Bible, and substituted for them another word, the word 'unique'. We ought to consider very seriously the casual nature of many of the documents which comprise the Bible. Much of the material which composes the works of the major prophets consists of isolated fragments which appear to have been included in the prophetic books largely by accident. The book of Judges includes at least one long narrative, describing Abimelech's hegemony based on Shechem, which is wholly concerned with Canaanite, and has apparently nothing to do with Israelite, history. The book of Psalms embraces not only religious hymns and poems but also stage directions, footnotes giving guidance to pilgrims, and rubrics for liturgical use of the contents. Some of St Paul's epistles are written with the conscious intention of their being preserved and studied for some time to come (e.g., Romans and perhaps 1 Corinthians). But several of them (and not the least important) were quite clearly written on the spur of the moment without any idea on the part of the writer that they would be studied for centuries later by millions of people. Second Corinthians, that fragmentary, improvised, unscripted document, is the great example here, but so in its way is Galatians. Many of the personal epistles (Philemon, 2 John, and 3 John) were clearly written originally as mere fugitive pieces, to deal with very temporary circumstances. If we regard these documents primarily as evidence, their casual nature does not in the least impair their value; on the contrary, it enhances it as witnessing to Christian belief and practice all the more effectively because undesignedly. But if we are to think that all the books of the Bible are specially inspired (whatever meaning we give to that word) in the way that other documents are not, the casual nature of many of them creates a serious difficulty. Paul dashes off a letter to the Church of Corinth to be carried by Timothy, and this forms the whole or part of 2 Corinthians and is inspired. Next day he dashes off another letter to the church of Beroea and sends it by Aristarchus; this does not happen to survive and is not inspired. An anonymous writer taking the name of Peter writes to the Church (let us say) of Rome; his letter survives and is inspired. Another writer, Clement, writes (perhaps earlier) to the Church of Corinth; his letter survives but is not inspired. To argue like this is to reduce the word 'inspiration' to meaninglessness; it is simply an invisible indefinable something which is attached to certain documents because they happen to have been included in the Bible. Inspiration is the compliment which the ancient Church paid to the Bible; but, like most compliments, its real meaning will not bear close examination.

The true and fundamental nature and function of the Bible are best summed up in the word *witness*. The Bible is the supreme witness to the origins and significance of the Christian faith, the only primary, indispensable witness for it. In this sense we can endorse the opinion of the Anglican divines of the sixteenth and seventeenth centuries when they insisted so strongly that the Bible (and particularly the New Testament) was the successor to the apostles. It is that collection of documents which enshrines, embodies and witnesses to the Christian faith as the apostles taught it, even though many of the documents of the New Testament were not written by apostles. To put this point in what may seem an uncongenially modern way, the Bible is a body of evidence. If anybody wants to know what the Christian faith was like at the beginning, how it started, and what our Lord and what his apostles did and taught, he must read, or have somehow conveyed to him, this heterogeneous collection of evidence called the Old and New Testaments. There is no other genuine way of obtaining this knowledge. To suggest that there is another source of this knowledge, the teaching of the Church, is futile, because the Church itself has no other source of doctrine except the Bible. Between the incarnation and ourselves stands immovably this body of evidence called the Bible.

Now the Bible has many of the features which any body of evidence is likely to have, whether it be the evidence collected in a book to reconstruct a famous battle of the past, or the evidence produced before a jury to enable them to decide the guilt or innocence of an accused person. The evidence, as we have already seen, is heterogeneous, consisting of a widely different number of forms of literature written by a large number of people, in three different languages, and dating from different times within a large span of history. Some of this evidence is more valuable than other parts. Deutero-Isaiah and the four Gospels and the Epistle to the Romans are much nearer the core of the information conveyed by this body of evidence than are such peripheral works as Esther, Song of Solomon and Jude, some of which are so remote from the subject to which the Bible as a whole witnesses as to be almost worthless. But then any large body of evidence will contain parts which are less valuable than others and some material which is almost or entirely valueless. The important point is that the Church decided, at a period in history at which it was in a position to distinguish between authentic and unauthentic tradition (as it is not in a position to do now), that the Bible contained enough authentic and reliable evidence for all men to find through it saving knowledge of God as revealed in Christ. When all pretence and all cant and all pious fancy have been stripped away, that is the true nature and function of the Bible.

On this estimate of the Bible, there is no necessity to call it inspired (to do this would be only to darken counsel); but it is necessary to call it unique. The Bible is unique because of its subject and because of the primacy, the earliness, of its witness to its subject. The subject of the Bible is God's saving activity towards his people, in his chosen race and in his chosen Messiah. This is not the subject of those many religious or philosophical works which are as inspiring as the Bible, Plato's *Republic* or Aeschylus' *Agamemnon* or Lucretius' *de Rerum Natura*. The witness of the Bible to its subject is uniquely early, uniquely valuable because of its earliness. This cannot be said for many most inspiring works which have the same subject as the Bible, such as Augustine's *Confessions* and Dante's *Divina Commedia* and Pascal's *Pensées*. When, therefore, we reject for the Bible the epithet 'inspired' on the ground that it is impossible to find any satisfactory content for this word, we are justified in substituting for it the word 'unique', because we can give a clear and concrete meaning to this word.

IV

But in reducing the Bible in this way to its essentials as unique and indispensable witness, it is not necessary to conclude that we are putting it in the category of ancient documents and assuming that this is all that can be said about the matter. Just because of its unique nature and function, we can admit freely that the Bible is also the fountain of the Church's life and the Church's preaching, the peculiar and sacred source of doctrine and of historical knowledge about Christianity, the primal, original tradition of the Church enshrining in written form that gospel which is older even than the Church itself, the book which has all through the ages nourished the faith, inspired the piety, and formed the behaviour of thousands upon thousands of Christians. But it has achieved this lofty status and held this incomparable place in the history of the Church, not because it is an inspired oracle, or series of oracles, not even because it was deliberately written in order to be inspiring, but because it was chosen by the Church—and rightly chosen, for in a sense it imposed this choice upon the Church itself—to be the unique and indispensable witness to the activity of God towards men in Christ. Without committing ourselves to the dubious and (it is to be feared) meaningless statement that God is the author of holy Scripture, we can with confidence say that it was through the guidance of the Holy Spirit that the Church retained the Old Testament and canonized the New.

To sum up we may revert to the strongest reason for regarding the primary function and nature of the Bible as witness: this definition enables us to see that it is perfectly compatible with the nature and function of the Bible that it should contain errors. The great purpose of a body of evidence is the impression that the evidence makes as a whole. There may be mistakes and inaccuracies in places in the evidence. Some of the mistakes may be minor, a few may be major mistakes, or there may be a great many mistakes in subjects within the body of evidence which are not directly relevant to the principal subject to which the body of evidence is designed to witness. All that is required of the evidence is that as a whole it carry such a weight of truth, as to enable a decision to be made on the right side. This is all we know, and all we need to know, about the Bible: 'these are written that you may believe that Jesus is the Christ, the Son of God, and that believing you may have life in his name' (John 20.31). To claim to know more than this about the Bible is to move from the sure ground of faith into the marshland of fantasy.

V

Ever since the beginning of Christianity the Church and the Bible have been dancing-partners. The dance began with a slow and graceful waltz which in some of the flights of patristic interpretation became a polka and even, under the guidance of some, a jig. During the Middle Ages the dance changed to something more intricate, more formal and more ceremonial, a minuet, a cotillion, or even a fandango. At the Reformation the rhythm and the figures changed to a brisk gallop or an ecstatic tango, and since then the Church might be regarded as having alternated between an apache-dance in which the Church was continually throwing the Bible away and pulling it back again violently, and a rock-'n'-roll in which every limb of both partners moves feverishly and they are continually meeting each other in intentional but indecorous collisions.

The Christian Church began by taking a view of the Bible which was essentially oracular. As we have seen, it inherited from late Judaism just such a view of the Hebrew Scriptures. To the rabbis every verse, every line, every word, and even, in their more imaginative moments, every letter, was capable of concealing a hidden meaning independent, or almost independent, of its context and of the historical situation in which it was written. The early Christian Fathers were not forced into quite so unrealistic a view because they were not compelled, as the rabbis were, to turn the whole Old Testament into a law-code, irrespective of all other considerations. It was open to them to treat the historical books as history, the Wisdom literature as literature, the psalms as hymns, the proverbs as proverbs, and so on. On the other hand they felt obliged not only to treat all the prophetic material as prediction and not commentary upon contemporary society, but they were gravely embarrassed by the law-books, which they could hardly accept *in toto* as directly binding as law. In the end they compromised by regarding most of the Old Testament historical books, psalms, proverbs, prophetic and apocalyptic material as oracular prediction in which wonderful prefigurings of Christ, the Church, and Christian doctrine could be found in multitudinous disconnected utterances, but also retaining as much of the law-books as could colourably be used in order to assist in forming ecclesiastical law. Thus the third century saw not only the popularization of virtually unrestrained allegorizing under the presiding genius of Origen, but also the activity of Cyprian in the West in using the Old Testament legal books as blueprints for constructing patterns for the Christian ministry and the day to day life and behaviour of the Christian Church, and in the East the interesting spectacle of Gregory the Wonderworker attempting to regulate the life of his diocese on the southern shore of the Black Sea during the aftermath of a disastrous raid from the Goths by the precepts and ordinances of Leviticus and Deuteronomy. The New Testament caused the Fathers less trouble because it obviously did speak of Christ everywhere, and because it provided virtually no legal material at all. Even the legally-minded Tertullian found it an uphill task to turn the Sermon on the Mount and the epistles of Paul into church law.

This oracular attitude to the Bible, if anything, deepened and strengthened during the Middle Ages. The old idea that the Church entirely lost sight of the Bible during the Middle Ages must certainly be rejected. The Bible continued to form, as it always formed, the very heart of the thought, the spirituality and the art of the medieval Church. But a certain remoteness, formality, loss of touch, of living contact with the text, did undoubtedly become evident. The Bible was to the theologians a mine from which scholastic theology was to be constructed, to the masses a very rich store among other varied and numerous stores of popular religious images, to the lawyers the ultimate, but remotely ultimate, authority upon which canon law must ostensibly be based. And in the later Middle Ages there grew up, as a result of this remoteness, the theory of two sources of doctrine, the Bible and tradition; tradition was conceived as a source of authentic original doctrine or information about our Lord derived independently of the Bible from him or from his apostles. The Bible was recognized as authoritative, was enshrined conventionally in the archives of the Church, was respected, was known, but was known at a certain distance.

The Reformation certainly represented a return to the text of the Bible and a tearing away of some of the veils through which the medieval Church had looked at it. The Reformed traditions found in the Bible a fresh spring of insight into the Christian faith, a fresh delight in its pages, a fresh dynamic issuing from it for

Christian faith and life and worship. But the underlying oracular view of it was not abolished by the Reformation, only modified and limited. And when the first fine careless rapture of the Reformation was over an exaggerated biblicism, paralleled only in the writings of Cyprian, tended to seek in the Bible direct injunctions for ordering all the details of Church life, sacraments, ministry, worship, behaviour, which had an atrophying effect upon legitimate tradition and resulted in an impoverishment of Christian life and in the reading into the Bible of ideas and institutions which were not there. The Church of the Counter-Reformation, scared by the explosive results of letting loose unrestrained study of the Bible at the Reformation, took a timid and cautious attitude towards the Scriptures which has only in our day begun to be relaxed. Since the Reformation two events in the world of ideas have gravely altered our view of the Bible. One of them was the discovery of the development of doctrine by John Henry Newman. The other was the advent of biblical criticism. This last event made it perfectly clear that, whatever else the Bible might be, it was a collection of ancient documents having all the usual characteristics of ancient documents, inaccuracy, incoherence, and uncertainty, and it initiated an examination of the biblical literature by scholars all over the world more radical and unsparing than has ever been applied to any other literature anywhere. This examination has by no means reached its end. It leaves the Church with the embarrassing question of how it is to deal with this, its sacred book. How can you dance with a partner who spends half her time on the operating table and the other half in a clinic undergoing deep x-ray?

VI

The first necessity in any reappraisal of the Bible as a norm of faith must be to abandon any lingering vestiges of the 'oracular' view of the Bible. The gang of former pirates in *Treasure Island* used the Bible in order to add a certain numinous influence to the process of black-balling one of their members. We are still inclined to regard the pages of the Bible as having a numinous quality about them. Even though they were not written in numinous Hebrew and numinous Greek, we tend to translate them into would-be numinous English, and too often to read them in a would-be numinous voice. This illegitimate importation of numinousness into the text has from of old been the besetting sin of translators and expounders of the Bible. The Septuagint translators at Isaiah 51.20 found a difficult phrase in the Hebrew altogether too much for them. It meant in fact 'like an antelope in a net', but the best they would make of it was, 'like a half-cooked piece of beetroot', yet they included this nonsense in their translation because they presumed that it hid some profound inner meaning. There are many examples of the same procedure to be found in the translation of the Psalms in the Book of Common Prayer. This attribution of numinousness to the text of the Bible was covered and still is covered by a theory of what is called 'inspiration'. The coming of biblical criticism made it impossible to hold this theory for those who are unwilling to indulge in pure fantasy. No alternative meaning for the word 'inspiration' when applied to the Bible has been produced which has any connection with the root meaning of the word itself or with Origen's definition of it. We still cling to the word, speaking of the inspiration of Scripture and of the inspired pages of Scripture, but we can give no meaning to it which does not alter it into an entirely different concept unconnected with the traditional one. It would be much better to abandon the word altogether as a lingering vestige of the oracular view of the Bible, and substitute another. We have suggested that a good candidate for its position would be 'uniqueness'.

The Bible is not a vast accumulation of oracles. It is witness, evidence, record. It is a collection of very varied forms of literature; we can detect in it myth, legend, saga, folk-story, law of every sort, anecdote, history, prophetic comment upon contemporary happenings, poetry, proverbs, love-songs, religious drama, philosophical speculation, liturgical and personal hymns, biography, diaries, official documents, cultic and ritual regulations, moral maxims, philosophy of history and of religion, apocalyptic visions, gospels, acts, letters, sermons. These twenty-eight forms are certainly not an exhaustive list. This widely varied corpus of literature constitutes a collective witness to the activity of God towards man in the history of the response of the Jewish race to God's calling and its climax in the career of Jesus Christ. The Bible is the record of revelation, and this record takes the form of historical witness. It constitutes testimony to an unique activity of God, to an unique course of events which happened to an unique people, and finally to an unique Person. This is what causes the uniqueness of the Bible; what constitutes its uniqueness is not the form or forms of the biblical literature, which are in fact most of them to be found in many other literatures and cultures as well, but its subject.

Now as witness or testimony to the revelation of God to man, as a collection of documents witnessing to events, it is not necessary that the Bible should be either infallible or exhaustive or even complete or wholly consistent. It is in fact clear that the Bible is neither infallible nor exhaustive nor complete nor wholly consistent. It exhibits many mistakes and many contradictions and inconsistencies. The Bible does not record all the words that Jesus uttered nor all the deeds that he did. It does not tell us about the ultimate destiny of the tablets of the Law in the ark nor about the end of the career of Isaiah nor of Jeremiah, nor about the later life, after the ascension, of more than three of the original twelve apostles. It tells us almost nothing about some subjects on which we would dearly like information; such as the state of the soul after death and before judgement. But then a collection of evidence need not be infallible nor exhaustive nor complete nor consistent. In fact, in every other case involving collections of evidence, documentary or oral, we would be highly suspicious if the collection possessed all these qualities. If a counsel presenting evidence against an accused man in a law-court, or an historian presenting evidence to convince us that his interpretation of a piece of history was true, claimed that his evidence was infallible and exhaustive and entirely complete and faultlessly consistent, he would forfeit our confidence at once. What we look for in collections of evidence is not these qualities. We look for their general drift, the total impression they make upon us, their scope, their direction, we look at where the weight of the evidence falls. In one word, what we ask of collections of evidence is not infallibility but sufficiency. This is what we ask of the Bible and what we find in it; not inspiration and inerrancy but uniqueness and sufficiency. All we have a right to ask of a collection of evidence is that it shall give an adequate impression of its main subject so that those who read it shall grasp clearly the weight, the burden and tendency of the whole. However much we may deplore the Church's indulgence of fantasy in its treatment of the Bible, its futile allegorizing, its readiness to read into the text imaginary meanings, its baseless theories of inspiration, we can fairly admit that the Church did gain an adequate impression of the Bible's main subject, it did grasp the burden of the whole. Somehow or other, in spite of all misunderstandings and misinterpretations, the Bible has performed its proper function through the centuries of witnessing to the activity of God towards men.

VII

If we allow that the Bible is in its form and function a collection of evidence about the activity of God towards man, it follows from this that the Bible is not itself directly doctrine nor ethics nor ecclesiology but raw material for all these. The Church has as to its task the inferring of doctrine from witness. The Bible gives its account of how God has acted, its infinitely varied and heterogeneous account; it is the business of the Church to deduce from this the proper consequences for its doctrine and its life. That the Bible is only raw material and not the finished product is a truth which has often been forgotten during the long centuries of church history. The Bible is not a manual of doctrine, so that teaching about the doctrine of the holy Trinity, for instance, can be read off from the pages of St John's Gospel. Coherent and articulated doctrine on the nature of the Godhead consistent with the witness of the Bible has to be gathered by a review of all the biblical evidence, some of it of less importance, some of it of greater, some of it even inconsistent with other parts. The early Fathers of the Church assumed too naïvely that Christian doctrine in the developed sense of the fourth and fifth Christian centuries was lying around the Bible waiting to be directly incorporated in theological treatises. The Bible does not provide a blueprint for the organization and institutions of the Church and the ministry which only needs to be directly implemented by the Church. This was the mistake made by two persons as different as Cyprian in the third century and Calvin in the sixteenth, with momentous consequences in both cases. The Bible is not a handbook of ethics, though Puritans in all ages have made strenuous efforts to treat it as such. Ethical consequences can of course be drawn from the biblical witness to God's acts, but it does not follow that all the ethical precepts and examples to be found in the Bible can be indiscriminately transferred into contemporary experience by the Christian. No doubt Shakespeare's *Hamlet* could provide useful material for a manual for gravediggers, a textbook for actors and a casebook for those who examine psychic manifestations, but its main purpose is not concerned with graves or dramatic technique or ghosts. Still less is the Bible a sacred crossword puzzle or divine Old Moore's Almanack filled with inspired prediction of coming political and international events capable of decipherment by earnest Christians whose piety supplies their lack of education and common sense. The Bible is given to the Church as its raw material from which it is to produce preaching, teaching, and doctrine. The Bible does not preach itself. If you place a Bible in the market-place it does not expound itself; it does not behave like a gramophone. The Bible has to be printed, translated, disseminated. It also has to be preached and taught.

But this apparently bleak and formal estimate of the nature and status of the Bible as evidence must be modified by two important considerations. In the first place the things to which the Bible witnesses are no ordinary things. The activity of God in disclosing himself to man is not like an ordinary event of history, like a naval battle, or a parliamentary debate or a railway accident, not even like a long historical process such as the growth of parliamentary democracy or the coming of the Industrial Revolution. We call it an event because we do not want it thought that the Bible witnesses only to ideas or only to human religious experience; it witnesses to the activity of God seen in historical events and in the lives of historical persons. But the nature of God's activity involves the inclusion in this evidence of a wide variety of signs of his activity—hymns, prayers, rituals, meditations, prophetic utterances, remodelled legends and folk-tales, letters composed for casual and particular occasions and needs, and so on. We find God's activity reflected in a dazzling multiplicity of ways and of situations and periods, and we need discernment to see how it is reflected in each. The analogy of a collection of evidence will only serve us in a limited way, though serve us it can. No collection and no subject was ever quite like this one.

Secondly, we must gladly admit that the Bible always has been and still is more than a dry collection of ancient documents. It was written from faith to faith. It was intended for the use of a worshipping community, and outside the context of a worshipping community it is inevitably misunderstood, misinterpreted and misapplied. It is intended for the use of a living Church, so that it may feed the Church's spiritual life. It is the crystallization in written form of the gospel which created the Church before the New Testament existed. This gospel, this Word always sustains the Church; to this gospel and Word the Church is subject. The New Testament was canonized in order that this gospel and Word might not be confused or corrupted or lost through human forgetfulness or frailty. The Bible therefore has in some sense a creative relationship to the Church. The Word speaks to the Church through the Bible and from the Bible. The Bible always has acted as well-spring, light, dynamic, and begetter of faith towards the Church, not because of its form, but because of its subject. The Bible is not a dead book. It has constantly shown its capacity to renew the Church's life, to revive interest in its pages, to engross and even to intoxicate men with its subject. When we maintain that the Bible is in form historical evidence and that its relation to the Church's use of it is that of raw material, we do not in the least intend to decry the Bible's unique role in nourishing and creating faith nor its unique religious vitality.

VIII

But for most dances there must be two partners, and each partner must contribute his share to the dance. The life of Christianity depends upon the Church dancing with the Bible and the Bible with the Church. The Church may indeed be lost without the Bible, like a ship without a compass. But the Bible without the Church is dead, a collection of ancient documents and no more. The Church is constantly faced with the task of interpreting the Bible, in such a way as not to run away from it and not to worship it. We may go further, and say that the Church has not only to interpret the Bible, but also to live from it, to use the Bible as its spiritual and intellectual food in all the varied departments of church life, in prayer, in worship, in study, in good works, in behaviour. But all these activities are only different expressions of an underlying interpretation of the Bible. All the diverse ways in which different Christian denominations express their worship and conduct their institutions and envisage their ethics are all so many indications of the manner in which they interpret the Bible, whether legalistically or idealistically or moralistically, and we should be able to gauge the particular interpretation of the Bible adopted by any denomination by looking at its worship, its institutions and its ethics, as surely as we can guess the year in which a clergyman was ordained by looking at his bookshelves. Whatever the Church does, it must interpret the Bible.

In the process of interpreting the Bible the Church creates

tradition. The word 'tradition' used in this context should cause nobody alarm, because 'tradition' of this sort is an indispensable ingredient of historical Christianity. As a snail in moving slowly across a path leaves a trail behind it, so the Church in moving slowly through history makes tradition. It is a wholly inevitable process; from time to time Christian bodies have attempted to dispense with tradition, to teach doctrine which they describe as 'the Bible and the Bible alone', but all they succeed in doing is to create a tradition of trying to dispense with tradition. Tradition is, in short, the deposit left by the Church in interpreting the Bible. Tradition is the proof that the Church is indispensable to the Bible and at the same time that the Church must subordinate itself to the Bible, for tradition is variable and open to reform and retrenchment, whereas the Bible is not. Tradition includes not only the great classical dogmas of the holy Trinity and of the humanity and divinity of Christ, but also the whole varied and vexed history of Christian doctrine.

It is at this point that we can most appropriately turn to a subject which has already been mentioned as of great importance, one which is closely connected with any consideration of the Bible as the norm of faith. This is the development of Christian doctrine. It is necessary first to take a brief look at the various views which have been held, and still are held, on this topic. The traditional Anglican view on the subject of the development of doctrine has been that up to the fourth General Council, the Council of Chalcedon in 451, a steady accumulation of integrated doctrine can be traced and accepted. The classical doctrines of the divinity of our Lord and of the union of divine and human in his Person, and of the holy Trinity, three Persons and one God, were achieved and articulated during that period. They are now embodied either in creeds, such as the Nicene Creed and the Athanasian Creed, or in theological statements like the Chalcedonian Formula. Some Anglicans in the past have been ready to acknowledge as a proper development of dogma the deliverances of the next two councils which called themselves general, those of the Second Council of Constantinople (held in 553) and of the Third Council of Constantinople (held in 680-681). Perhaps some Anglicans today would still regard the pronouncements of these last two councils as a necessary and proper part of the development of doctrine. But beyond this point Anglicans do not agree that doctrine developed further in any ecumenical or official sense.

The Church, thereafter, they hold, was too gravely divided for any development like those of Nicaea (325) and Chalcedon (451) to take place. Newman in his 'Essay on the Development of Christian Doctrine' asked pertinently of this view whether its holders think that the Holy Spirit ceased operating after 451 or after 681? Why should development of doctrine have ceased so comparatively early in the history of the Church? To this query no official Anglican answer has ever been given. Very few have ever been unofficially attempted. In contrast to this, the Roman Catholic account of the development of doctrine is clear and, at first sight, consistent. The first four General Councils gave a solid but rudimentary beginning to the development of an integrated and harmonious system of dogma which has been proceeding steadily and majestically ever since, through councils, of which the recent Second Vatican is the twenty-first, and decisions of Popes. The three latest examples of development were the dogmas of the Immaculate Conception of the Blessed Virgin Mary (1854), of the Infallibility of the Pope (1870), and of the Corporeal Assumption of the Blessed Virgin Mary (1950). This account certainly cannot be accused of leaving the Holy Spirit without any function as regards doctrine since the fifth or the seventh century. On the contrary, dogma is being produced in recent centuries, on this view, at the unusually fast rate of three new dogmas every hundred years. But we are bound to question seriously the basis and principles of this view of development when we scrutinize its latest product, the dogma of the Corporeal Assumption of the Blessed Virgin Mary. This dogma has no serious connection with the Bible at all, and its defenders scarcely pretend that it has. It cannot honestly be said to have any solid ground in patristic theology either, because it is first known among Catholic Christians in even its crudest form only at the beginning of the fifth century, and then among Copts in Egypt whose associations with Gnostic heresy are suspiciously strong; indeed it can be shown to be a doctrine which manifestly had its origin among Gnostic heretics. The only argument by which it is defended is that if the Church has at any time believed it and does now believe it, then it must be orthodox, whatever its origins, because the final standard of orthodoxy is what the Church believes. The fact that this belief is presumably supposed to have some basis on historical fact analogous to the belief of all Christians in the resurrection of our Lord makes its registration as a dogma *de fide* more bewilderingly incomprehensible, for it is wholly devoid of any historical evidence to support it. In short, the latest example of the Roman Catholic theory of doctrinal development appears to be a *reductio ad absurdum* expressly designed to discredit the whole structure.

A very different picture is presented to us by the account of the development of doctrine given by a number of Continental Protestant scholars beginning with Sohm and Harnack, whose chief supporter today is the Swiss Modernist Martin Werner. They regard all doctrinal development as a continuous deviation away from the original purity of the gospel into Hellenization, legalism, into an unnecessary complication of the originally ethical or apocalyptic message by metaphysical concepts, and generally into unreal, barren speculation, rigidity and scholasticism. Sohm believed that the rot set in with the First Epistle of Clement (A.D. 96) whose writer has abandoned the first fine careless rapture of charismatic activity and personal relations governed by love for an official ministry and a concept of law. Harnack saw the original purely ethical message of Jesus, the religious genius who preached the Fatherhood of God and brotherhood of man, as gradually overlaid by Hellenization. Werner, the more radical, apparently thinks that Christianity had already seen its best days by A.D. 60. It was a purely eschatological message and when after a generation the world had not ended and the Second Coming of Christ had not taken place, inevitably corruption set in. The coming of the classic dogmas of the fourth and fifth centuries was sheer disaster. If you take Harnack's line, you regard the doctrine of the Arians in the fourth century as a deviation encouraged by Greek philosophy, and the thought of Athanasius as an unsuccessful attempt to return to true doctrine frustrated by false philosophical presuppositions. If you adopt Werner's thesis, you regard the Arians as the heirs and restorers of the true doctrine. The weakness of all these points of view is, of course, that each scholar starts from a different assumption of what was true Christianity, what was the norm from which deviation erred. Their criticism of the history of Christian doctrine has often been valuable, but their theories suffer from an apparently fatal subjectivism.

We may however draw one common conclusion from all these views of the development of Christian doctrine. Dogma cannot simply be read straightforwardly off the text of the Old Testament or the New Testament. The early Church did not teach the doctrine of the Athanasian Creed nor of the Nicene Creed nor of the Chalcedonian Formula. These doctrines do in some sense represent something new in doctrine. Newman saw this point and his genius ensured that everybody else should see it too. What are we to do about it?

IX

The New Testament does not supply us with a Christian doctrine of God. All it supplies us with is the materials for composing such a doctrine. In the New Testament we find writers who have inherited the conception of God at which late ancient Judaism had arrived, and who also have certain convictions, expressed in very diverse ways, about the activity and the significance of Jesus Christ. But these two sets of conceptions are nowhere in the New Testament made consistent with each other so as to form a coherent doctrine of God different from the Jewish doctrine. The task of achieving this coherent statement of the implications of a belief in Christ for the doctrine of God was a long and arduous one, and was only gradually achieved by a system of trial and error by the early Church during the first few centuries of its existence. Similarly, there is no doctrine of the incarnation in the New Testament. The verb (but not the noun) first appears only in Melito, and the noun in Irenaeus, if we are to trust his Latin translation as rendering by the word *incarnatio* some such Greek word as *ensarkōsis* or *ensomatōsis* rather than the less specific *oikonomia*. The concept may indeed be perceived to be gradually forming itself in the pages of the New Testament, especially at John 1.14. But it can hardly be said that any other book of the New Testament speaks in terms of incarnation, though it is of course easy to see that materials for a doctrine of the incarnation are readily at hand in Matthew, in Paul, and in Hebrews.

The process whereby the doctrine of the Trinity and the doctrine of the incarnation were achieved was not a simple one of directly interpreting the biblical evidence, as an intelligent candidate at an examination today might gather all the various texts together and expound how they contribute to these results. It was a very complex process, only gradually completed, at the cost of much heart-searching, many false trails, and immense controversy. It was not even formally a matter of interpreting the New Testament alone, for all the Fathers thought that they were also interpreting the Old Testament in arriving at the dogmatic conclusions to which they contributed. And, further, we cannot dispute the contribution made to the result by the fact that all those who helped to form these dogmas were themselves worshipping Christians and were almost always writing for worshipping Christians. The specifically Christian experience of God was one important ingredient in the formation of these dogmas. And there is one more element in this process to be noticed, the contribution of ancient philosophy. No coherent Christian doctrine of God—not even Barth's—has been achieved without calling in the aid of philosophy in some form, simply because the Bible does not afford enough material to produce a consistent doctrine without using some non-biblical form of thought as well. The use of the *homoousion* in the Nicene Creed, and of the concept of *physis* in the Chalcedonian formula are only two examples of this. It must be conceded that other forces besides purely and strictly the evidence of the Bible were at work in the formation of Christian doctrine; and not only this: it is difficult to see how Christian doctrine could have been formed in any other way. Not only did the Church allow the experience of the worshipping community and the usages of contemporary non-biblical thought to influence it, but the Church was quite right in doing so; it was yielding to a proper historical necessity.

Christianity therefore consists, not simply of the 'theology' of the New Testament (nor of the Old Testament), because in the strict sense there is no such thing as a 'theology' of the New Testament etc., but only materials in the Old Testament and the New Testament for a Christian theology. Christian doctrine is formed by the witness of the Bible being reflected upon, interpreted, and lived out in a worshipping community by the aid of contemporary philosophy. The reason why the Old Testament was accepted by the Church approximately as the Jews had handed it down and why the New Testament was canonized was because they were thought to give indispensable historical witness for the proclamation of the Christian gospel, and as a necessary development of this for the formation of Christian doctrine. They were not intended to be, they were not used as, the sole elements, the sole basis, in the intellectual development of the Christian message. They were not used in a vacuum, *in abstracto*.

In discussing Christian doctrine, then, or in teaching or preaching it, to move directly from the witness of the New Testament to the present day is to create an unreal abstraction. It is in fact done by almost nobody who today attempts to present Christian doctrine, and it is an extremely difficult, if not impossible, task to perform. To rely on the Bible and the Bible alone, uninfluenced by any dogma, entirely excluding the testimony of Christian religious experience in handling Christian doctrine, demands powers of abstraction of a very high order, and if the task were achieved the results would probably strike most people as grotesque. Even those who call us to believe in 'the Christ-event' or 'the pure gospel' or 'salvation by faith alone' consciously or unconsciously appear to assume the dogmas of the divinity of Christ and of the incarnation. This is only another way of saying that the Bible only comes to life or makes sense when understood within the tradition of a worshipping community. *Mutatis mutandis* this is probably also true for the Old Testament within the tradition of Judaism. Deliberately to abandon a dogmatic tradition, or a tradition in which doctrine develops, to produce a Christianity which would be discontinuous with that tradition but would still attempt to preserve the witness of the Bible, if such a feat were feasible, would result in a construction so abstract and unreal as to be not recognizable as Christianity. In fact, it would not *be* Christianity.

This means that the Bible is dependent upon the Church. It is not only inseparable from the Church, it is dependent upon it. Used outside the tradition, the life, the experience of the Church, the Bible becomes opaque; indeed it begins to disintegrate into diverse and insignificant fragments. Viewed simply as a collection of ancient documents, the New Testament at least appears fragmentary, contingent, and inarticulated. What could be more casual, more like a telephone conversation overheard in fragments, than 2 Corinthians? How abruptly the Gospel of Mark plunges us into the concerns and preoccupations of the primitive Jewish Christian Church, and with what mysterious abruptness it ends! I say nothing of the insoluble obscurity of some of the Psalms, nor of those many isolated passages in the books of Isaiah, of Jeremiah, and of Ezekiel whose historical context and reference cannot be conjectured with any certainty, and perhaps will never be known. We cannot even determine with entire certainty the exact limits of the literature that comprises the Bible. The Christian Church has never made up its mind about the precise status of the Apocrypha, and in recent times it has become an open question whether we should include the last eight verses of Mark's Gospel and the *pericope de adultera* in the Scriptures at all. Moreover, the New Testament pretty clearly overlaps with the literature of the sub-apostolic period both in quality and in time. Can it honestly be said that the second epistle of Peter has some superior quality of relevance or insight which the epistles of Ignatius lack? Indeed it is likely that Ignatius' epistles were written earlier than 2 Peter, and 1 Clement may be an older document than 1 Timothy. There is in fact no rounded completeness in the New Testament. What gives it its apparent unity is its use by the Church as a collection of documents designed to provide historical testimony.

Newman in his famous book *The Development of Christian Doctrine* stated clearly and honestly the conclusions which have just been put before you. He did not, of course, express them as radically as they have been expressed here, but I think that his position was fundamentally similar to this one. He spoke of the acorn developing into a tree, of the spring developing into a river, of something whose small beginnings are no measure of its later expansion. He realized that the great dogmas enshrining the Christian doctrine of God and of the work of Christ (the incarnation) were a development from the ideas and the doctrine represented in the New Testament. He firmly grasped the nettle of development. An acorn cannot be a norm to a tree. A spring cannot be regarded as a norm for a river, but only a starting-point. He in effect relegated the Bible to the position of foundation and starting-point to that development, but no more. He shifted the norm from the Bible to the Church. For him the criterion of orthodox development became, not whether the development was agreeable to Scripture, but whether the Christian body creating the development has a right to declare that it is agreeable to Scripture. When you have found the true Church, then you have solved the problem of right development. What that Church declares to be agreeable to Scripture must be agreeable because that Church has declared it so. True doctrine is the doctrine taught by the true Church, and it is true because the Church says so. In view of the greatly enhanced appreciation of the fragmentariness and casualness of the Bible which we have acquired since Newman's day, would we not be best advised to follow Newman's example, and to articulate a full-blown theory of the development of doctrine?

X

Curiously enough, Irenaeus and Tertullian had already in a sense anticipated Newman's argument. Faced with the rival interpretations of the Bible sedulously conducted by Gnostics, they had tried to move the argument altogether off the field of the Bible, and had appealed to the rule of faith of the Church. The Church had taught its rule of faith from the beginning, and the Scriptures, when the Church wrote them, were no more than a restatement of this rule in another form. The heretics had therefore no right to argue about the Scriptures, and could, formally speaking, be refuted without them. So Irenaeus implied in at least one passage in the *adversus haereses*, and so Tertullian explicitly argued at the beginning of his *de praescriptione haereticorum* and elsewhere. (Irenaeus, *adv. haer.* 3.4.1; Tertullian, *de praescr. haer.* 14–18, 19, 20, 31, 37; *Apol.* 47.10; *adv. Marc.* 1.1.6, 3.1.2; 5.19.1; *Adv. Herm.* 1.1; *de carne Christi* 2.3.5). But both authors are half-hearted in this argument, and spend much more time arguing from scripture than arguing about the superfluity of scripture, and both unselfconsciously support the rule of faith by appeal to scripture. I think that their attempt to appeal to the Church's tradition instead of scripture rests upon a similar fallacy to that which also underlies Newman's argument. How are we to know the true Church? By looking at the apostolic succession of bishops or teachers, said Irenaeus and Tertullian. But here we have only to ask, apostolic succession going back to what? The answer must be, to Christ and his apostles. But who are they, and why should we take any notice of them? Because the Bible tells us that.... Here we are back again at the appeal to scripture. Newman's answer to the question, 'How can we know which is the true Church?' was not as simple as to say directly, 'By seeking the one most closely adhering to scriptural principles', though some of his arguments approach this position. But if we ask a more fundamental question of Newman we shall attain the same result. 'Why should we look for a Church at all? What *is* the Church, that we should seek it? If we do not simply accept the Church on its own valuation, to what can it point to substantiate its claims?' The only answer to that can be, 'Because the Bible tells us that the Church is the community of Jesus Christ.' The *petitio principii* is therefore revealed in the statement that the test of orthodoxy in development is not agreement with the scriptures as a norm but the exclusive authority of the Church which conducts the development.

Further, the Bible was deliberately chosen by the Church as a norm. It was never regarded as simply the earliest example of Christian literature. Non-biblical Christian literature was, after all, well known by the Church Fathers from an early date. Tatian and Irenaeus knew Justin's work; Tertullian knew Irenaeus' books, as did Origen. Origen knew Ignatius' Epistles and 1 Clement, and so on. Even though for several centuries the line between canonical and non-canonical literature was blurred, the Fathers always treated as normative that which they identified as scripture. These scriptural documents were very quickly credited with inspiration and inerrancy and thought of as supplying prefrabricated a complete system of doctrine, but originally they were chosen as constituting historical witness, as crystallizing in the permanent written form the oral tradition about the acts and significance of Jesus Christ because, by the lapse of time, purely oral tradition was becoming unreliable and corrupted. And this function of historical witness, this quality of *Einmaligkeit*, has always attached to the Bible and must always attach to it. The very choosing of some books to be in the canon implies that the canon must (as the Greek word *kanōn* implies) be a norm.

In fact it is not difficult to see that the Old Testament, as a collection of documents, is the only collection adequately witnessing to the history of God's dealing with the ancient Jewish people, and was deliberately preserved by the Jews for this purpose. And the New Testament constitutes, *as a collection*, unique historical witness to the life and career of Christ and to earliest, primitive Christianity. I say 'as a collection' because of the fact, already noticed in this book, that the latest parts of the New Testament overlap in time with the earliest parts of non-biblical Christian literature.

We have stated earlier that the Bible is dependent upon the Church. We now perceive that the Church is also dependent upon the Bible. Without the Bible as independent, carefully-preserved historical witness, the Church could not substantiate its claims nor explain its origins. Without the Bible, it might conduct a fascinating and dizzy development of doctrine into all sorts of new exciting forms and dogmas, but it would have no means of showing that these new developments had anything particular to do with God or with Jesus Christ. By canonizing the Bible, the

Church placed the Bible over itself as a norm of its belief and doctrine and preaching, as a deliberate control. It thereby acknowledged that it could not teach or preach whatever it liked, that it was responsible to the historical teaching of Christ and the preaching of the apostles. In this act of canonizing these documents the Church also gave up a certain control over its own inherited tradition which it had received in an oral form and which it handed on in a written form. It acknowledged that it could not ever henceforward turn back the clock of history and stand where it stood in the early years to supplement the Bible or to substitute something in its stead.

But the normative function of the Bible is based upon something even deeper. Involved in the very life of Christianity, and at the heart of it, is the historical existence, the appearance as an identifiable personality, of Jesus Christ, and the continuity of this historical personality with the personality of the risen Jesus seen and met by the apostles and the early disciples. We cannot eliminate from Christianity what von Hügel called the 'element of happenedness', this mooring of Christianity to a particular point in history. The reason for this is that the content of the 'Christ of the Church's faith' is provided by the historical personality of Jesus. In fact, the distinction between 'the Christ of the Church's faith' and 'the Christ of history' is unreal. The first rests upon and gains its form from the second, and the second would be insignificant and meaningless without the first. This fact cannot be by-passed and must not be explained away, however awkward it may be, and may always have been, to historians, and however troublesome it may have been and may still be to philosophers. At this fact we reach the core of the Christian faith, of God's self-communication to man.

This historical attachment has an important consequence for our understanding of the development of Christian doctrine. It means that this development can never depart very far from the historical witness of the Bible; it means that development is in a sense bound by historical limits. It means that development will not proceed in a steady line of ever more remote and complex, albeit logical, articulation, the theologians of each generation busily building, like sea insects, new layers of coral, till the whole towers into a vast and stately mass of carefully structured doctrine. On the contrary, development is likely to proceed rather in an alternating, or even a circular, movement, now moving away from the given historical data, now returning as the line of history, so to speak, pulls it in. It is of course, as I believe some contemporary Roman Catholic theologians have been observing recently, premature to speak confidently of the development of doctrine regularly in any one direction until we can be sure that we are standing at the end of the process of development. In fact we are ourselves involved in the process whose movement we are trying to plot, and this makes all prediction uncertain. But if we are to make predictions about the development of doctrine by observing its course of development hitherto, which is the only ground upon which we can make such prediction, then it would be very unwise to assume that Newman's prediction of a steady, unwavering line of continuous development is the most likely one. His schematic view of unwavering continuous doctrinal development in the past will not fit what we know of the past history of Christian doctrine. He simply ignored all the discontinuities, the periods spent in blind alleys, the returns to earlier doctrine, the prunings of tradition, the revivals of neglected elements, the attempts to suppress such features of Christianity as eschatology or sacramental life, which later take their vengeance in a violent *revanche*. These things make Newman's scheme of steady expansion and articulation by dogma after dogma appear artificial and unreal.

Development need not be confined to what is formally called 'dogma'. We need not assume *a priori* that it is only through the pronouncements of General Councils that doctrinal development can take place. Much of what the Reformers of the sixteenth century contended for is now accepted by almost all traditions within Christianity, yet the Reformers never formulated a 'dogma'. Almost all Christian traditions are now in the process of assimilating the results of historical criticism, and clearly this process will have considerable effect upon their doctrine; among other gains, they are through this assimilation learning the importance of an understanding of history for theology. But this assimilation has not been achieved by formulating 'dogma'. The dogma-producing method may have served other ages well. But the attempts of the Roman Catholic Church to produce dogma during the last hundred years or so do not encourage us to think that this is the best way of managing the development of doctrine in our time.

We cannot, therefore, deny either the dependence of the Bible on the Church or of the Church on the Bible. The Bible is involved with the life and tradition of the Church and the Church's dogma and doctrine are involved with the Bible, because the Bible is a norm consisting of historical witness to the activity of God towards his chosen people culminating in the coming of Jesus Christ. The Bible is, however, only significant within a tradition; it is intended as a norm for that tradition, but only for that tradition and not for any other. This is not an impossible or self-contradictory situation. An analogy, though not a perfect analogy, is provided by the relation of the judge to the law in the political system of this country. He does not make the law; he does not attempt to control or manipulate the law; he interprets it, and in the process he creates a tradition of judicial decisions which are thenceforward valid. So the Church does not control the Bible but interprets it and in the process creates an authoritative doctrinal tradition. (The definition of the Church and the limits of dogma are dealt with later in this book.)

XI

Finally something must be said about the principles which should govern our use of the Bible as a norm today. We live in a period of confusion, of the blurring and the mutual fertilization of hitherto distinct theological traditions, at a time when the scientific investigation of both Old Testament and New Testament is in full swing, and there is no obvious prospect of either discipline reaching final and agreed conclusions on any important subject. It is one thing to declare theoretically that the Bible can be a norm for Christian doctrine; it is another to discover the principles by which it can be used as a norm in this quite new and in many ways perplexing situation. I believe that the following principles could well be explicitly acknowledged by all scholars:

1. We must take seriously a fact which has always been conceded tacitly by both ancient Judaism and early Christianity, as the evidence of lectionaries suggests, and which has been widely allowed by almost all students of the Old Testament for nearly a hundred years. This is the fact that the witness of the Bible is of differing value and importance in different parts of it. Even though Origen believed in the existence of a 'special sense' latent in every passage of scripture, he would not have argued that Ehud is as important as Amos. And nobody after him, whatever their formal exegetical principles may have been, would have been bold enough to

maintain the thesis of the equality of these two. The text 'a pomegranate and a knop, a pomegranate and a knop, in the borders thereof round about' (Exod. 28.34) cannot be of equal value with the text 'Comfort ye, comfort ye my people, saith your God' (Isa. 40.1). These are obvious examples of this principle. But we are sufficiently mature today in the new understanding of the Bible brought by historical criticism to apply this principle logically to the New Testament also. One verse in 2 Peter is not a sufficient basis for the doctrine that we are all destined to share God's nature (2 Pet. 1.4) rather than God's life, as the rest of the New Testament teaches. One passage in the Epistle of James (5.14f) is not enough to justify the practice of extreme unction as a sacrament instituted by the apostles, nor two passages in Acts sufficient to give the rite of confirmation that supreme value which Anglicans sometimes seem to attach to it (8.14–17; 19.1–7). We must look for widespread testimony for any doctrine, and if possible for testimony in those parts of the New Testament which are at the heart of the New Testament as well as from those which are on the periphery and are later and less authoritative. We must face the consequence of realizing that the New Testament was not written all at once in a short time by a few apostles, but that its documents spread over quite a long period, perhaps as long as seventy years, that the Pauline Epistles come first, then the synoptic Gospels, then Acts and Hebrews and Revelation, then the fourth Gospel, then the deutero-Pauline letters and the Catholic Epistles. And we must be prepared to regard the fourth Gospel as canonized interpretation of the significance of Jesus rather than as a reliable account of his acts and words.

2. Secondly if we are to use the Bible as a norm for Christian doctrine we must recognize honestly the diversity of witness within the New Testament itself. Instead of forming sentences beginning with the words 'the Bible says', or 'the New Testament says', we should face the fact that there are in the New Testament a number of different, independent interpretations of the significance of Jesus, not always consistent with each other. There are the distinct interpretations of Mark, of Matthew, of Luke-Acts, of Paul, of the Johannine literature, and the separate contributions of Hebrews and of 1 Peter and of Revelation, not to mention possible distinct sources within these sources. This is not to say that the New Testament must be regarded as an incoherent medley of dissonant

statements. It is a series of separate interpretations of the same Person and the same events, having certain assumptions in common—e.g., the assumption about the eschatological significance of Jesus—but also differing on many points, the whole constituting a rich and many-sided testimony to the deep and mysterious influence of Jesus Christ upon those who knew him in the flesh and those who first heard the gospel about him. The New Testament is not a single looking-glass or window. It is more like a series of lenses of different composition and power through which we look in succession at the same object.

3. The third principle to be observed in treating the Bible as a norm is a logical consequence of the last one. We must recognize that the Bible does not, as the Fathers of the early Church and many others after them thought it did, provide us with prefabricated, ready-made doctrine, already processed and packaged. It is for us to compare the different aspects which we see through different lenses with each other and to decide upon the colour and shape of the object shown to us by them. It is for us to sum up the total impression made by the different interpretations and to express this in the form of doctrine. What the Bible gives us is not doctrine in any form but witness. The Bible is not a manual of doctrine; no Trinitarian dogma, no 'fact of the incarnation' lies ready to hand in its pages, capable of being read directly off its text. The Bible is not a text-book of ethics; if you wish to solve an ethical problem you will probably find in the Bible at least one direct contradiction on the subject and you will have to assess the evidence carefully. The Bible does not provide a blueprint for the ministry; though all denominations, even those who believe that there should be no distinctive ministry at all, have claimed to find their ideas about ministry confirmed in the Bible, I do not believe that we can find in its pages authority for any single exclusively valid ministry. The Bible is not a liturgical directory, it is a singularly sterile task to search its pages for light on either baptismal or eucharistic services. Neither is the Bible a customary to direct our ecclesiastical affairs. It provides the raw material from which we can draw or by which we can measure doctrine on all these subjects.

We must behave responsibly towards the Bible, recognizing its nature and function, and also recognizing its limitations. We ought to acknowledge frankly where it does *not* shed light. I have already suggested two fields where we must not ask for specific guidance from the Bible, the form of the ministry and the form of eucharistic worship; a third is the nature of the next life. What the Bible supplies us with is not an inexhaustible, inerrant, infallible treasury of all possible theological and ecclesiastical information, but—to use a good Anglican word—sufficiency. It supplies us with enough material for our salvation, enough testimony to guide the Church in the house of its pilgrimage. It does so in its own way which we must recognize and respect. Catholics may have erred in finding too little in the Bible, but Protestants have certainly erred in finding too much in it. As those of us who are concerned with teaching doctrine today consider our task, which is not the least difficult of the tasks that face theologians today, we have to keep in mind this duty of the Church to preserve a creative, but also an honest, relationship to the Bible.

NOTES

1 For most of all the foregoing statements and of my account of Philo and of Origen I refer the reader to chapters 1–4 and 7 of my book *Allegory and Event.*

3 *Dogma*

I

THE NATURE OF CHRISTIAN DOGMA

The history of theological thought in the twentieth century is one full of interest, variety, surprise, and promise. It has seen the appearance and disappearance of Liberal Protestantism and Modernism; it has seen neo-Thomism, the rise of neo-orthodoxy with the work of Karl Barth, biblical theology, the Liturgical Movement, the eclipse of literary criticism of the Gospels by the methods of form criticism, the influence of Rudolf Bultmann, the effects of the flight from metaphysics in philosophy, existentialism, and linguistic analysis, the Ecumenical Movement, the Second Vatican Council and all that has flowed from it, and now, most recently, the return to a kind of eschatology in the work of Moltmann and Pannenberg, and in the writings of Küng and of Rahner and of several others the enterprise of taking philosophical and theological categories coined by Protestant theologians and filling them with a Catholic content.

The situation now makes it possible for both Catholic and Protestant theologians to build a theology based upon the concept of the Word of God. All Christian theology must start with this thought. Ever since the Reformation Protestant theologians (though Anglicans have usually formed an exception here) have based their doctrines and systems upon this ground. But it is only recently that Roman Catholic theologians have found themselves free to give it a central place in their thought. As the basic historical phenomenon in Christianity is the Church preaching the Word, as this is the fact which has to be explained, from which all historical judgement or examination of Christianity must start, so the concept of the Word of God must be the basic concept for all Christian theology. If the Church is asked what is the Word which it is preaching, it must refer the questioner to the Bible, and in particular to the New Testament. In the New Testament we find a Church preaching a gospel or a Word. The earliest, the most primitive and in some respects the basic documents of the

New Testament are not the Gospels, but the Epistles of St Paul. Here we find indeed Jesus Christ at the centre of the Church's message, but specifically Jesus as Risen Lord, as Saviour, as Son of God. And in these Epistles the phrase 'Word of God' does not mean merely a message, a transcript of some propositions communicated or commended to us by God, but the activity of God towards us in Christ, our encounter with God as he makes an act of self-disclosure to us which is at the same time an act of reconciliation and redemption. It means the moment at which, the means by which, the *drama* of God's redemption in Christ meets us and involves us. At its deepest level, where Paul expresses its innermost meaning, as in Rom. 5, 1 Cor. 1, and 2 Cor. 5, it means nothing less than God's self-communication in Christ. We shall return to this point later in this book.

This is the right point at which to begin Christian theology. Various religious traditions have in the past been inclined to begin at other points. The Roman Catholic Church has tended to begin theology with the authority of the Church. The subject of the Church's authority is, of course, an important one and Protestants have too often tended to neglect or ignore it. But it cannot be the basic, primary subject. If any Christian tradition takes the attitude that the Church has the right to know its own gospel, to determine its own Scriptures, and to demand of the inquirer that he shall believe the Word simply because the Church says so, this position can always be turned by asking, 'What is the Church and why should I accept its authority?' It is impossible to answer this question without referring to the Bible as at least an historical authority. We are then reduced to the original position of finding in the Bible the picture of the primitive Church preaching the Word.

The Anglican Communion, on the other hand, has at least during the last century tended to take as the starting point for its theology the words of Jesus as recorded in the Gospels. This is a very natural tendency, which appeals at once to unreflecting minds. But it is a wrong tendency. Our final authority should not be, and cannot be, Jesus simply as an historical figure, Jesus in the days of his flesh, Jesus as a teacher, even Jesus as an earthly example. To put the matter in its crudest form, our only reason for listening to him as a man is because we think that he is more than a man. Some little time ago an effective and moving television story was made of the life of Jesus. It was a completely unconventional presentation of the subject, and it ended with the death of Jesus on the Cross and his cry, 'My God, my God, why hast thou forsaken me?' When viewers had recovered from the immediate emotional impact of the story presented in this way, they must have realized, if they were capable of intelligent reflection, that the story was in one way a complete fraud. It was like giving a picture of the Napoleonic wars but omitting to mention the battle of Waterloo. For, whatever we may think of the resurrection, if there had been no resurrection, or if we are to be meticulous we should perhaps say, if the first disciples had not thought that they saw Jesus risen, and if all Christians ever afterwards had not believed them, nobody would have had the slightest interest in Jesus of Nazareth. No Epistles would have been written, no Gospels compiled; neither Josephus nor Tacitus nor Suetonius would have mentioned him. We are interested in the words of Jesus because he is the self-disclosure of God, and the fact that he is the self-disclosure of God is logically, though not chronologically, prior to his words. We cannot in all cases be sure that the words attributed to Jesus in the Gospels were his *ipsissima verba*. This is a brutal and disconcerting truth which has by no means yet percolated to the grass roots of the Christian community in any of its denominations. It does not mean that uncertainty is thrown upon all the recorded words of Jesus, as simple Christian clergy and laity tend to think when this perplexing fact is first presented to them. But it does mean that a theology which takes the words of Jesus as its starting point and basis is rendered even less satisfactory in the twentieth century than it has been in previous ages. We might add that the words attributed to Jesus in the Gospels are comparatively few and cannot possibly be made to cover even the main points of Christian doctrine and ethics.

This argument, however, does not mean to go to the length of ignoring the historical Jesus, the Jesus who walked the lanes of Galilee and the streets of Jerusalem, or of declaring that this figure, though theoretically identifiable, is theologically insignificant. This is far from being the case. The thinking and preaching of the Christian theologian must start from Jesus Christ as preached by the primitive Church, Jesus as Risen Lord and Saviour. But an essential and inseparable part of this Risen Lord is Jesus of Nazareth, Jesus who is identifiable as an historical figure, whose character, if not his biography, can be reconstructed with confidence. The early Church did not preach an apocalyptic cipher, an eschatological event void of content, when it preached Jesus as Lord. Paul is very sparing in his quotations of the words of Jesus, but nobody can fail to see that Paul knew of the *character* of Jesus, that he knew, for instance, that he was unselfish, loving, compassionate, full of faith and courage; and the same holds true for the book of Acts, the Epistle to the Hebrews, and the First Epistle of Peter. Behind the Risen Lord we can see the Jesus of history. Those persons to whom Jesus appeared after his death did not merely see a blinding vision, they recognized a known person. And the character of that person is the historical content of the message concerning the Risen Lord. The Gospels very extensively enlarge and illuminate our knowledge of that person and that character. And without a knowledge of the character of Jesus the preaching of the early Church would have been powerless and empty. But it is still true that we must start our theology from Jesus as Risen, Jesus as exalted Lord. True, it is *Jesus*, not an apocalyptic *x*, who is the Risen Lord. In that word is all that the Gospels can tell us about him and beyond that the whole complex and rich history of the Jewish people which led up to him. But unless we begin our theology with the Word of God as apprehended in Jesus Christ, we have no particular authority for being interested in Jesus at all.

We can perhaps take one further step in this argument and ask, 'Why do we believe that Jesus is the Word of God?' And here the answer can only be that the total picture of Jesus in the New Testament gives us this impression, together with the experience of Jesus by the Church, contemporary and past. It may well be that in order to understand the divinity of Christ we must approach his divinity through his humanity, instead of attempting to regard the two as parallel and in some sense independently observable, as the Church of the Fathers was inclined to do. But this is not to take the humanity of Jesus alone, the behaviour of Jesus as an historical character isolated from any other aspect of him, and to build on this as the ultimate theological foundation. Our theological foundation must be to take the whole Jesus, Jesus Christ as proclaimed and believed in by the primitive Church, Jesus Christ after the resurrection, and to build on that. Even though our approach to his divinity is today through his humanity, we do not build on his humanity alone. His humanity is such that it compels us to ask questions which go beyond it until we perceive that he is not simply Jesus the craftsman of Nazareth but Jesus

Christ the Son of God who has risen from the dead and is our Saviour and Lord. That is why the starting point for our theology must be the Word of God as it is presented to us in the New Testament, and particularly in the Epistles of St Paul.

The doctrine of the Word of God must indeed be the starting-point for our theology, but our theology cannot possibly end here. There still exists a naïve belief in most Protestant traditions that it is possible to confine Christian doctrine entirely to the limits of the Bible and almost entirely to the vocabulary of the Bible. It must be said at once, without infringing the right of the Bible to be the norm of Christian doctrine, that it is utterly impossible to confine Christian doctrine to the limits and to the vocabulary of the Bible, and that no Christian body has ever successfully done so, no matter how much it may have deluded itself into thinking that it has succeeded in this enterprise. Two considerations (to take only two) should prevent our falling into this delusion, both of which will be dealt with at greater length in later essays in this volume. First, the Christian Gospel as we find it in the New Testament is presented in an eschatological framework which it is utterly impossible for us to reproduce faithfully and literally today; this truth was recognized by the Church as early as the second century, when it changed from an eschatological to a christological presentation of its gospel. Even if we make the futile attempt, as some very *simpliste* Christian traditions still do make, to work ourselves into a state of mind in which we can believe that the Second Coming of Jesus Christ will take place in a very short time, we have done nothing to explain away the fact that if Christians of the earliest period held the same belief (and they clearly did) they were obviously mistaken. If nearly two thousands years ago the belief in an early return of Christ was erroneous, why should we believe in an 'early' return of Christ today? We may take refuge in the conviction of the author of 2 Pet. (3.3–10) that the word 'early' in God's sight may include periods of thousands of years. But this is only an ingenious way of saying that the phrase 'early return of Christ' has now become meaningless. Whatever else we do with the eschatological language of the New Testament (and various suggestions about what can be done will be made in a later essay in this book), it is futile and absurd to believe that we can return to the same attitude towards it as that adopted by the Christians of the first generation. We must apply reflection to the eschatological language of the New Testament; we cannot simply reproduce it without explanation. In other words, we must create doctrine. We must develop our thought beyond the limits of the New Testament.

The second consideration is that the New Testament does not supply us with a consistent doctrinal system. The Church has to work this system out for itself, though the only source of raw materials for this system is the Bible; we may perhaps derive our method and our logic from other sources, but the only conceivable source of the doctrine itself is the Bible. The Bible does not supply us with a complete and consistent and philosophically viable Christian doctrine of God. It presents the reader with the doctrine of God of late ancient Judaism on the one hand, and on the other with a number of statements about somebody called Jesus Christ. But it makes only the most rudimentary progress towards integrating these two things, towards producing a doctrine of God which is specifically and recognizably Christian. He does not tell us what precisely is the difference made to our doctrine of who God is by the phenomenon of Jesus Christ. As long as Christians were no more than a sect within Judaism, or as long as any Christians today are content to live in a cocoon of self-absorption without attempting to make any intellectual contact with the outer world, then the question of the Christian doctrine of God need not be raised. But Christianity, quite rightly, makes intellectual claims. It long ago found itself in a position in which it was bidding for the allegiance of well-educated and intelligent people who had no contact with Jewish culture at all, people who would inevitably and with every justification challenge it to produce a consistent Christian doctrine of God. The process of enlarging, articulating, and developing the witness of the New Testament, of building upon the doctrine of the Word of God, began. There was no alternative. This process is called the process of the formation of dogma. It was a process which led the Church beyond the limits and the vocabulary of the Bible.

Many people assume that the process of the formation of dogma is the same as the process of the formation of the creed. If this assumption is meant to apply to the creed known as the Apostles' Creed, it is false. The Apostles' Creed is a curious production. As a matter of strict historical pedigree, its origins are distinct both from the New Testament and from the Rule of Faith, though it was generally assumed during the second and third centuries to be a rudimentary summary of the Rule of Faith. But we shall see how far it is from being a strictly dogmatic formula when we realize that the Apostles' Creed mentions neither the doctrine of the Trinity, the doctrine of the incarnation, nor the doctrine of the atonement. It can hardly be said to observe what the Second Vatican Council usefully described as 'the hierarchy of truths'. What, for instance, is the position of the article which mentions the Descent into Hell and of that which mentions the Resurrection of the Body? What do these two doctrines mean? If we can painfully transpose them into some statement which is not purely fantastic, where do they rank in order of importance in our presentation of Christian doctrine? The fact is that the Apostles' Creed is, as I have said elsewhere, a kind of doctrinal washing-line. On a washing-line there are displayed indiscriminately alongside foundation garments other articles, like handkerchiefs and headscarves, which, while useful and perhaps decorative, cannot be described as indispensable. If therefore we are to consider the nature of Christian dogma, we will not advance our investigation by turning to the Apostles' Creed.

There are of course other formulae which we can consult in order to understand the nature of Christian dogma. Some of them are considered in the essays which follow this one. At this point, however, this essay will take an arbitrary step and instead of following the logical course of examining one by one the major traditional doctrinal formulae will put forward for the consideration of its readers a thesis concerning Christian dogma.

There are only three necessary and fundamental dogmas in the Christian faith, only three basic convictions flowing from our encounter with God in Christ which give Christianity an unalterable and permanent shape and without which Christianity would not be Christianity. They are the dogma of the Trinity, the dogma of the incarnation, and the dogma of the atonement. They could be described as the doctrine concerning the nature of God himself, the doctrine concerning God's relations with history and the doctrine concerning God's relations with man. No other Christian doctrine can be considered equal in importance to these. All other Christian doctrines worthy of the name flow from these fundamental three. Development of Christian doctrine takes place and must take place round these three dogmas, and these only. Indeed the three can themselves be regarded as the product of a development, in as far as the Trinity is not mentioned in the New Testament and the word 'incarnation' does not occur till the second century. If they are the product of development, however, it is only that form of development which explores and discovers what lies behind and beneath the data supplied by the Bible, not a type of development which works to prolong to their furthest extent the ideas to be found in the Bible so as to reach conclusions ever more and more remote from the text, even though still connected with it by a logical argument. In order to understand what is meant in this essay by the word 'dogma' we must examine the three doctrines in rather more detail.

The doctrine of the Holy Trinity, of God as three Persons but one God, is usually regarded as the example *par excellence* of Christian dogma. By most clergy of all denominations it is regarded with respect, but with distant respect. They do not profess to understand it. They seldom or never preach on it. They accept it as handed down to them from the past, and leave it, not disowned, but disregarded, thinking of it as either a venerable relic or as something which may be true but which is beyond them. But in fact it is a doctrine which was only reached after nearly four centuries of trial and error, after the best intellects of the Christian Church had exercised themselves upon the subject as upon something which was of the highest importance to Christians. It represents a necessity to which the Church found itself driven after deep heart-searching, thorny controversy, and much vicissitude. It is the considered answer of the Church to the searching and unavoidable question addressed to it by the educated world, 'What difference does your Jesus Christ make to your knowledge of who God is?' It is the fully-fledged, mature statement by the Church of the specifically Christian doctrine of God, only achieved after many alternative answers had been tried and found wanting. It is a doctrine which has been honestly hammered out upon the anvil of history. There is about it a cogency, a profoundly basic quality, which Karl Barth has expressed incomparably in his exposition of this dogma in the first volumes of his vast work on Church doctrine.

But this foundation dogma of the Church's faith has never been expressed in a single, final formula accepted as formally unalterable by the whole Church. The Apostles' Creed makes no mention of it whatever, as we have observed. The Nicene Creed contains the doctrine of the consubstantiality of the Father and the Son and the statement that the Holy Spirit proceeds from the Father and (or through) the Son and that he is worshipped and glorified with the Father and the Son. But it makes no mention of three Persons in one Godhead. It does not mention the word 'Trinity'. The so-called 'Athanasian' Creed does indeed contain a concise and lapidary statement of the doctrine of the Trinity, but this formula was produced in the West in the fifth century and has never been accepted by the Eastern Church and in its present form is never likely to be. The doctrine of the holy Trinity can of course be collected over and over again from the writing of eminent theologians all down the ages. But they have all expressed the doctrine in a rather different way from their predecessors. The manner of presenting this doctrine to be found in the work of Athanasius and of Hilary of Poitiers in the middle of the fourth century is noticeably different from that in which the Cappadocian fathers, Basil of Caesarea, Gregory of Nazianzus, and Gregory of Nyssa, present it later in the century. Augustine's exposition of the doctrine in his *de Trinitate* early in the fifth century differs in some respects from all these, and we could go on to show that the same applies, for instance, to this dogma as presented by Thomas Aquinas, by Gregory Palamas, by John Calvin, and by Karl Barth. But nobody could doubt that it was the same dogma that all these men both believed in and expounded.

Further, we can justly say that the language traditionally used to express the doctrine of the Trinity is for our purposes today in many respects unsatisfactory. The most obvious example of this is the word *person*, which in its traditional use to mean the separately existing entities of Father, Son, and Spirit within one Godhead is widely different from its use in ordinary English usage today to mean a separate centre of subjective self-consciousness, with all the rich shades of meaning conferred on this concept by the development of the study of the human individual since the Renaissance. In a Trinitarian context today the use of the word 'person' is gravely misleading. Only less unsatisfactory is the use of the word *substance* or *essence* to express that which the three separately existing entities have in common. It is not easy for contemporary thought to accept the word *substance* to express that which makes God God. It is not surprising that modern versions of the Nicene Creed tend to speak of the Son as 'of one Being' with the Father.

It should, however, be noted that the very theologians who were most responsible for achieving the formulation of the doctrine of the Holy Trinity were fully aware, indeed acutely aware, of the inadequacy and provisional nature of the language which they found it necessary to use about God as Holy Trinity. It can readily be shown[1] that Athanasius, Hilary, Basil, the two Gregories and Augustine knew perfectly well that the language which they were using to express the dogma of the Trinity was unsatisfactory, that it was only being used *faute de mieux* and that it must be regarded as provisional. Unlike the rationalists of the fourth century (who were to be found among the extreme Arians) they had no serene confidence in the power of language to express truth about God. But they did not doubt that there was a reality to be expressed and that they must attempt as well as they could to express it, so that the truth about God should not be obscured or lost.

This is why it is most appropriate to call this dogma of the Holy Trinity, as we should call other dogmas, a *mystery*. This mystery is not a mystification; we cannot apply to it the phrase *omnia exeunt in mysterium*, if by that is meant that if you think rigorously about God you eventually reach a stage when you lose all landmarks, all contact with experienced reality, and are simply lost in a fog of uncertainty. A mystery means in this sense a reality which we know to be a reality but which we cannot completely express in words because it is too great for us, and in the Christian sense of the term it means a reality which can be to some extent also apprehended in prayer and in worship as well as in logical discourse. Even the most intransigent of creeds, the 'Athanasian', though it appears to teach that those who do not give intellectual assent to its considerably developed doctrines will burn everlastingly in hell, does state that

> the Catholic Faith is this, that we *worship* one God in Trinity and Trinity in Unity.

This mystery can be expressed differently at different times, according to the changing demands of philosophy and science and culture. It is open to re-exploration and restatement. We today perhaps would say that the doctrine of the holy Trinity means that in the nature of Godhead there is an outgoing and return in love, the Holy Spirit expressing this concept of return, rather than being best apprehended in terms of procession or gift. But our understanding of this dogma or mystery, though not wholly nor finally expressible in words, retains a recognizable shape which is imposed on it by necessity arising from the unchanging elements of Christianity itself.

The next basic dogma of the Christian faith is the dogma of the incarnation, the dogma that Jesus Christ is both fully God and fully man. Like the dogma of the Trinity, this doctrine was only reached gradually. For a long time, partly because the best minds in the Church were preoccupied with the task of working out the Christian doctrine of God, the necessities of this dogma were not fully realized. There operated here too a process of trial and error. Some of those who were quite orthodox on other subjects failed to realize that their attitude to the humanity of Jesus Christ was incompatible with the evidence of the New Testament and with a thoroughgoing belief in the incarnation of the Son of God. It was only in the middle of the fourth century that theologians began to be aware of how unsatisfactory it was to assume that Jesus Christ as man did not have a human mind. To the end of the patristic period all writers of the ancient Church found it more difficult to imagine realistically that Jesus was fully man than to allow that he was fully God.

At first sight it looks as if in this case there does exist a carefully devised formula for expressing this dogma, accepted by both the Eastern and the Western Church at a general Council. I refer, of course, to the Chalcedonian Formula of the year 451. In this Definition the Church appears to have provided itself with a final and unalterable form of words in which the dogma of the incarnation has been permanently stated. But closer inspection of the facts will throw doubt upon this assumption.

In the first place, it is doubtful whether the Chalcedonian Formula is completely compatible with an acknowledgement of the entire humanity of Jesus, even though it states that he was consubstantial with us according to his manhood. The concept of the hypostatic union adopted by this Formula from Cyril of Alexandria still leaves unanswered a difficult question. In this account Godhead and manhood are joined together in a single, unique entity and we are supposed to assume that the human nature has a divine *hypostasis* (though not a divine mind). What does *hypostasis* mean here? If it means that the human nature of Jesus Christ is not the same as our human nature, then it is difficult to see how a full incarnation has been achieved and how what is fully human in us can have been redeemed by a Saviour who is not fully human. If to speak of the human nature possessing a divine *hypostasis* does not mean that Christ's human nature is not like ours, what does it mean? Does it mean anything? Is not the Formula at this point involved with a term from Greek philosophy which does not further our grasp of the incarnation because it is not accurate enough to meet our needs today?

In the second place, the Chalcedonian Formula has been, so to speak, by-passed in our own day. Competent theologians among all the major Christian traditions, including A. Grillmeier, the outstanding authority upon the Council of Chalcedon, admit that the teaching and even the formula of those opponents of the Chalcedonian doctrine such as Dioscuros and Severus of Antioch were orthodox. Even representatives of the Eastern Orthodox churches have allowed, after two recent conferences held at Bristol and at Rhodes, that the christological doctrine of the so-called Monophysites of the central tradition was intending to express the same truth, though in different words, as the creators and champions of the Chalcedonian Definition intended to convey in their formulae. The facts entirely undermine the position of the Chalcedonian Formula as an ecumenically acknowledged and universally binding and permanently irreversible statement, though they do not prevent us from admiring the Formula as an admirable achievement within its limits, as we similarly may admire the 'Athanasian' Creed.

The dogma of the incarnation, then, has not been finally and permanently expressed in any form of words. In our own day what had been thought to be a permanent and magisterial expression of it has proved to be (relatively speaking) provisional and temporary, subject to the erosion of time. But behind the differing formulae we can recognize an enduring and permanent shape for this dogma, and once again, as in the case of the dogma of the Trinity, a shape necessitated by the facts of Christian history and Christian experience. Christians cannot believe that Jesus Christ is not fully man and they cannot believe that he is less than fully God, however widely their expressions of these convictions may vary according to time and place and language. And these convictions are quite compatible with the belief that this particular dogma is in special need of new expression in our age, for our age has seen the rise of the science of historical criticism, and historical criticism has very seriously affected this dogma of the incarnation which is more deeply concerned than any other with God's self-disclosure in history. But what must be newly expressed is not itself a new doctrine. The shape remains the same. It may very well be that we shall have a deeper and fuller understanding of this shape as we strive to express it in terms produced by the revolution in historical study. But if our new terms radically alter the shape, then we shall have reached a point where Christianity has ceased to be Christianity.

Our doctrine of the Church and our doctrine of the activity of the Holy Spirit in the Church and in the world must flow from this dogma of the incarnation. The incarnation does not only mean that Jesus Christ was incarnate; it means that he *is* incarnate. The place where he is to be encountered incarnate today is the Church. And the reason why we must call the Holy Spirit God is because the incarnation was not an isolated event, a closed incident in long past history, but continually occurs now and is now available for all men. Only if God is as Holy Spirit Lord over history and capable of dwelling in history and quickening it and transcending the limits of time which history imposes can the incarnation be a contemporary reality as well as a past reality. From this dogma also must flow our doctrine of the sacraments which are the moments and means whereby what has happened once is applied as contemporary to the people of God. Everything that is concerned with God's impact upon history must logically flow from our doctrine of the incarnation. This is not to say that the doctrine of the Church, the activity of the Holy Spirit, and the sacraments are less important than the doctrine of the incarnation. It is rather that these essential doctrines form a constellation at the centre of which is the dogma of the incarnation.

The third and last of the three basic Christian dogmas is the dogma of the atonement. Nobody has ever claimed that there exists a single universally accepted formula to express this dogma. It is a remarkable fact that the first full-scale theological work to be devoted exclusively to this dogma did not appear till the year 1097 (Anselm's *Cur Deus Homo?*) Calvinists have at times come near to claiming that their penal substitutionary theory of the atonement is a universal and compulsory explanation of this dogma. But their claim cannot be taken seriously and must be resisted strenuously whenever it is made. There is no ecumenical formula, there is not even an universally agreed explanation, to define the dogma of the atonement.

And yet the doctrine of Christ's atonement for our sins must be called a dogma, a mystery, one of the great component parts of the Christian religion, one of the underlying realities of which Christians are aware, one of the ingredients and immediate implications of living Christian faith, witnessed to overwhelmingly in the Bible, attested thousands of times in Christian tradition. This is indeed the most existential of Christian dogmas. The tradition within Lutheran piety which continually stresses the words *pro me*—a tradition deriving directly from Luther himself—is entirely true to Christian literature, history, and experience. When Christians have ceased to believe that in some sense Christ died for them, they have ceased to be Christians. This dogma too is intimately linked with sacramental thought and practice. Both the two main sacraments of baptism and of the eucharist are in a sense a re-calling of Christ's death. And with the dogma of the atonement must be associated all Christian doctrine about justification, about guilt, and about grace. This is the dogma which deals more directly than any other with God's relationship with man. It is in a sense the most intimate and inward of the dogmas of the Christian faith.

Perhaps the dogma of the atonement is the best illustration of the nature of Christian dogma, just because nobody has ever succeeded in defining it, and few have even attempted to do so. The early Fathers of the Christian Church obviously felt themselves under no necessity to define this dogma, although nobody could doubt that they believed in it. Their attempts to explain it are usually far from convincing. The Easterns tend to give the impression (though the impression is no doubt a false one) that the atonement is a kind of biological trick, a piece of blood-transfusion whereby the divine Logos took humanity to himself and thereby communicated immortality to it, and after the age of Tertullian almost all writers seek with deplorable consistency to avoid the scandal of the cross in their account of the significance of Christ's death. The Middle Ages saw the rise of theories revolving round the concepts of satisfaction, contract, and law. The Reformation era favoured above all penal and substitutionary theories. The moral theory came into its own in the nineteenth and twentieth centuries. Today theologians often favour a theory based on the vague but alluring idea of the 'Man for others'. The Church will always be considering the significance of *huper tōn hamartiōn hēmōn* and probably will never reach an agreed formula upon the subject and never feel the necessity of doing so. But it would be obviously absurd to conclude that this means that the doctrine of the atonement is non-existent or meaningless or ineffectual or peripheral. On the contrary, it is at the very heart of the Christian faith, it is 'borne in the bosom of revealed religion', it is a basic dogma of Christianity. But it has never been crystallized into a single formula or definition. Its permanent shape is unmistakably there. But it is a shape which is amenable to perennial restatement and reconsideration and new application.

What gives these dogmas their shape is ultimately the historical shape of Christianity itself. They are not the product of sheer speculation delighting in its own activity. They are not the result of a popular cult making religious demands motivated by curious pressures in the folk consciousness. They are not the outcome of an Hellenization of Christianity. The Christian religion itself has certain indelible historical characteristics which ultimately constitute the necessity that caused these dogmas to take the shape which they did. It is this historical shape which continually prevents Christianity lapsing into a syncretism like Hinduism whereby it constantly absorbs and adapts itself to new developments without serious reference to its original form, or running into the sands of vague philosophical theories or formless mysticism. But though the shape of these dogmas is enduring and cannot be altered without altering the essence of Christianity itself, in no case can their shape be finally defined in words possessing a permanent and exhaustive validity. The final reason for this is that God himself cannot be defined in this way. In the language of the 'Athanasian' Creed, God is 'incomprehensible'. This does not mean that he is unknowable and that all we can discover about him is a perplexing chaos of uncertain conjectures. It means that he cannot be exhaustively known by us. We cannot know him as we know another object, a house or a map; we cannot master him as a scientist masters a new theory in connection with his subject. We can know him enough to be reconciled to him and redeemed by him, but he can never be epistemologically at our disposal. And so these basic underlying truths which are a necessary part of his self-disclosure in history are not truths that can be exhaustively and precisely stated in human language, like the truth that the earth goes round the sun or the proposition that any two sides of a triangle are together longer than the third side.

There are no other dogmas than these three, if we are to use the word 'dogma' in the sense which has been given to it in this essay. It is not the business of the Church to multiply dogmas. Dogma must arise necessarily and inevitably out of the historical shape of Christianity itself, and must be a basic truth, at the top of the 'hierarchy of truths'. The Church is mistaken when it imagines that its business is to codify dogma, to attend to the ever more elaborate articulation of a system of dogma. The Church does not have control over dogma and cannot determine whether or not it will indulge in the exercise of dogma-producing. The Church must place itself under the demands of the gospel, and allow itself to be restrained by the necessities of the historical witness of the Bible. The gospel does certainly demand some articulation, some development; the Bible is not complete without the Church. It is the Church's task to discover the necessary rounding-off and logical sub-structure of the biblical witness, but here necessity must be the guide and not arbitrary piety nor rationalist demand for a tidily complete system of doctrine. Origen, Gregory Palamas, and Thomas Aquinas may produce their systems, and these may have stimulating effects upon Christian thought. But systems must not be turned into dogmas. By this criterion all the dogmas achieved by the Western Church since at latest the Fourth Lateran Council of 1215 must be regarded (as far as dogmatic status is concerned) as unnecessary and frivolous, since they cannot seriously be thought to achieve the status of dogma, and all the dogmas of General Councils held in the East after the Council of Chalcedon must be relegated to the position of at best doctrines of lesser importance. They cannot be thought of as basic necessities of the Christian faith. The Anglican tradition which recognizes as essential and binding no dogma later than those achieved by the fifth century, though it cannot be the last word, represents a more valuable insight than it has in recent years been given credit for. By that period the theologians of the Church had, so to speak, taken the measure of the Church's intellectual task. The necessity of working out a Christian doctrine of God and of elucidating the Church's belief concerning the incarnation (a necessity which, once the full Godhead of Christ had been established, followed ineluctably from the other) had been fairly faced. Intellectually the Church had come of age. No other dogmas achieved by debate and controversy, by trial and error, could ever be quite as central as these.

Newman was quite right in calling attention to the fact that doctrine does develop. This realization constitutes his greatness as a theologian. But he was wrong in his account of how doctrine develops, and it is to the credit of the Roman Catholic Church that it has never officially accepted his theory of development. Doctrine does not develop in a steady line of organic biological growth. The process of the development of doctrine is not like the formation of a coral reef, whereby thousands of insect-like theologians contribute to the logical erection of an impressive theological structure ever growing as more parts are added by development to the existing system. This is a fanciful picture which does not correspond to the realities of history with its discontinuities, vicissitudes, ebb and flow of opinions, reversals of trends, uncompleted reformations and new movements of thought which traverse and confound the old. Christian doctrine is the result of the continually changing, adjusting, reinterpreting intellectual life of the Church as it lives with the mysteries with which it has been entrusted. There is indeed in the history of Christian doctrine a movement onward and outward and forward, but there is also a movement of return in obedience to the pull of the historical witness of the foundation documents of Christianity. If we are to find a picture to describe this process, biological growth is not a correct one. It would be better to substitute for it the picture of a dance or a dialogue as the life and thought and worship of the Church interact with the Bible. Certain things are indeed learnt, certain gains made, in the course of this dialogue. But we have no right to claim that we can see a steady, logically-articulated process of growth. Apart from any other consideration, it must be conceded that if there is a process of development we are in the middle of it; we cannot see the end. It is temerarious to speak as if we can with confidence predict the end of an historical process which includes us, the speakers, in its course. We must remember the folly of the Hegelian historians of the last hundred years who haughtily rejected ecclesiastical allegiance as they surveyed history, but were confident that they knew the course which history in future would pursue, men such as von Ranke, Mommsen, Bury, and even the gentle Hodgkin. We cannot foresee the end of the history of Christian doctrine; we cannot plot its future course. The conversation which the Church has been holding with the Bible for nearly two thousand years will only end in heaven.

II

THE AGE OF THE FATHERS

What is the Age of the Fathers? How can it be defined? It is easy to see where it begins: roughly speaking, where the New Testament ends. But how far does it extend, and what Fathers does it cover? Some Anglicans recognize the first four Councils, others the first seven. Some people would argue that the Age of the Fathers ends when the point is reached at which East and West begin their separate theological development, so that Fathers like Athanasius, Basil the Great, Cyril and Leo can be included in the Age of the Fathers, whereas writers such as Augustine, who was immensely influential, but only in the West, and Leontius of Byzantium, who left a considerable mark but only in the East, cannot be included. But this neat scheme will not survive application to the historical facts. Origen has never been regarded as a Father of the Church, but his thought was for a long time widely influential in both East and West. Maximus the Confessor lived long after the theological development of East and West had gone their separate ways, but his thought had far-reaching influence not only in the East but also in the West. Again, for those Christian traditions who do not accept Chalcedon, it is absurd and unreasonable to end the Age of the Fathers with that Council. For them the second and third Councils of Constantinople are not milestones or finishing tapes but disasters, and they have their own Fathers developing their own theology in a quite different Age of the Fathers. For the Orthodox Churches the Age of the Fathers lasted at least as late as the seventh Ecumenical Council in 787. For the Western Church it is very difficult indeed to fix a terminus for the Age of the Fathers. Is it the early Middle Ages, with Pope Gregory the Great as the last of the Fathers and the first of the medievals? Or is it—as many people prefer to think—as late as the twelfth century, when Bernard of Clairvaux continues what looks very like the patristic tradition? It is significant that John Calvin in his *Institutes* quotes Bernard nearly as often as any other ancient author after Augustine. If we try to define the last of the Fathers, we cannot do so without making an arbitrary decision. All we can say is that all Christian traditions recognize that at some point the Age of the Fathers ceased, and all can point to a succeeding age. But no final choice about the date of the terminus can be made.

Secondly, we ought now to recognize that the Age of the Fathers was not a Golden Age, not at least in the sense that we are bound to reproduce it in an archaistic manner, so that, for instance, if we are to have ordained women, they must be deaconesses in the ancient tradition and none other; nor even in the sense that we should always in every situation ask what the Fathers did, and then try to do it. For instance, if the proposal were made to accept non-episcopally ordained ministers in a reunion scheme, it would not be legitimate to reject this scheme simply because the Fathers did not employ such a ministry. We must not allow ourselves to be restricted and limited by so rigid a regard for, not merely historical precedent, but narrowly patristic historical precedent. The conditions under which the Fathers lived were totally different from ours; they lived in a different society, in a different culture, their ways and forms of thought were very largely different from ours, everything that conditioned their customs and affected their way of living was different. To take examples of their practice, or even of their ideas and modes of self-expression, and introduce them, unmodified, as sheer authoritative unalterable rules or directives for our church life in the mid-twentieth century, would be naïve and unwise and lacking in historical sense. We would not dream of doing this in the case of the medieval Church, perhaps because we are close enough to it to realize that we cannot reproduce it. It is only the romantic mist thrown by distance over the patristic period that prevents us seeing the impossibility of reproducing patristic practice or life.

But, further, even though we recognize that there were some men of gigantic intellectual power in the Age of the Fathers, and many men and women of great saintliness and great virtue, and not a few who showed themselves ready to die for their faith, we must also be realistic enough to admit that the people who guided the destinies of the Church in the Age of the Fathers were often sinful, and always limited. There certainly were heroic periods during the patristic time, especially during persecutions, but there is no reason to think that either ordinary Christians or eminent Christians were better then than they are now. There are too many disgraceful episodes, large and small, in early church history to allow us to assume this, such as the rush to apostasize during the Decian persecution, the series of events attending the outbreak of the Donatist controversy, and the treatment accorded to John

Chrysostom by Theophilus and to Nestorius by Cyril, and to Hosius of Cordova by the Arians. A reading of the acts of ecumenical councils in the early Church is not calculated to enhance our opinion of the Age of the Fathers. And even at this distance of time we can discern that there were many instances in the Age of the Fathers when bewilderment and uncertainty took the place of decisive action and confident knowledge of the true doctrine. The Church, for instance, was singularly ill-prepared for the patronage given it unexpectedly and embarrassingly by the Roman imperial government early in the fourth century. Nobody had ever imagined what would happen or what response would be the proper one, if the emperor supported the Church instead of persecuting it, and when the miraculous event happened the Church in many ways surrendered too easily to the seductive temptations which accompanied state patronage. Again, we can hardly understand the Arian controversy until we realize that during the first few decades of this conflict nobody, or almost nobody, knew with certainty what was the proper, adequate, orthodox answer to the burning question about Christ's divinity. The trouble was not so much that orthodoxy was at stake as that nobody really was sure what in this case was orthodoxy.

But there is a deeper objection than either of these to regarding the period of the Fathers as a Golden Age. How far are we justified in canonizing any era? If we do so, are we not bound in the end to petrify or ossify the Church's life and structure? Christianity is a living thing. Christians are under the rule and guidance of the Holy Spirit, who is not given by measure and is not bound by anything, not even by sacraments, not even by tradition, not even by Scripture. We can, of course, learn from the past, but we must not be restricted by the past, by any past era. To take one era, however we determine it and exalt this above all others, is to court just this sort of false development. It is not at first sight obvious to twentieth-century eyes why we should pay more attention to the ideas and traditions of the patristic period than we should to those of later periods, or the middle ages, of the explosive and turbulent sixteenth century, of the eighteenth or nineteenth centuries. We have been influenced by all of them. If we push the concept of the pre-eminence of the Age of the Fathers to its logical limit, are we not forced to assume that the Fathers and their contemporaries enjoyed some advantage in apprehending the Christian revelation which we do not, that they had access to some light which is denied to us, and that we should imitate them because this is the only way in which we can receive this light? But this conclusion should be rejected by all Christians who believe in Christianity as a not purely historical phenomenon, who believe in the Holy Spirit as God who transcends or is sovereign over time and who pours his light on all men indiscriminately ever since the coming of Jesus Christ. In short, is not a limitation of the Age of the Fathers, and a recognition of it as having a peculiar claim on us, a covert way of reducing Christianity to no more than *Religionsgeschichte*?

A final objection to attributing a special position to the Age of the Fathers is the uncertainty as to whether we can make sense of their dogmatic decisions and doctrinal formulae today. The philosophical sub-structure of all the classical development of doctrine and definition of dogma in the patristic era was either Platonic or Aristotelian. The metaphysics, psychology, and cosmology which they learnt were widely different from ours. One example which occurs to mind is the distinction made by Aristotle between *protē ousia*, meaning concrete occurrence of substance or essence in an individual person and thing, and *deutera ousia*, meaning the general category or type of substance under which the *protē ousia* can be logically classified and which it expresses in an individual form. This is admitted by everybody to have underlain the patristic distinction of *hypostasis* and *physis* used so widely in Christological exposition. If we do not accept Aristotle's definition as corresponding to any agreed description of reality given by science or philosophy today, what reality is left to the patristic Christological distinctions based on it? There is no reason at all why we should *a priori* accept Aristotle's definitions; the patristic use of them does not give them any added authority. Or we could instance the Fathers' obsession with the impassibility of God, which produced such curious phenomena as Hilary of Poitiers' theory that Jesus Christ experienced *passio* but not *dolor passionis*[2]; or the widespread patristic tendency to treat concepts such as humanity, and even knowledge, as a kind of *ousia*, in a paraphysical way, so that Athanasius in his *de incarnatione* can sometimes give the impression that he regarded the atonement as a biological operation, an inoculation of human flesh with divinity, a transfusion of divinity into the blood of Adam's race.[3] Many of these concepts are not only strange but virtually meaningless to the mind of the people of the twentieth century. It is impossible, or rather useless, to reproduce them unaltered in contemporary theological discourse. It is difficult to see how they can even be translated or transposed. It has often been thought that a process of what might be called 'transposition' can be employed on the doctrinal definitions of the Fathers, so that the substance of what they meant could be maintained while the form of its expression was altered. But it is doubtful whether this can be applied in all cases, or even in the majority of them. Suppose we can decide what the Fathers were originally intending to say, and suppose we discover that their original intention was so much involved in the philosophical assumptions underlying it that it cannot be successfully expressed in modern terms, what then? In any case to erect into a norm of doctrine definitions and dogmas which appear to need so much reinterpretation and restatement, and which sometimes may disappear in the process of being restated, seems a perilous and unwise proceeding. To regard the Age of the Fathers as providing useful or necessary norms for interpreting the Bible or for teaching Christian doctrine seems to be a romantic rather than a realistic policy.

These are serious and weighty difficulties, which have largely arisen from scientific study of the Fathers conducted over the last sixty years, or from the questionings which the contemporary climate of opinion causes to arise in our minds. But against these arguments we must set certain facts which are as real and as weighty as any objections which we have been considering. They combine to form a strong argument against the suggestion that we can with impunity either ignore or dismiss the Age of the Fathers.

In the first place, it is unscientific to imagine that we can jump directly from the Bible or from the New Testament to the thought of the nineteenth or twentieth century, easily ignoring the doctrinal development which took place immediately after the period covered by the New Testament. This is only another way of stating that all the arguments against canonizing the literature of the Fathers are just as valid against canonizing the literature of the New Testament, or indeed of the Old Testament. It is no more feasible to reproduce the thought of the New Testament directly and unmodified in the twentieth century than to carry out the same process on the thought of the Fathers. It can in fact only be done in an eclectic manner, by choosing one or two strands of New Testament thought, such as the existential element and ignoring most of the others. But even this operation is virtually impossible to carry out with reference to the patristic development of doctrine. In fact the word 'unscientific' is too mild to apply to the attempt to move directly from the first century to the twentieth, ignoring the second and following centuries; it is, viewed in the coldest light of objective investigation, impossible. The work of the Fathers stands immovably between us and the Bible—'immovably' is not too strong a word here.

Consciously or unconsciously, the vast majority of believing Christians of all traditions look at God and at Jesus Christ through the spectacles of Nicaea, and probably through those of Chalcedon as well. We do not think of God as the God of the Jews, into relationship with whom Jesus Christ has somehow to be brought, as the author of 1 Clement and Justin apparently did. We do not in our heart of hearts think of Christ as the apocalyptic figure who has come down from heaven as the Great Angel and who will subject himself to the Father in the end—an end which is rapidly approaching (1 Cor. 15.27, 28; 2 Thess. 1.8–10; Rev. 14.14–20). We do not think of him as the hidden Messiah whose crucifixion and rising from the dead has precipitated the last, brief crisis (Mark), nor as the Man from Heaven, antitype to Adam, who will soon slay Anti-Christ with the breath of his mouth (1 Cor. 15.45–49; 2 Thess. 2:8), nor as the Second Moses who is God's Son by his obedience (Hebrews), nor even quite as the Logos-cum-Son-of-God of John. We do not accept a Pauline Christology separately, nor a Johannine Christology separately, nor that of Hebrews nor of Matthew nor Mark nor Luke nor 1 Peter nor James nor Revelation separately. Our Christology is basically the Christology of early Christian tradition or, to put it in a simpler and more straightforward way, what the Fathers made of the Bible. This is not only a fact which nobody can ignore but it is fairly easy to explain why it is true. If the New Testament is approached out of the context of a community which uses it and of the tradition created by that community, if it is examined in the pure dry light of scholarship, without presuppositions and simply as an historical document, it begins to crumble. The lineaments of the historical Jesus begin to disappear altogether beneath the layers of later interpretation discovered or imagined by the critics; the Pauline Gospel becomes an ill-assorted series of Hellenistic or Gnostic speculations; the *kerygma* of the early Church is discovered to be no more than a series of diverse *kerygmata* patched together into a late and implausible reconstruction by Luke. Every heresy known to the later Church —Docetism, Adoptionism, Gnosticism, Arianism—is found lurking in the pages of the New Testament. The Holy Spirit sinks into a mere divine influence. Jesus Christ becomes a patchwork quilt of such diverse and incompatible ingredients as to lose all significance. If the New Testament—or, for that matter, the Bible —is approached or expounded in isolation from the tradition of the Church, it collapses, just as the tradition of the Church, if taught and presented without reference to the New Testament or the Bible, becomes empty and self-condemning. In our belief in God as revealed in Jesus Christ we very largely accept the interpretation of the Bible given to us by the Fathers, and we do so because we must. We have virtually no alternative, unless we are to build up an entirely new Christianity from the foundations, a task which neither Luther nor Zwingli nor Calvin nor Cranmer dared to attempt. Indeed, for anyone to attempt this task in the twentieth century would be as absurd as it would be unrealistic, and the resulting Christianity would be pitiful and unrecognizable.

This is not, of course, to say that the Bible or the New Testament is just a miscellany of facts to be interpreted in a dozen different ways by a dozen different traditions, a wax nose to be twisted into whatever shape fancy chooses. The Fathers were bound by the Bible, in spite of the spurious freedom which their allegorical interpretation tended to give them. The Bible supplied the materials for their faith, and in thus supplying materials the Bible restricted their interpretation and formed their convictions. But it needed interpretation; it was not self-expounding. It arose out of a living tradition and depended upon a living tradition for its effectiveness, indeed for its life. Christianity is a religion of a book, but it is not a religion written in a book; it is not a written legal code. The book is the book of Christianity because it witnesses to a perennial living reality which would render futile any attempt simply to reconstruct it from a book. There was a give-and-take in the patristic use of the Bible; a dialectical relationship. Earlier I have compared the relationship to a dance. The Fathers danced with the Bible, and that dance has set a pattern to which our feet move too.

Indeed, I venture to suggest that this patristic interpretation of the Bible, and not the Bible alone, is the underlying bond which gives to Christians today that sense of unity which is expressing itself in the Ecumenical Movement. The Bible is indeed one of the things which all Christian bodies involved as participants or spectators in the ecumenical movement possess in common. But then the Bible is also the possession of many bodies not involved in the Ecumenical Movement, such as the Christian Scientists, Jehovah's Witnesses, the Mormons, the Unitarians, and indeed the evangelical sects which regard the Ecumenical Movement as anathema. If one listens to the ecumenical debate today, one would hardly guess that all the participants were united by the Bible; for actual hermeneutics differ vastly between different Christian traditions. The biblical exposition of a Greek Orthodox theologian will be very different from that of an American Baptist, and the exposition of a member of the Church of England will contrast sharply with that of a member of a body as geographically near as the Church of Scotland. What gives to the sharers in the Ecumenical Movement a sense of unity with their fellow Christians in spite of all apparent disunity is that they all share the common tradition of the Fathers, the common acceptance of the shape which the Church of the first four centuries gave to the Christian faith. This tradition, as accepted and lived out by the divided portions of Christendom today, is of course a fragmented tradition, but in spite of all the vicissitudes of history it still lives as a common tradition, and it is the force which makes for unity and pushes the divided communions towards each other and convinces them that, to adapt the words of Pascal, they would not be seeking unity if they had not in some sense already found it.

It is therefore necessary for us to define our relationship to the Fathers. We cannot ignore them or dismiss them without being naïve and unrealistic. I take it that the policy of simply reproducing the Fathers' words, whether embodied unaltered in creeds or in formulae like that of Chalcedon or in doctrinal treatises, and expecting them to be effective and intelligible, is no longer practicable. We must find for ourselves some other relationship than the one implied in that policy.

The first possible relationship which occurs is that which I have already described as 'transposition'. We can try to reproduce the substance of what the Fathers intended to say in the terms of our own day. Certainly this cannot be done in a completely literal and *simpliste* way. But the concept is not completely invalid. It is as well to remember that the Fathers themselves engaged in a vast and comprehensive process of 'transposition', and we do not for the most part conclude that they were attempting a hopeless task or that they failed in this enterprise. They were, consciously or unconsciously, transposing the gospel or the Christian message—or the witness of the Bible, or what they thought was the witness of the Bible—out of Jewish ways of thinking into Greek ways of thinking. This is what the great German scholar Harnack, following in the steps of the much less famous English scholar, Hatch, has taught the learned world. They did indeed accomplish a Hellenization of the gospel. They had no alternative. By the third century it was impossible for any intelligent Christian to promote his faith among intellectuals by simply repeating and publicizing the old primitive traditional inherited terms. The most obvious and perhaps the most fundamental and important example is eschatology. The Christian writers of the second century preserve most of the traditional eschatology of primitive Christianity, all its symbols and much of its structure, even though they do not, because they cannot, reproduce the dynamic of the eschatology of Paul or of Mark. Irenaeus, for instance, in his *adv. haereses* apparently believes that the utterances of the prophets about a miraculously renovated earth and a reconciliation of the tensions and hostilities within nature are to be literally fulfilled.[4] Tertullian has a programme for souls to fulfil after death which is recognizably derived from traditional elements, even though it is rather a confused scheme.[5] But Irenaeus in his *Demonstration* (*Epideixis*), which was probably written later than his larger work, has abandoned a belief in the literal fulfilment of these prophecies and takes them as referring figuratively to the present condition of the Church.[6] And by the time Origen was writing, in the second quarter of the third century, a simple unmodified presentation of primitive eschatological ideas, and an interpretation of the significance of Christ exclusively in such terms, was impossible for the intellectuals. Consequently, when Origen taught and wrote for the intellectuals, he undertook a transposition of eschatological terms as thorough and sweeping as has ever been done. As far as eschatology was concerned, Origen engaged in a process of *Entmythologisierung* which even Bultmann could hardly surpass, and this revolutionary reinterpretation of this very central part of the Christian faith inevitably involved far-reaching changes in other parts of it. This 'transposition' did of course cause protests and rouse opposition, and did have some very unfortunate results later. But the immense popularity which Origen's work enjoyed during the next century and a half, and the immense influence which it exerted on patristic thought, make it clear that this example of 'transposition' took place when the time was ripe for it, when the choice was not between preserving the primitive Christian eschatological structure and eschatological dynamic or transposing them, but between transposing them or abandoning them.

We have recalled Harnack as one who forced scholars everywhere to recognize that the Fathers did carry out this transposition from primitive Jewish thought to Greek thought, and perhaps in this lay his greatness. He inclined to think that in the process of transposition the Fathers had lost or diluted or corrupted the message. We live today, however, in a post-Harnack age, even though there still appear to be many teachers of church history and of the doctrine of the early Church who do not realize this and who continue to reproduce the old Harnackian shibboleths unaltered and unexamined. But today we would not dream of reconstructing the original message or gospel in the terms in which Harnack reconstructed it, and we can therefore scarcely subscribe to his theory of dilution or corruption by Hellenization if we do not agree with his account of what was the pure gospel from which the degeneration took place. And we are far more conscious today than he ever was of the profoundly Jewish character and form of the primitive gospel, and therefore of the ineluctable necessity of this character and form submitting in the lapse of time to change. I venture to think that most of us have consciously or unconsciously agreed that some sort of 'transposition' was forced upon the Church and that by the third century most intelligent Christians realized this, especially that pre-eminently intelligent Christian, Origen. And unless we have convinced ourselves that the very essence and pure heart of Christianity disappeared at about that time, that in effect Christianity collapsed in the second or third century, leaving only a deceptive shell or larva to survive through the succeeding thousand-odd years, we presumably agree that the process of transposition which was well under way by the end of the fourth century was by and large a successful one. There are still, I believe, some who hold that true Christianity disappeared early in the history of the Church, only to be rediscovered by Martin Luther in the sixteenth century, or possibly by Martin Werner in the twentieth. But I confess that I cannot subscribe to that view. Indeed, it seems to me that the Nicene dogma about the place of Jesus Christ in the Godhead was a successful example of the 'transposition' of the original eschatological Gospel into the terms of Greek metaphysics, and that Arianism, to which it put a terminus, was a dangerous example of the wrong way of mixing Jewish and Greek doctrinal elements, for while it used a good deal of earlier Christological material and could make a fair show of appealing to tradition, it rested ultimately upon the Greek assumption that God could not communicate himself.

I believe that more arguments could be produced to show that in effecting this 'transposition' the Fathers did not abandon the original heart and essence of Christianity nor render themselves insensible to the important truths which Jewish thought and the witness of the New Testament had to teach them. One could instance their surprising rejection of a cyclical view of history, brought into prominence by Fr A. Luneau's book on *L'histoire du salut*, and the refusal to abandon a formal belief in the full humanity of Jesus in spite of the attractive alternative offered by Apollinarianism, whatever we may think of the actual terms in which they imagined what the Jesus of history had been like. But perhaps enough has been said to suggest that the enterprise of 'transposing' the ideas of the Fathers into terms of our own day need not seem so hopeless if we reflect how large and difficult a process of 'transposition' they themselves carried out with considerable success. One recent example of just such a 'transposition' into modern concepts can be found in *The Shape of Christology*,[7] by Professor McIntyre of Edinburgh. He suggested that the patristic concept of *anthropotes*, of humanity as a universal existing in all examples of human beings, and as adopted or taken by Christ at the Incarnation, which we certainly find a very difficult concept today, can be reinterpreted in Sartrean terms which make it at once more intelligible and more acceptable to us. Here, I suggest, is one example of successful 'transposition' of a patristic Christological term.

But we need not take the concept of 'transposition' as the only image or model or policy for the relationship of the thought and work of the Fathers to the thought and work of the Church today. We can think of our relationship to the Fathers in terms of dialogue. As we study the Fathers we conduct a dialogue with them, putting questions to them and seeing what sort of answers they give, just as they themselves in a sense conducted a dialogue with the Bible, putting questions (sometimes the wrong questions) and receiving answers (sometimes very curious answers). We take our stand alongside the Fathers, aligning ourselves with them, trying to understand what were the intellectual and moral and cultural pressures which were acting on them and to illuminate their motives and intentions. We study not only their texts but their background and intellectual heritage. We accept them as partners in the same work as that in which we are engaged, but at a much earlier period of its development, and we ask them what were their problems and needs and desires. We seek to discover how far their reactions and fears and expectations were the same as ours; and if they were to any extent different, we want to know why they were different. It is perhaps only with the outstanding minds among the Fathers that we can conduct a dialogue in this way. But recent work upon such men as Irenaeus, Origen, Basil, Augustine could reasonably be described as the initiation of a fruitful dialogue with these authors. One could hardly conduct a dialogue with Hippolytus or Cyprian or Epiphanius.

Yet another model which has been suggested as useful to illustrate our relationship with the Fathers is that of a present experience. The Fathers could be regarded as an experience which every theologian ought to undergo, because it is the common experience of the whole Church. It is, too, as has already been suggested in this paper, an experience which in a sense is always with us. It has become part of our mind as far as Christianity is concerned. One could express the same thought in another way by saying that all Christians, and especially all Christian intellectuals, have experienced the same patristic trauma. Some people apparently are influenced all through their lives by some deeply impressive psychological experience which occurred when they were very young and susceptible. To take an historical example from the Fathers themselves, St Patrick when he was sixteen was captured and carried away into slavery by Irish pirates. This frightful experience deeply influenced the rest of his life, so that when he was an old man, an authoritative bishop capable of dealing out excommunications, he could still sometimes write of himself as if he were a helpless and friendless boy. So all theologians almost inevitably have encountered the patristic experience which they can never remove entirely from their minds. We still accuse each other of Marcionism, of Nestorianism; we still either embrace or recoil from Augustinianism. We still tend to smell out Donatism or Gnosticism or Sabellianism in our opponents' views, and so on.

Perhaps this is only another way of saying that the Fathers are necessarily a paradigm for us. They first encountered the problems, made the mistakes, felt their way round the pitfalls, explored the blind alleys, drew the conclusions, which to a large extent we all meet and must meet if we are true to original Christianity and can use right reason. There is a story of the Irish mathematician, Rowan Hamilton, who was a child prodigy and at the age of about twelve asked his father about the relation of divinity to humanity in Jesus Christ; on being told to work out the problem for himself, he came back with four successive answers, representing Nestorianism, Eutychianism, Monophysitism and finally the Chalcedonian solution. The story sounds apocryphal, but it is a kind of parable of the fact that we all must necessarily travel over much of the ground travelled by the Fathers and that they must accompany us as we travel it, whether as cheering forerunners or as awful examples.

These different ways of conceiving of our relationship to the Fathers are not mutually exclusive. There is no reason why we should not think of our relationship in all three ways, as engaging in a work of transposition, as carrying on a dialogue, and as having a present experience. These models may, however, suggest that though our attitude to the Fathers must be more flexible and complex and varied than our predecessors before the rise of historical criticism imagined that it could be, still we cannot ignore or dismiss the Fathers, and the possibility of a fruitful relationship with them is entirely open.

NOTES

1 And in fact it has been shown in an article called 'Dogma and Formula in the Fathers' which the author wrote for the Sixth International Patristic Conference which met in Oxford in September 1971; the article will appear in the published Proceedings of the Conference.

2 *de Trin.*, x. 14–23.

3 E.g., *de incarn.*, viii. 3; xliv. 1–7.

4 E.g., *adv. haer.*, v. xxxiii. 1–4; 35. xxv. 1, 2; xxxvi. 2.

5 E.g., *adv. Marc.*, III. xxiv. 3-5; IV. xxxiv. 13–14; *de anima*, xxxv. 3; lv. 4, 5; lviii. 1; *de resurrect. mort.*, xvii. 2, 8; *Scorp.*, vi. 7.

6 *Dem.*, 61.

7 *The Shape of Christology* (1966), pp. 105–12.

4 *The Doctrine of God in the Early Church*

I

Many years ago when I was learning theology I was often given the impression, both by those whose lectures I was attending and by the books which I was given to read, that the New Testament is, unfortunately, slightly unorthodox in its doctrine of Christ. First of all, until one reaches the blessed haven of the Fourth Gospel, the New Testament appears to be deplorably unwilling to come into the open on the subject of Christ's full divinity. Then there are those unhappy passages in Paul where he does not seem to realize that he is subordinating the Son to the Father in a manner scarcely compatible with orthodoxy (e.g. 1 Cor. 15.28; Phil. 2.9–11), and passages in the Epistle to the Hebrews to the same effect (e.g. Heb. 2.10; 5.8; 12.2), and those texts which seem to indicate that Paul did not distinguish clearly between the Son and the Spirit (Rom. 8.26, 34; 2 Cor. 3.17); one might add the strange fact that the author of Acts (and with him presumably the apostles in their speeches retailing the *kerygma*) seem to know nothing of a pre-existent Son in the traditional sense.

More significant even than these examples however is the dominant and widespread tendency in the New Testament to speak of Christ in terms of function rather than in terms of status. 'Christ Jesus, who was made unto us wisdom from God and righteousness and sanctification and redemption' (1 Cor. 1.30), and 'God ... has at the end of these days spoken unto us in his Son, whom he appointed heir of all things, through whom also he made the worlds' (Heb. 1.1, 2). These are christological statements highly typical of the New Testament. There are indeed passages which attempt, instead of merely indicating Christ's function, to sketch his status, i.e. to relate his being to the being of the Father. It might be said that the title 'Son of God given to Jesus very widely in the New Testament represents an attempt to define his relation to God. But the title is so vague and is patient of so many interpretations that it can hardly be said to do more than postulate some close relation between God and Jesus. Hebrews, after calling his 'the [or a] Son', describes him in the next verse to the one just quoted as 'the effulgence of his glory and the very image of his substance', in words borrowed from the literature of Hellenistic Judaism. Paul in one famous passage describes Christ as 'being in the form of God' and as not counting it a prize to be equal to God (Phil. 2.6); he suggests that Christ knows the mind of God (1 Cor. 2.16); and in Colossians Christ is described as 'the image of the invisible God, the first-born of all creation', and it is said that 'in him dwelleth all the fulness of the Godhead bodily' (Col. 2.9; cf. 1.15). The furthest that the New Testament goes is, as has already been indicated, in the Gospel according to St John, where the famous christological sentences of 1.1–18 appear, and where Thomas finally cries out to Jesus, 'My Lord and my God' (20.28). It is all the more startling to find the carefully-chosen title *Logos Theou* (Word of God) which has been applied to Jesus in the Prologue of the Fourth Gospel reappearing in that apparently most Semitic of all books of the New Testament, the Revelation of St John the Divine (Rev. 19.13). But these attempts to define the status of Jesus in relation to God, to relate the being of Jesus to the being of God, are comparatively rare in the New Testament. They cannot be said, even in the Fourth Gospel, to constitute a coherent or recognizable specifically Christian doctrine of God. Taken as a whole, the New Testament must be judged to give us many fruitful ideas about the function of Jesus, about his agency as Lord (Kyrios), Mediator, Son of Man, High Priest, Sacrifice, Second or Last Adam, Good Shepherd, Servant, Victor, King of the armies of Heaven, Second Moses, New Temple, Pioneer, and in many other roles. But it does little to define effectively his ultimate relation to God. And this is pre-eminently true of the title which was so important or so frequently given that it became a kind of personal name, the Messiah or Christ. The Christology of the New Testament, in a word, is primarily *functional*.

It is also *dynamic* and *dramatic*. It indicates the significance of Jesus Christ in terms of movement and drama. He is represented in Paul, in Hebrews and in John as coming down from heaven, sharing our existence for a while, enduring death and then returning from the dead, lingering a short moment on this earth and then returning to Heaven to sit at God's right hand. His career is like a parabola, which comes from infinity, cuts a horizontal line on a graph, dips in its curve below that line, cuts the line again in curving back again, and then returns to infinity. His significance is couched in terms of battle and victory, of a drama, with, at the Resurrection, the *peripeteia* which the pattern of traditional Greek drama often included (see 1 Cor. 1 and Revelation *passim*). 'Drama', after all, means a doing, a movement, an act, a resolving of a tension created by the clash of great forces, usually moral forces. '*Tetelestai!*', says the Johannine Christ: the drama is done, the tension resolved. Dynamic and dramatic terms come much more readily to the pens of the writers of the New Testament than metaphysical terms or expressions defining Christ's status in relation to God. Christ is not only the centre of the drama, not only the Agent. In a sense he *is* the drama, he is not so much the Agent as the Act. In those passages where St Paul speaks of a new creation given in Christ (Rom, 8.19–22; 2 Cor. 5.17; Gal. 6.15), or where he speaks of Christ becoming sin or becoming a curse for us (2 Cor. 5.21; Gal. 3.13; cf. Rom. 8.1–4), one can catch a glimpse of a deeper concept even than these, the thought that Christ represents God's move to commit and pledge himself into human existence, the picture of a divine self-abandonment and self-involvement which goes further in daring exploration of Christ's significance than any other statement in the New Testament. But still that significance is expressed in dynamic and dramatic rather than in static and philosophical terms.

And if the New Testament describes Christ as the Act of God, we are left in no doubt that this is the *last* Act. The thought of the New Testament is eschatological through and through. The situation is not merely that when we have finished considering other aspects of Christian doctrine in the New Testament, its doctrine of God, its doctrine of the person of Christ, of the Atonement, of the Holy Spirit, of the Church, of faith, of grace, of man, and so on, we come at last to its doctrine of the Last Things. The doctrine of the Last Things dominates and pervades the whole thought of the New Testament, from Mark's echoes of primitive Christian eschatology, through the eschatology of Paul and of Hebrews to the 'sublimated eschatology' of John and the apocalyptic eschatology of Revelation. Even if we accept the interpretation of Luke's thought given in Conzelmann's *The Theology of Luke*, the author of Luke-Acts is deeply influenced by eschatological thought if only by way of reaction. This is one of the constants in all the varied interpretations of the significance of Jesus Christ to be met in the New Testament, and this could even be said to be the last word about Jesus in the New Testament. He has come, to precipitate the last great crisis in the relations between God and man. With him the last hour, the ends of the ages, the beginning of judgement, eschatological salvation, are here. He is of such limitless significance that the only important event that can happen after his appearance is the end of the world. The fact that the Holy Spirit is active and operating is a proof that the Last Age is here, for the Holy Spirit in the New Testament is an eschatological phenomenon. The Church now stands between the Cross and the End, in the overlap of the Age to Come with the present age. This is the framework in which the thought of the Gospels of Matthew and of Mark and of the letters of Paul are set, and in spite of a lessening of eschatological tension in Luke's work and a transposition of it in the Johannine literature, and a tendency to push eschatology into the future in the later literature of the New Testament (the Pastorals and 2 Peter), this is still the framework in which is set the whole thought of the primitive Church generally. Jesus Christ has come once, to usher in the Last Age. He will come again, to consummate it. There is no pressure, there is no time, to work out his exact relationship to the Father. As Hamlet might have said, the rest is eschatology.

II

There is on the whole no observable tendency to change this state of affairs until we approach the middle of the second century. As the researches of Daniélou have revealed to us, the very earliest Christian literature outside the New Testament was still of an intensely Jewish kind. What he has called 'Judaeo-Christian' literature was expressed in such uncompromisingly Jewish terms that the later Church preferred to forget it, and it has only survived either in fragmentary form or in translations into obscure languages spoken by people remote from the world of the Mediterranean basin, like Ethiopian and Sclavonic. It is not surprising, then, to learn that this very early genre of Christian literature exhibits an extremely Jewish type of Christology and in particular that it has a tendency to represent the pre-existent Christ as an angel, the highest of the angels. This angelomorphic Christology is probably also to be detected in the closing verses of the fourteenth chapter of Revelation and is certainly to be found in Hermas. The collection of literature classed as 'sub-apostolic' does not show any advance upon the New Testament as we know it today. Jesus is called the 'Son', the 'Servant' (or 'Child'), the 'Beloved', as well as the Christ. It is clear that there is felt among these writers no need to advance beyond the traditional early Christian christological terms. Ignatius of Antioch describes Christ as the Logos, it is true, in his curious phrase 'the Word proceeding from silence' (Magnes. 8.2), and in 1 Clement he is described as the Creator (1 Clem. 59.3),[1] but neither of these uses goes as far even as the Fourth Gospel to define his relation to the Father. The most usual title of all, 'Lord' (Kyrios), indicates both his presence with the patriarchs, wise men and prophets under the old dispensation and the religious and spiritual authority which the Church has ascribed to him from the beginning. But hitherto it cannot be said that any serious attempt has been made to formulate a specifically Christian doctrine of God. The Church is so far content to take over the Jewish monotheistic doctrine of God and to hold in juxtaposition to this a belief in Jesus as an eschatological Saviour without attempting seriously to reconcile the two.

But as the Church emerged further and further from a purely Jewish milieu into a Gentile one, whose intellectual and spiritual atmosphere was dominated by Greek philosophy, it became increasingly difficult, and finally completely impossible, to present the gospel in the terms in which the Christians of the first century had presented it, and in the face of other totally different conceptions of God from the Jewish one, both those of Greek philosophy and of pagan religions, it became urgently necessary to produce some sort of a coherent doctrine of God which should be neither purely Jewish nor obviously polytheistic but specifically and recognizably Christian. On the one hand the gospel presented within the frame of Jewish-Christian eschatological expectation meant nothing, and can have had very little appeal, to the educated Gentile who was not a proselyte or godfearer and had never heard or read the Old Testament. On the other hand, the expectation of a Parousia which had so much conditioned the thought of the primitive Christian Church was now being clearly revealed as mistaken. The early Parousia had not taken place. Was it possible to continue to preach a gospel which expressed its claim and appeal in this frame of reference any longer, and that to people who were anyway quite unacquainted with this peculiarly Jewish form of thought? Obviously it was not.

There are indeed a few heroic souls who are prepared to argue that this was possible, and that it was at this point that the Church abandoned the true gospel by abandoning the eschatological framework of early Christian thought. But this theory would mean that the Church which outlasted three centuries of persecution by the Roman Government, persuaded that Government eventually to co-operate with it and then proceeded to take over the whole cultural tradition of Europe, in spite of the collapse of the Western Roman Empire, and later extended its influence widely over the whole world, had very early in this extraordinary career, almost before it began, abandoned its true message and corrupted its life-blood. Acceptance of an historical improbability as gigantic as this can safely be left to a few doctrinaire scholars. It is enough to say that the Church of the second century made the great decision—implicit no doubt in its tradition from the first—that the ultimate significance of Christ did not depend upon an early Parousia, and produced Christology instead of eschatology, produced something like a consistent Christian doctrine of God. It was the first, but by no means the last, great transposition of Christian doctrine. It appears to have been made in its earliest form virtually without the assistance of that document which was deliberately preparing the way for such a transposition, the Gospel according to St John; and we can see how much it suffered from the lack of this Gospel.

This first attempt at a Christian doctrine of God is to be found in the works of the Apologists who wrote at various times between about A.D. 140 and about A.D. 200. They do not of course agree in every detail, and we are heavily dependent upon one of them, Justin Martyr, more of whose work survives than in the case of any other, but there is a basic theological structure visible in the thought of each, whether we choose Justin or Aristides or Tatian or Theophilus or Athenagoras or Minucius Felix. The doctrine of God can be described thus: God, the absolute Being beyond all being, as recognized by the Greek philosophers, always had immanent within himself a principle or energy which could be called his Reason (or Logos): when he desired to make himself known he first caused this Reason to become separate, though not divided, from himself, so that it formed a separate entity which could be called (at least, in Justin's thought) a second or another God; then through this Reason he created the world, and the human race in it; then this Reason instructed the wisest and greatest of the men of the chosen race in most of the details of Christianity, by appearing to them personally in various temporary forms; finally this Reason himself became a man in order that the Proof should appear along with the Truth. He overcame demons, taught righteousness, offered himself as a sacrifice on the Cross, died, rose again, and now offers eternal life, or incorruption, to all who believe in him.

These are the main lines of the theological structure presented by the Apologists. We may well be amazed at its narrowness and disproportion. It runs a serious risk of presenting Jesus as a demigod who came to give us information about a basically unknowable High God. It relegates the incarnation to the status of a kind of acted parable endorsing a long history of the teaching of Christian doctrine. It leaves no satisfactory position for the Holy Spirit, whom the Apologists mention with somewhat embarrassed carefulness but who really upsets their theological scheme. Finally, their Trinity, if we are to call it a Trinity, is a Trinity adopted by God for purposes of creation and revelation. The Apologists do not envisage the existence of permanent distinctions within the being of God. In terms of theological jargon (which has its proper uses) theirs is an economic and not an immanent Trinity. Fundamentally their thought starts with the One God of Jewish belief, and then attempts to fit Jesus Christ into this Godhead by identifying him with the Logos of contemporary Middle Platonism; the Holy Spirit is left to hover uncertainly in the background. This was a Christian doctrine of God, though in many ways a very inadequate one. It was, however, designed to attract the intellectuals of the period, who were well acquainted with Greek philosophy, and who would be favourably impressed by the fact that this Christian philosophy solved a problem acutely felt at the time, the problem of how the Absolute, identified with God, could under any circumstances and by any means come into contact with this world of change, of becoming, of decay, of transitoriness which we sublunary beings experience.

That the Apologists were correct in calculating that their theological scheme would appeal to the age in which they lived is proved by the number of eminent pre-Nicene Christian theologians who reproduce it, in one form or another, in their writings. We can list Irenaeus, Tertullian, Hippolytus, Novatian, Arnobius and Lactantius, and Victorinus of Pettau[2] as retaining this basic scheme for their theology. It might almost be said that up to the Arian controversy this was the orthodox Christian doctrine of God. But the scheme was not left without improvements and without a distinct restoration of balance to it. Irenaeus, though this remained the basic structure of his thought, shifted the emphasis from the cosmological to the soteriological part of the scheme, and greatly enriched and strengthened this. He was not interested in the question of how God could come in contact with the world, but concentrated upon presenting Jesus Christ as the self-manifestation of God. The chief cause of this very healthy shift of emphasis was Irenaeus' wholehearted acceptance, and indeed championship, of the Fourth Gospel. This Gospel, which must have been composed about A.D. 100, had before Irenaeus' day been regarded with suspicion by the Catholic Church; it had been used in Gnostic circles, and no doubt the Catholics, not without some justification, tended to regard it as a Gnostic gospel. But Irenaeus realized that if it was Gnostic, then it was a Gnostic gospel to end Gnostic gospels, adopted it enthusiastically, allowed its thought to influence him profoundly, and provided it with an apostolic author guaranteed by a chain of historical testimony which looks to modern scholars much too good to be true. St John's Gospel is the document which above all others was written to effect the transposition from primitive Christian eschatology to later Christian Christology without losing the essentials of the gospel. In Irenaeus' hands it had the effect of providing balance and proportion for the new Economic Trinitarianism which this doctrine badly needed. Further, Irenaeus found rather more satisfactory means of handling the doctrine of the Holy Spirit so that his Trinity really is a Trinity and not, like Justin's, a thinly disguised Binity. In short, Irenaeus succeeded in bringing the newly-minted Christian doctrine of God into better accordance with the witness of the Bible itself. But his Trinity is still no more than a strategy on the part of God. He does not envisage eternal distinctions within the Godhead; indeed he refuses to speculate on such themes; they are, for him, too reminiscent of Gnostic speculations.

Tertullian in his turn contributed to restore balance and proportion to the tradition of economic Trinitarianism. He devised a terminology for Trinitarian theology in Latin which all later ages were to use. He envisaged the Godhead as a unity distributed into a Trinity of three Persons equal in *status* (quality) but not in *gradus* (rank) so convincing that many scholars in the past have assumed that he anticipated the Trinitarian doctrine of the fourth century Church, or even that he is a witness to its continuous existence since the time of the primitive Church. He too gave a much fuller recognition to the place of the Holy Spirit in the Trinity and found better ways of expressing the Spirit's function. He too placed proper stress upon the incarnation, indeed, he speaks in almost Swiftian language about the coarse, earthy reality of Christ's life as an infant, and he realizes that to deny the reality of Christ's humanity is to deny the saving effect of his death. But when all is said and done, Tertullian in his Trinitarian thought remains a man of his age. The Trinity is still for him a strategy devised by God for purposes of creation and revelation. There was a time, he specifically says, when the Father was not a father. He does not anticipate the fourth century, he does not break out of the restrictions of economic Trinitarianism. The same may confidently be said of Hippolytus and of Novatian, though neither of them returns to the inadequacies of the Apologists' doctrine of God, and they have both learnt well from Irenaeus and from Tertullian. Arnobius and Lactantius, writing in Latin just before the outbreak of the Arian controversy, stand as sharp reminders that Western theologians still regarded economic Trinitarianism as basic Christian orthodoxy. Indeed these two authors not only are quite unacquainted with the work of Origen, who had died fifty years before they wrote, but even in the inadequacy of their Christology compare unfavourably with Tertullian and Novatian. The same may be said (though with greater excuse, for he clearly had much less education) of Victorinus of Pettau, their contemporary.

It is interesting to note that there were attempts in the third century Church to provide an alternative doctrine to economic Trinitarianism without calling in a philosophically conceived Logos-doctrine. The later Church so decisively rejected them that they only now survive in fragments quoted by those authors who wrote against them. They had no influence, except by way of reaction, on the traditional Christian doctrine of God, but they serve to remind us how fluid was the whole situation even in the third century, and how much this history of the formation of the Christian doctrine was a matter of trial and error.

III

Between the emergence and refinement of economic Trinitarianism as a coherent Christian doctrine of God on the one hand, and the christological turmoil of the fourth century on the other, there lies another, and very different, attempt to produce a philosophically intelligible and acceptable Christian doctrine of God, the doctrine of God set out by Origen. When we reach the Christian Platonists of Alexandria we come for the first time to a point when the Christian faith is consciously and deliberately establishing communication with contemporary philosophy and accepting its aid. Christian theologians hitherto had of course used philosophy, but they had done so without acknowledgement, in spite of themselves, and they had often disparaged philosophy. A catena of passages from the Epistle to Diognetus, from Tatian, from Hermias, from Tertullian, and from Hippolytus could be produced to prove this. But Clement of Alexandria and Origen welcomed the aid of philosophy—the right sort of philosophy—and acknowledged that the study of philosophy could lead to truth. Origen was indeed one of the leading philosophers of his day, and was acknowledged as such by his contemporaries, especially when the Emperor Alexander Severus and his mother condescended to interview him. Indeed the whole aim of Origen's intellectual activity might be summarized as the supplying of the Christian faith with a philosophical framework. It was this objective that led Origen, by far the most sophisticated and intellectual writer whom the Church of the first three centuries produced, to formulate a doctrine of God which was at once perfectly defensible as consistent with Christian orthodoxy and strikingly different from any which had been produced before his time.

Origen began by positing God as the absolute One, beyond all being, simple, untouched by becoming or change or transitoriness or multiplicity. The immutability of God is indeed the cornerstone of all Origen's doctrine. He identified this absolute unchanging One with the living God of the Old and New Testaments; he did not achieve this by a kind of unequal yoking of the two. This absolute One was, in Origen's view, goodness itself, and self-revealing goodness. But in order to communicate and reveal himself this absolute One had to possess within his being an organ whereby he could communicate with the world of multiplicity, of transitoriness, of becoming and change. This organ was the Son or Logos, who was entirely God, a second *hypostasis* or person within the Godhead, who had been begotten or produced by the absolute One from eternity and is always so begotten. But this Son was a mediator-God by his very nature, a mediating organ within the Godhead lower in rank than God the Father, and representing one stage of the movement of God towards mutability and multiplicity. The Spirit was a third stage, still fully God but less in rank even than the Son and produced by the Son. Still, all three constituted one God, a Godhead which had grades within it. If, however, this God was a self-communicating and self-revealing God, he must always have been so (otherwise he would have been changeable). Therefore there must always have been rational spirits to whom he could reveal himself, for God would not communicate or reveal himself properly to anything less than rational spirits. Therefore all souls of all people have existed from eternity and will exist for eternity, indestructible. But at some point these free rational spirits all (with one exception), using their free will, fell, turning from God. In order to recover them, God created the physical universe, into which these souls can be born with physical bodies and begin, as in a kind of cosmic Approved School, their ascent back to God. The majority of them do not achieve this return immediately, but after this life have still to endure a long series of further (intellectual and spiritual, no longer incarnate) existences or worlds until they all finally return to their original state of obedience to God as pure spirits. The one exception to this pre-mundane Fall was a spirit which had always clung steadfastly to the Logos, and continued to do so. When the Logos determined to become incarnate he caused this unfallen soul to be born with a physical body like any other soul, and the resultant human being (soul+body) was Jesus Christ, who continued all through his earthly existence to adhere unswervingly to the Logos. After the Resurrection and Ascension the human body of Jesus disappeared, though his soul continued to cling to the Logos. This Logos who thus became temporarily incarnate is, as he always has been, the mediating organ through whom all men may attain to God, and, as God's immutability requires strict universalism, through whom all men and all demons, including the Devil, eventually in some distant future after passing through many existences (though only one incarnate existence) will assuredly return.

This, in its barest outline, is Origen's doctrine of God. It is immensely well-constructed, immensely ingenious, a carefully planned and well integrated combination of Middle Platonism, at the point where it is about to become Neo-Platonism, with the Christian faith. Its advantages are obvious. It has broken out of the restrictions of economic Trinitarianism, boldly envisaging the Trinity as immanent, not as a strategy adopted at one point by God in order to create and reveal, but as a picture of the very nature of the eternal God himself. Jesus Christ in this scheme is a real human person whose bodily existence is no sham. The human soul of Jesus is the link between God the Logos and Jesus the man, a most ingenious, a most elegant, solution of a difficult problem. The whole sweep of human history, the whole story of all created things, are gathered into an account of God's self-communication and self-revelation in Jesus Christ, and are given a philosophical explanation of the highest respectability. This certainly is a nobly consistent doctrine of God, and one that can claim to be authentically Christian as well. Beside it even the most improved form of economic Trinitarianism looks narrow and amateur. It is not surprising that Origen's theology gathered many disciples and admirers during his lifetime and was very widely influential for centuries after his death.

Origen's system has one more apparent advantage, which in fact on closer inspection reveals one of his most seriousness weaknesses. It does away entirely with eschatology. Of course Origen made some gestures towards, and paid some lip-service to, traditional eschatology, but in effect he had abolished it. Not only does he allegorize biblical eschatological terms into present religious experience (a device learnt from the Gnostics), achieving the distinction of demythologizing seventeen hundred years before Bultmann, but it is obvious that, however Origen may protest, if beyond this life, this world, there are countless further intellectual or spiritual existences in store for us, it does not very much matter how this world ends. Eschatological phenomena like the Parousia, the general resurrection, and the judgement lose their significance when placed in vistas as vast as this. Whether eschatology can be disposed of in as sweeping a way as this or not will be discussed later, but this devaluation of eschatology necessarily leads us to ask whether Origen did not similarly devalue the incarnation. In this system the incarnation is a closed episode in history. The Logos has ceased to be incarnate. But Origen did not crudely attempt to by-pass the incarnation. He insists that everybody must begin with the *Heilsgeschichte* as a genuine history; we must all begin by believing in the incarnate Christ, though the more advanced Christian is encouraged to move beyond this rudimentary form of belief to belief in and contemplation of the post-carnate Logos. The incarnation can justly be said to be central to Origen's system. But it is of course a central piece in a very vast edifice of speculation, and we can reasonably ask if the very vastness of the whole does not reduce the significance even of the centrepiece, leaving it comely but dwarfed, like Trinity Church, Wall Street, in New York, crouching between its neighbouring sky-scrapers.

Consonant with this reduction of the incarnation is Origen's emphasis upon the cosmological side of his system. In a sense he has reversed the trend set by Irenaeus and Tertullian and switched the weight of his thought from Christ incarnate as a redeemer to the Logos in the universe as the revelation of God. This was the price he paid for accepting the aid of philosophy so fully. His speculations about the relation of the persons of the Trinity to each other and to the world are sophisticated and ably constructed, but they appear to be called for more by the necessities of his philosophical assumptions than by the data of Christian revelation to be found in the Bible. In particular his Logos-mediator is an unsatisfactory feature. God the Son in Origen's system is by his nature, by his position in the Godhead, a mediator; he is the mediating part of the Godhead, and with the Holy Spirit he constitutes an immanent Trinity, indeed, but a graded one. The three Persons are co-eternal together, but not co-equal. This was in the end to prove the gravest weakness of all in Origen's system. The mediatorial activity of Jesus Christ is not therefore a gracious and paradoxical self-giving into human history and human nature on the part of God, but a device within the Godhead for reducing itself sufficiently to be able to communicate with what was not God.

IV

The greatest crisis which the Christian doctrine of God had to encounter in the process of its formation was the Arian controversy, which is usually reckoned to have lasted from 318 to 381. It is still customary for the authors of textbooks of church history to describe this controversy as if there existed from the beginning of it an authentic orthodox doctrine of the relation of the Son to the Father, recognized by large numbers of people as such, to the general effect that the Son was consubstantial and coequal and coeternal with the Father, and that the story of the controversy is the story of how this doctrine was first asserted by a General Council in 325 and then attacked and suppressed by a large number of people who ought to have known better. In support of this theory there is sometimes alleged the fact that in the middle of the third century bishop Dionysius of Rome appears to have attacked bishop Dionysius of Alexandria on the grounds that, among other misdeeds, the latter had refused, or neglected, to attach the epithet 'consubstantial' to the relation of the Son to the Father. It is concluded from this that the see of Rome at least, and probably most of the Churches of the West also, had known the correct, orthodox doctrine of the consubstantiality of the Son for a long time before the Nicene Council declared it. But this view is not at all likely to be true. If Dionysius of Rome insisted upon the necessity of the word 'consubstantial' it is much more likely that he did so because he was anxious to preserve the teaching of Tertullian that the Father and the Son are equal in *status*, i.e., quality, and are *unius substantiae*, of the same God-stuff or divinity, but that he also adopted the economic Trinitarianism of Tertullian and of Novatian. As the account of his remarks is given to us in Greek we cannot be sure what were the exact words of the Roman bishop.[3] If the contention were true that Nicene orthodoxy had long been the accepted doctrine of God within the Church or within a great part of it, we would be faced with an historical enigma. A doctrine upon which the orthodox, traditional, teaching of the Church was clear to a great many people, and had been clear for a long time, was the subject of bitter, confused controversy which convulsed the whole Christian Church for over sixty years, involving the calling of at least four General and many less important Councils, the composition of a large controversial literature, the expulsion and reinstatement of many bishops, the appearance of several new theological groups or parties, and the frequent interference of the Roman imperial government. If there was no serious subject for controversy, if there was no honest doubt on the subject in minds of men of integrity and intelligence, how could such a controversy have taken place? But if we assume, on the contrary, that what made the Arian controversy so acute and prolonged was the fact that when the doctrinal questions were first raised nobody knew the answer, that the controversy is a story of the process of what has been called 'trial and error' in determining Christian truth operating in a most important subject, then the whole affair becomes much more understandable.

Abandoning therefore the myth of the Church of Rome, or any other Church, being at the beginning in sure possession of the truth about the subject, we must look briefly at the various traditional doctrines which existed when the controversy broke out and also at those which developed as the controversy ran its course. Any attempts at stating the Christian doctrine of God without invoking the aid of a Logos-doctrine had now been entirely suppressed in the Catholic Church, and were generally branded indiscriminately as Sabellianism, The last important such attempt, that of Paul of Samosata, bishop of Antioch, had been condemned in 268. Economic Trinitarianism was still a live option, whether the more balanced and refined version expressed by such writers as Irenaeus, Tertullian, and Novatian, or the rather cruder type to be found in the second-century Apologists, and in the works of Arnobius and Lactantius and Victorinus of Pettau, who wrote only a few years before the Arian controversy broke out. The most influential and most sophisticated variety of doctrine of God was that of Origen: his theology was now very influential indeed in the Eastern Church and had been so for some time. Dionysius of Alexandria (*ob.*264) had been a great Origenist. The bishops who opposed and condemned Paul of Samosata had been Origenists, if we are to judge by a circular called the *Letter of Hymenaeus* produced by some of them. The writings of Eusebius of Caesarea produced just before the Arian controversy broke out, the *Praeparatio Evangelica*, and the *Demonstratio Evangelica*, give us a valuable picture of how a devoted Origenist expressed himself at that time. Clearly the issues which were to be brought into the limelight during the controversy were already agitating men's minds. Eusebius is concerned to define the relation of the Son to the Father's being (*ousia*). He never uses the word 'consubstantial' (*homoousios*), and is inclined to suggest that the best formula is to say that the Son or Logos is the image of the being (*eikōn tēs ousias*) of the Father. On the subject of *when* the Son was begotten, whether eternally or at a point in time, Eusebius carefully hedges. He subordinates the Son to the Father even more than his master Origen did; the Son is produced and wholly dependent on the unbegotten, incomparable Father, who is beyond all and without beginning. One can see how easy it would have been for Eusebius to slide gently from Origenism into Arianism; by the time (much later) he has written his book *Against Marcellus*, the slide has been accomplished.

The doctrine of Arius himself cannot be identified with either of these two traditions, though it offered some similarities to both. Its origins are obscure, and need not concern us here. He began from the doctrine of the incomparability of God the Father. Nothing whatever in the universe can be put in the same category as he. He has indeed within his being, among other energies, Logos or Reason, but this power at no point became separate from him. At a point in time, or at any rate not in eternity nor as an eternal process, God produced an entity or organ called the Son, through whom he created the world and communicated with it for purposes of redemption. This Son was not produced from the Father's being, but was made out of nothing, was not consubstantial with the Father, and could not even correctly (but only by way of courtesy) be called the Logos. After creating the world as God's Agent, communicating with the chosen race on behalf of God, becoming incarnate in order to redeem men, being crucified and raised, and ascending to the Father again, the Son became permanently divine and could be addressed as God. He was never immutable by nature, and has become so only by his steadfast loyalty to the Father's will. The Spirit was a lesser creation of the Father, after the Son, and was not easily distinguishable from the highest angels. There certainly had been a time when neither the Son nor the Spirit had existed.

Unusual though this doctrine was in some ways, it had points of appeal to both existing traditions. It clearly began by accepting a firmly monotheistic God in the Jewish tradition and fitted into relationship with him the Son and the Spirit, thoroughly subordinated in a manner which could be represented as scriptural. This would appeal to all economic Trinitarians. Though Arius' doctrine was not at all like that of Origen, the fact that Arius had uncompromisingly set the Son in a mediating position between God and the world might hold a certain appeal to Origenists. Arius strongly attacked the idea that the Son could be regarded as consubstantial with the Father. To many in both existing traditions this doctrine of the Son's consubstantiality appeared virtually to imply the identification of the Son with the Father, and this nobody would assent to.

On the other hand, Arianism as expounded by Arius in other ways seriously offended the theological convictions of many people. To describe the Son as a creature made out of nothing, and to declare that there had been a time when he had not existed, was difficult to reconcile with the idea, held by most exponents of economic Trinitarianism, that the Logos had always existed within the Father's being even before he had taken part in the strategy whereby the Trinity was developed, and flatly contradicted Origen's exposition of God as a Trinity. Arius' doctrine traversed in a difficult and confusing way many existing ideas about the Christian doctrine of God, and brought the whole subject to a decisive issue without making any serious contribution to its solution. In as far as it seemed to support existing doctrines it merely served to show up their weakness. In as far as it denied existing doctrines it challenged their exponents to produce alternative accounts of the subject which would at once satisfy everybody and do justice to the scriptural evidence, in the circumstances an almost impossibly difficult task.

What happened is well known. The Emperor Constantine convened a General Council in 325 which resoundingly condemned the views of Arius, and produced a creed which declared that the Son was 'begotten ... out of the substance of his Father ... begotten, not created, consubstantial with the Father', and which denied that there was a time when the Son did not exist or that he came into existence out of nothing or that he was of a different entity (*hypostasis*) or substance (*ousia*) from the Father, or that he was created or changeable or variable. The next two decades after the Council showed that its language was not regarded as representing a satisfactory doctrine of God by many bishops, especially in the East. The cause of Arius, who died not long after the Council, was largely forgotten and his actual doctrines were championed by very few, but the question was left open, and the most resolute attempts were made, first to discover an alternative account of the doctrine of God to that of the Nicene Council, and then to achieve universal agreement on a formula which would leave the question open, or at any rate rule out attempts to define the relation of Son to Father by relating the substance of the Son to that of the Father, and allow full toleration to believers in a thoroughly subordinationist account of the Trinity.

The controversy which resulted from this confused situation produced a whole spectrum of differing views about the relation of the Son to the Father. There was a school of Origenists who objected to the Nicene Formula as virtually identifying the Son with the Father and preferred as their slogan a phrase taken from the works of Origen himself, 'unchangeable image' of the Father. Not very different from them was a group, later dubbed the 'Semi-Arians', who thought that the right phrase was not 'consubstantial' but 'like in substance' (not *homoousios* but *homoiousios*). There was an influential party which rejected all reference to substance in the matter and attempted to enforce the term 'similar according to the Scriptures', apparently in order to leave room for an openly subordinationist doctrine. The extremes were represented by right-wing pro-Nicene figures such as Marcellus of Ancyra and Photinus of Sirmium who reacted so violently from subordinationism as to deny the separate existence of the Son within the Trinity, and left-wing Arians, whose chief theologian was Eunomius, a consistent, extremely rationalist, doctrinaire Unitarian, who was as anxious as Toland to represent Christianity as not mysterious, and who believed that the Son should be described as having a different substance from the Father's.

The view which finally prevailed was that which had been from an early period in the controversy expounded and championed by Athanasius, bishop of Alexandria. It constituted a kind of theological revolution, for it put an end to both economic Trinitarianism and Origenism. Athanasius was not seriously interested in philosophical speculation nor in the problem of linking an incomparable God with a world of transience and decay. He may indeed be said to be the first to produce a completely Christian doctrine of God, because he did not start from the Jewish monotheistic God and then try to fit the Son and the Spirit somehow into proper relation with his being, and yet he was deeply concerned with salvation, with Christ as representing God to us. He began by postulating God as a Trinity within whose being the Father, the Son and the Spirit have always been distinct entities without detracting from the unity of the Godhead. God did not require any intervening agent to create the world; he created direct. Athanasius here decisively abandoned the old Logos-doctrine which had been at the root of economic Trinitarianism, and he did so for the very best reason, in the interest of his doctrine of redemption. In Athanasius' thought the Son is not a cosmological device, nor even a mediating organ within the Godhead; instead, he fully represents and conveys the Father. In the Son we have the Father. Jesus Christ is not simply an agent for conveying to us messages, even messages of salvation, from God. He is the self-communication of God. Here we have the centre of Athanasius' doctrine, and here we see both what was at stake in this controversy and what was the root fault of Arianism. Arians, one suspects, could never quite believe that God is capable of communicating himself. This, after all, is the great scandal and the great claim of Christianity, that in this historical figure Jesus of Nazareth God does communicate himself, and many philosophers and historians and theologians since the fourth century have found it impossible to accept this doctrine and have sought to find ways of modifying or evading it.

Athanasius insisted firmly that the redeeming function of Jesus Christ must be reflected, and must be expressed in theological terms as reflected in the immanent relations of the Father and the Son in the Trinity, and presented this crucial conviction wholly, or almost wholly, in terms of Greek metaphysics. They were the terms in which the whole controversy was conducted. He taught that the Son is co-eternal with the Father, that he is from the Father's substance (*ousia*), that he is similarly constituted to the Father in all points, that he should be called 'consubstantial' with the Father, i.e., that he has the identical being (not just the same sort of being) which the Father has, with only this difference, that he issues from the Father and is not actually the Father, for the Father is the root and source of the Son. In the case of the Son 'to be begotten' means to share completely by nature in the Father's entire nature. The Father has always been Father and has always implied a Second, the Son.

In his *Letters to Sarapion* Athanasius did attempt to extend his Trinitarian doctrine to the Holy Spirit, as he realized he logically must. He did not carry this task far, partly because his main interest was always christological, partly because he, like all the Fathers, found it extremely difficult to produce scriptural evidence for the divinity of the Spirit as a separate entity (*hypostasis*) within the Godhead, and partly because he had not worked out any philosophical structure to assist him. The completion of this task was achieved by Basil of Caesarea, Gregory of Nazianzus and Gregory of Nyssa, three closely related theologians who are usually called the Cappadocian Fathers and who wrote and taught between 370 and 390. They not only turned their attention particularly to the subject of the divinity and co-eternity of the Holy Spirit, but they were able to supply a philosophical structure, borrowed partly from the Neo-Platonic philosophy of the age, to expound and justify the full-blown Trinitarian doctrine which they were commending. The formal seal of the Church's approval of the work of these pro-Nicene theologians was given in the Creed of the Council of Constantinople of 381, which declared that Jesus Christ was 'born of the Father before all ages ... true God from true God, begotten not created, consubstantial with the Father', and described the Holy Spirit as 'the Lord and Giver of Life who proceeds from the Father, who is worshipped and glorified along with the Father and the Son'. This Trinitarian doctrine was to be filled in and rounded off in various ways by later theologians, notably by Ambrose and by Augustine. But in this formula of Constantinople of 381 the Christian doctrine of God had reached in its essentials the mature form which it has retained ever since in the creeds and belief of the Catholic Church.

V

The doctrine of God achieved by the Church of the fourth century appears to be a far cry from the doctrine about God to be found in the New Testament. An eschatological drama involving a Saviour-figure who is the Act of God has been replaced by a construction of Greek metaphysics consisting entirely of speculations about immanent relations of entities within the Godhead. This certainly does represent a development in Christian doctrine, as Newman perceived and as Harnack declared, and also, at least in the terms used, a Hellenization of the original Jewish Gospel. Dynamic terms consisting mainly of vivid imagery have been replaced by philosophical categories. Function has been pushed into the background in favour of status. One can sympathize with theologians like Schleiermacher and Ritschl who turned their backs on the doctrine of the Trinity or reduced it to insignificance.

But it would be a mistake to imagine that the traditional doctrine of the Trinity has really been substituted for the gospel, or was ever intended to be. The gospel of Jesus Christ and the doctrine of the Trinity are two quite distinct, though not necessarily incompatible, things. The one is the message as taught with all its existential power and with the full benefit of the imagery of the New Testament. The other is a consistent doctrine of God developed in the light of the significance attached to Jesus Christ by the writers of the New Testament, a theological construction designed to draw out the doctrine of God which lies behind the evidence of the Old and New Testaments. The very people who were most responsible for producing the final form of the Christian doctrine of God protest constantly that they do not want to add to the faith, that they are only interpreting the Bible. To speak of the doctrine of the Trinity 'replacing' the evidence of the Bible, is therefore, strictly speaking, inaccurate. The former is an interpretation of the latter.

Was it a necessary interpretation? It is enough to have listened to the fumbling and inadequate explanation of the status of Jesus given by anyone belonging to one of those sects who reject the doctrine of the Trinity in favour of 'the teaching of the New Testament' to realize that *some* interpretation was necessary. The very fact that the final, Nicene, form of the doctrine was only achieved after four centuries of groping, of trial and error, shows that only dire necessity drove the Church to formulate this doctrine. A hundred and fifty years ago almost all scholars would have believed, and would have argued, that the doctrine of the Nicene Creed had been handed down from the apostles themselves and had always been known in the Church. We now realize that this was a quite unhistorical and grossly over-simplified view of the matter. But the very record itself of doctrinal development, doctrinal speculation, alteration, controversy, dissidence, vicissitude, the crudities, the redressings of balance, the new starts, the fact that the line of development is anything but straight and smooth, the impression we gain of men wrestling with new and difficult problems and trying now this answer and now that—all this makes the final result more impressive. Doctrinal agreement achieved this way is more authentic than the glib theory of a mere publication of inherited tradition. The achievement of the Nicene Creed was not a simple, straightforward restating of the New Testament in other terms, an inference so obvious that nobody could fail to make it, as the Thirty-nine Articles and the Westminster Confession suggest, but a formula wrung out of three or four centuries of debate and reflection and experience. To the question 'What difference to our concept of God does Jesus Christ make', there is no simple, ready-made answer, lying unmistakably on the surface of Scripture, or anywhere else. The answer in the end was of course given in terms of Greek philosophy, in Hellenized terms. It is pointless to regret this fact. It would be as profitable to regret that the Parthenon was made of stone, and not of steel and concrete. There were no other terms available to the Church during that period. Even if it had proved possible to express this doctrine coherently and rationally in Jewish terms (and it is very doubtful if it could), these terms would have been of no use to the Church, because they would not, they could not, have appealed to the intellectuals of the ancient world. During the Arian controversy there were plenty who disliked the use of Greek terms, and wanted to eliminate any reference to *ousia* (substance). But the only alternatives they had to offer were either to confine the definition to the words of Scripture—a perfectly futile suggestion considering that the controversy was about the meaning of the words of Scripture—or to drop any attempt at definition at all. Of course the use of Greek philosophical terms meant that the definition would be in some respects unsatisfactory. All definitions are unsatisfactory because human affairs are mutable and human words become obsolete. To describe God in words of any language or era is to court eventual inadequacy and obsolescence. What the Nicene Creed was trying to describe was not wholly expressible in words. But this does not mean that the attempt should never have been made, for, once Arius had raised the question in the way that he did, some definition had to be made. Nor does it mean that the definition was not within its limits and according to its measure successful. It was in some ways remarkably successful.

In the first place it secured that one powerful factor which operates in the making of Christian doctrine was satisfied, the existence of a worshipping community. Christian doctrine was not invented by a series of theological back-room boys who devised speculative theology for their own aggrandisement and the mystification of the ordinary honest Christian. It was not even invented by a number of university professors who lived in an unreal, hothouse atmosphere where ideas counted more than experience or life. It was largely invented by bishops and presbyters who had congregations to cater for, congregations with perfectly normal, humdrum problems, some of whom might, for most of the period involved, have to surrender their property, their liberty, or their life rather than surrender their beliefs. The theologians of the early Christian Church were all writing in an authentically existential situation. And part of this situation was that they worshipped God along with those for whom they wrote. All their theology was pastoral and arose out of a pastoral situation. How was the fact that Christ was worshipped to be safeguarded and expressed? Was he a demi-god, a lesser god, a being to whom (to use a later expression) *douleia* but not *latreia* could be offered? There were plenty of demi-gods in the world of late antiquity, many of them addressed, like Christ, as *theos* and *kyrios*. But Christianity knew that it was not paganism. In the fourth century it had just fought a successful battle against paganism. It knew that it was a monotheistic religion. Was the worship of Christ to be abandoned, therefore? Origen in his austerer moods sometimes appears to suggest this, but such a policy would have been totally unrealistic, would have contradicted one of the most primitive cultic traditions of the Church, and outraged Christian sensibility and opinion everywhere. Athanasius and his friends in their polemical writings constantly refer to the Church's practice of worshipping Christ. It was only by pushing back the person of Christ into the immanent Trinity, into the very life and nature of God himself, that the worship of Christ could be safeguarded and integrated into Christian thought. There was no other policy available. Once again we realize that in its doctrines of the Trinity the Church was attempting to express the inexpressible, because it was forced to do so, to speak only in case silence might betray the truth.

And, remote though the doctrine appears to be from the words of Scripture, it did, and does, safeguard the sense of Scripture better than any alternative formula which has hitherto been produced. Those who have read much of the work of the ancient Fathers of the Christian Church may indeed be excused if they conclude that careful and judicious interpretation of Scripture was not their strong point. Their determination to see the Old and the New Testaments as on an equal level of relevance, and their use of allegory to read advanced Christian doctrine into almost every part of both Testaments, the irresponsibility of their approach, the unscholarly way in which they handle the texts, deprive us of confidence in their capacity to interpret the details of Scripture rightly. The very fact that Proverbs 8.22 was the central text over which the controversy about Christ's divinity may be said to have been fought, and that the great text which agitated those who disputed about the divinity of the Holy Spirit was Amos 4.13, is eloquent testimony to this. But though they were often utterly astray about the details of exegesis, when it came to assessing the main message, the burden, the drift, the weight of Scripture, what Irenaeus calls the *hypothesis* and Tertullian the *ratio* and Athanasius the *skopos*, their judgement was usually sound. They knew perfectly well, for instance, that the Synoptic Gospels at least unequivocally represented Jesus as wholly human, even to his mind, and that a cyclical theory of history was impossible to reconcile with the Bible. On the main question, therefore, as to whether Jesus Christ was the self-communication of God, or rather whether he was the self-communication of God in such a way as to remain permanently the self-communication of God, the final judgement of the fourth-century Church was entirely sound. This is what the Bible intended to teach. This was the impression left on the mind of those who had known Jesus in the flesh, of those who had formed the primitive Church and of those who had worshipped God in the Christian Church ever since. And the Nicene doctrine of the Trinity alone could ensure that this conviction was safeguarded. This was the point for which Athanasius—who was no injured innocent but a violent and often unscrupulous party-leader—fought so fiercely. He did know that this was what Scripture taught about the significance of Christ. And he knew that none of the other forms of expounding the Christian doctrine of God —Origenist, economic Trinitarian, Arian, Semi-Arian, Eunomian —could permanently ensure this truth. The Arian controversy, which put searchingly to the test so many well-meant theological efforts, had clearly shown this.

We call the doctrine of the Trinity a dogma, but we need not intend by this a doctrine which requires no reinterpretation, no re-examination, no restatement, a belief the formulation of which has achieved so final a form that the Church need never reconsider it. George Tyrrell used to describe dogmas as invitations to thought and to discussion, as signs of a mystery which needs exploration and probably new understanding. If we think of the doctrine of the Trinity as an invitation to examine the subject of the difference made to the doctrine of God by the career of Jesus Christ, and if we resolve to take seriously the full implications of this subject, we shall do well. But however long we may explore this doctrine the conclusion is difficult to avoid that the dogma of the Trinity has given the Christian faith a particular shape which has affected its development ever since and which it cannot lose without ceasing to be Christianity. This dogma represents the point at which the Church's doctrine of God reached maturity, attained the full measure of the Church's experience of God. The words may grow old and meaningless. The reality behind them will not pass away.

NOTES

1 'Thy Name, the source of all creation', but the word *Logos* does not appear here.

2 *De Fabrica Mundi*, 7 (CSEL, ed. Haussleiter, p. 7, 10–11).

3 The source of our information is Athanasius, *de Sententia Dionysii*, *passim* and especially 13.1–3 and 18.2; *de decretis* 26.1–7 (quotation of Dion. of Rome 2–7); *de synodis* 43 (ed. H. G. Opitz, Berlin, 1935–41); see also C. L. Feltoe, *Dionysius of Alexandria* (Cambridge 1904), pp. 177–82. Athanasius says that Dionysius of Rome in his book against the Sabellians denied that the son is a creature or that he came into existence or that he was formed or made and that there was a time when he did not exist. All this, even the last phrase, is compatible with economic Trinitarianism, if it is granted that the Son existed from all eternity within the Father's being. Other language in the words quoted by Athanasius suggests economic Trinitarianism. In the words quoted as his, Dionysius of Rome does not use the word 'consubstantial', but in his reply, clearing himself, Dionysius of Alexandria did mention the word and accept it.

5 *The Chalcedonian Formula: a Declaration of Good Intentions*

The traditional Christian doctrine of God achieved during the first five centuries of the Christian Church's existence, the doctrine of God the Holy Trinity, has on the whole, at least till very recently, weathered the storms created by the advent of historical criticism pretty well. Those theologians whose philosophical basis was idealism positively welcomed the doctrine of the Trinity, and Karl Barth, in what is perhaps the finest exposition of this doctrine produced since the Middle Ages, gave it powerful support. The same cannot be said for the Chalcedonian Formula. Here criticism has been during the last century and a half much more widespread and more penetrating, and defence less convincing. Harnack described the Formula as 'the bankruptcy of Greek theology'. William Temple had no difficulty in accepting a doctrine of the Trinity, in suitably modified idealist terms; but in his contribution to the composite volume *Foundations* he criticized the Chalcedonian Formula severely, even though in his later work, *Christus Veritas*, he came to regard it as possessing negative virtues. Barth defended the Formula stoutly, but hardly with the same depth and conviction which which he had rehabilitated the doctrine of the Trinity. Brunner found the Formula wholly distasteful, as an arrogant attempt to explain that which should be believed by faith. H. R. Mackintosh regarded it with dislike, as a conversion of the gospel into metaphysics abhorrent to all good disciples of Ritschl. Most recently Pannenberg has defended the doctrine of the Trinity, but has found it impossible to accept the Chalcedonian Formula.

The reason for this is obvious. The Chalcedonian Formula, in that it attempts to define the relation of divinity to humanity in Jesus Christ, is much more concerned with history than any expression of the doctrine of the Trinity could be. It must speak about Jesus as an historical figure. But the last century and a half have seen a revolution in historical method. The Chalcedonian Formula is clearly more vulnerable, more readily measured against something like an agreed or objective picture of the historical Jesus, dim though the outlines of such a figure must inevitably be. We may well discern what the Fathers of the ancient Church were intending in producing the Chalcedonian Formula, and we may perhaps applaud their intentions. But it is impossible not to question their success in carrying out their intentions, in view of the inadequacy of their capacity for historical thought. This essay is intended to amplify this theme.

The tradition of thought which ascribes two natures, one divine and one human, to Jesus Christ, is, as has often been pointed out, an old one. It is Melito of Sardis who first uses the term, and Origen who first gives it distinctness;[1] but earlier authors such as Ignatius of Antioch, had used language that could readily be adapted to a 'two-natures' theory. It has often been remarked that Rom. 3.4, 'his Son, who was descended from David according to the flesh and designated Son of God in power according to the Spirit of holiness by his resurrection from the dead, Jesus Christ our Lord', also lends itself to such an interpretation. In fact, however, there is no explicit doctrine in the New Testament of two natures in Jesus Christ, and this doctrine was developed, like the doctrine of the Trinity, under the pressure of intellectual needs of an age much later than that of the first century.

We can detect a general necessity and a particular problem, both of which contributed to the formation of this 'two-nature' theory. In the first place, once the battle against Arianism had been won, the next Christological problem was logically that of the relation of divinity and humanity within Christ. Once it had been established that Jesus Christ was God, was not a hybrid being, more than man but not fully God, and that it was necessary in order to support full Christian faith and worship to postulate a distinction of being within the one Godhead, then the question of the relation of Godhood to manhood in Christ clamoured for attention. Were the champions of the Nicene doctrine, for instance, abolishing Christ's humanity by asserting his divinity? Was his humanity a mere front for his divinity? Athanasius and Hilary of Poitiers, and many others after them, were accustomed to speak of Christ's manhood as a tool or instrument which his divinity used for its own purposes. Did not this suggest that his humanity need not be taken seriously? Again, the Church constantly spoke of the incarnation of Jesus Christ. If Christ was a kind of superior angel the problem of his incarnation might raise little trouble; he would then have represented a kind of temporary epiphany. But if he was 'God of God, Light of Light, very God of very God, being of one substance with the Father', then the question of how he could be envisaged as God incarnate became an acute and searching one. Already towards the end of the Arian controversy the appearance of Apollinarianism had shown that the subject of how the incarnation was to be envisaged was the next question on the theological programme. The solution offered by Apollinarius of Laodicea was a brilliant and a seductive one; it only asked Christians to believe that Christ's mind was divine and not human, and on this assumption it gave a logical and attractive account of the incarnation. It is much to the credit of the ancient Church that it rejected this apparently simple and satisfying explanation. But it was significant that the question should have been raised even before the Arian controversy was over. For most theologians of the period a 'two-nature' theory of the incarnation seemed an obvious and useful basic assumption from which to begin considering this subject. It did not, of course, solve all the questions. But it appeared to provide a satisfactory line of approach.

The particular problem which made a 'two-nature' theory appear peculiarly acceptable during the second half of the fourth century and later arose out of the Arian controversy itself. During this controversy the Arians were anxious to prove that the Son of God, as a being not consubstantial with the Father and of no comparable divinity to his, was shown by Scripture to be limited in several ways, weak and incompetent in comparison with God the Father, and subject to change, unlike the immutable and impassible Father. They consequently brought up again and again those passages in the Gospels where Jesus is particularly represented as subject to human limitations and failings, where he clearly experiences human passions, and where he acknowledges his inferiority to the Father. They pointed to the fact that he was obliged to eat in order to live, that he needed sleep, that he admitted ignorance of some facts, such as the exact time of the Second Coming, that he exhibited anger and even, during the Agony in the Garden, fear, and that he once said explicitly 'My Father is greater than I' (John 14.28). The champions of the Nicene viewpoint found these arguments difficult to counter. They tried sometimes the argument that Jesus only pretended not to know some facts, that he only pretended to be afraid, and so on.[2] But even in the fourth century this was not a very convincing argument. They found it much more satisfactory to say that the verses referring to Christ's limitations, weakness, human passions etc. referred to his human, and not his divine nature. They thereby emancipated the Son, the pre-existent Word, from this Arian disparagement. They even insisted that the great key-text of the controversy, Prov. 8.22, 'The Lord created me the beginning of his ways', referred to the human nature of the Word incarnate, and not to his divine nature. They thereby rescued themselves from an expository snare, but they did so at the expense of committing themselves irrevocably to a 'two-nature' interpretation of the incarnation. This theory, in fact, entered the fifth century as a kind of vested interest. There was very little likelihood from the outset of the christological controversies of the fifth century of any theologian starting from any other basis, however he might in the course of debate modify his ideas about the the relations of the two natures.[3]

Every theological student knows how in the year 451 the Chalcedonian Formula, designed to end a long controversy, set out the relation of the two natures, divine and human, in the one Christ:

> Following, then, the holy Fathers, we all unanimously teach that our Lord Jesus Christ is to us One and the same Son, the Self-same Perfect in Godhead, the Self-same perfect in Manhood; truly God and truly Man; the Self-same of a rational soul and body; consubstantial with the Father according to the Godhead, the Self-same consubstantial with us according to the Manhood; like us in all things, sin apart; before the ages begotten of the Father as to the Godhead, but in the last days the Self-same, for us and for our salvation (born) of Mary the Virgin Theotokos as to the manhood; One and the Same Christ, Son, Lord, Only-begotten; acknowledged in Two Natures unconfusedly, unchangeably, indivisibly, inseparably, the difference of the Natures being in no way removed because of the Union, but rather the property of each Nature being preserved, and (both) concurring into one Prosopon and one Hypostasis; not as though He were parted or divided into Two Prosopa, but One and the Self-same Son and only-begotten God, Word, Lord, Jesus Christ ...[4]

It should be clear to anybody who reads this complex and subtly-designed formula carefully that it is not indulging in hair-splitting definitions and distinctions simply for the sake of baffling the uninitiated, but that, on the contrary, it is intended to safeguard the concept of the incarnation against a number of misconceptions and misinterpretations, and that it does in fact succeed in doing so. It firmly rules out, for instance, the idea that Jesus Christ was a mixture between manhood and Godhead, a divine man or a human god. It rejects the notion that God became man in the same way that men become rabbits in fairy-tales, or that Ulysses' followers were turned into pigs by Circe; the Athanasian Creed was later to put this point, 'not by the conversion of the Godhead into flesh'. God did not turn into a man. The Godhead was not reduced in order to become man, nor the humanity inflated to become God. It insists positively and emphatically upon the unity of Christ. He was not the result of an uneasy linking of divinity and humanity. He was not a man liable sometimes to act as God, nor God occasionally succeeding in behaving like a man. He was one person with one physical and psychological structure. But on the other hand, the statement does its best to guard against the idea that because of the incarnation we can simply substitute the word 'God' for the word 'man' in describing the activities of Jesus Christ. If the union is acknowledged 'unconfusedly' and the difference of the natures is not confused but the property of each nature is rather preserved, we cannot say, without further qualification, 'God ate fish', 'God went to sleep in a boat', 'Jairus' daughter was taken by the hand by God'. And finally, the statement declares as emphatically as it can that Jesus Christ was completely man and also was completely God and yet was one, not two.

The intentions of this declaration are unimpeachable. If we believe that God communicates himself in Jesus Christ we must formulate some doctrine of the incarnation. The framers of the Chalcedonian Formula saw the immense importance of the doctrine of the incarnation. They saw that its deepest significance must be preserved; they foresaw many of the dangers to which such a doctrine is exposed. They did not indulge in elaborate metaphysical constructions devised out of an irresponsible spirit of speculation. Nor was it a mere walking of a tightrope in order to satisfy different points of view. The Formula carefully and solidly enshrined much of the constructive christological thought which had preceded it, using some of the ideas of both the Antiochene and the Alexandrian schools.[5] It makes sense, it is a logically coherent construction. It is a Formula which attracted some of the best minds of the next three centuries to its defence. The history both of those who defended it and of those who attacked it should make it impossible for any fair-minded person to dismiss it as hopelessly unrealistic or as purely polemical. The men who composed it knew what they were defending, and were seriously convinced that it was vital to the Christian faith that the dogma concerned should be defended. We must give them credit for good intentions. But we have to ask ourselves whether their method of expressing these good intentions, i.e., the use of the theory of two natures, was so satisfactory that we today can use it to express the same intentions in a quite altered intellectual atmosphere and in quite different circumstances.

In the first place, it is no use concealing or ignoring the fact that the revolution in theological thinking brought about by the advent of historical criticism must make a considerable difference to our estimate of the value of the Chalcedonian Formula. The time is past when a large and scholarly book, such as Sellers' *The Council of Chalcedon*, could be written in defence of the Council's work without any reference being made to the effect of historical criticism upon our estimate of the Council's doctrine. It should be clear that most of the Fathers had different ideas from ours as to what constitutes evidence for the divinity of Christ. High upon their list of evidence would come the Virgin Birth, the miracles performed by Christ, and the wonderful manner in which Jesus Christ in particular and the early Church in general fulfilled the predictions made by inspired men in the Old Testament, and prominent among these inspired men they would have placed Moses, David, and Solomon—Moses as the author of the legal books, David as the author of the Psalms, and Solomon as the author of most of the Wisdom-literature on the Old Testament and of the book of Wisdom in the Apocrypha. These arguments seem to us today weak and uncertain. However we may estimate the historical evidence for the Virgin Birth, it appears to us to be a most unsatisfactory basis upon which to rest arguments for the divinity of Jesus Christ, if only because it plays so small a part in the total witness of the New Testament to the incarnation. Paul and the author of the Fourth Gospel are probably the two authors within the New Testament who come closer to formulating a doctrine of the incarnation than any others, and who between them supply the greater part of the material upon which a doctrine of the incarnation may be based. These two authors either did not know the story of the Virgin Birth, or if they did they did not think it important enough to give it any place at all in their work.

We might regard the Virgin Birth as a kind of corollary of the incarnation (though there are difficulties even here), but as a basis for a theology of the incarnation the Virgin Birth is most unsatisfactory. Much the same argument can be used about the miracles of Jesus. Quite apart from the question of whether they all happened exactly as they are recorded in the Gospels (a point which cannot be taken for granted about all of them), it is most unconvincing to regard them as direct testimony to the divinity of Jesus Christ, in the way in which they are regarded in, e.g., the *Tome* of Leo. The New Testament itself seems to take a more indirect and ambivalent attitude to the miracles of Jesus than this. Finally, our new understanding of the Old Testament makes it almost entirely impossible to think of the prophecies—or what the Fathers regarded as the prophecies—as serious witness to Christ's divinity. We cannot believe that Moses or David or Solomon wrote anything like the large amount of literature in the Old Testament attributed to them by the Fathers, nor that the majority of texts assigned to these figures really were predictions in the natural sense of the word at all. Even when we consider the utterances of those whom we acknowledge to be prophets, the great majority of their savings we must envisage as addressed primarily to their contemporaries and not as constituting direct prediction concerning Jesus Christ or his Church in any serious sense. We have the advantage of a much better Hebrew and Aramaic text of the Old Testament than had the Fathers, and we are not impeded in our understanding of the Old Testament, as they were, by the necessity of relying on an indifferent Greek translation of the original, or even, in the case of some of the Latin Fathers, on an indifferent Latin version of an indifferent Greek version of the original text. This last difference is perhaps the most serious of all, for here we cannot appeal to the New Testament against the Fathers. The writers of the New Testament were pretty well at one with the Fathers in their estimate of the predictory capacity of the Old Testament, at least in principle. If therefore our estimate of the evidence for Christ's divinity to be found from an inspection of his career differs in so many respects from that of the Fathers, plainly we cannot uncritically accept their account of the relation of divinity and humanity in his person.

What we find wanting in the fathers as they handle the Gospels in their exposition of both the divinity and the humanity of Christ is the capacity for historical imagination. We need not regard this as a serious moral charge against them. Nobody in the ancient world possessed this capacity, except in a very rudimentary way. Every age of Christian art, for instance, until the nineteenth, represented the people of the Old and New Testaments as dressed in the garb of its own day, as virtually its contemporaries as far as culture, behaviour, and background were concerned. In one sense this was an admirable trait, since it ensured that the contemporaneousness, the perennial modernity, of Christianity was properly appreciated. We have incurred loss as well as gain in the painstaking archaism of much religious art of the nineteenth century. But it meant that almost no eminent theologian was capable of reconstructing the ideas and aims and feelings and motives of the men and women of the first Christian century and the centuries before it more than in a very restricted way. We find, for instance, Origen conjecturing that Judas had to identify Jesus with a kiss at his arrest because, owing to the manifold activity of the Logos, the man Jesus changes his appearance frequently and was consequently difficult to recognize,[6] and Hilary of Poitiers teaching that Jesus suffered the Passion (*passio*) but not the pain of the Passion (*dolor passionis*),[7] and John Cassian declaring that Jesus Christ was capable of experiencing neither genuine temptation nor ignorance nor fear,[8] yet all these Fathers unequivocally insist upon the real humanity of Jesus Christ. Historical perspective, a proper appreciation of the past, scarcely existed in the culture in which Christianity was born and expanded. It is unlikely then that the Fathers could have had as acute an appreciation as we have of what it means to say that Jesus of Nazareth was a man of the period known to scholars as late ancient Judaism, nor anything like the understanding of his limitations as a man such as we are bound to accept.

The Fathers, under the influence of this 'two-nature' theory, constantly tended to see divinity and humanity as two elements existing side by side in Jesus Christ, as if one could observe his divine nature operating in some of his words and acts and his human nature operating in others. This is, in fact, precisely the attitude taken by Pope Leo in his famous *Tome*. The divine nature shines in his miracles; the human nature appears as he collapses under blows,[9] and so on. This may be a possible way of dealing with the incarnation in theory, but it is very difficult to accept when we look at the actual picture of Jesus as presented in the Gospels, even in the Fourth Gospel. Here we see Jesus first and foremost as a man, and if we are to believe in him as God we can only come to his divinity through his humanity. The Fathers were inclined to write as if we can observe the divinity of Jesus side by side with his humanity, united with it indeed, and not in contradiction to it, but directly observable independently of his humanity. This is true (as indeed most of the criticism made in this essay is true) as much of the so-called 'Monophysite' as of the Chalcedonian Christology. We must remind ourselves again and again that the subject of the Christological debates of the fifth century was an historical character, and that this fact deeply affects our estimate of the success of the formulae emerging from those debates.

It is true that the Chalcedonian Formula insisted very strongly indeed upon the unity of Jesus Christ. Those who drew it up were convinced that Nestorianism, which had been condemned at the Council of Ephesus twenty years earlier, had dangerously imperilled this unity and had tended to split Christ into a Jesus and a Christ and make in effect two Sons tenuously united by an ill-defined thing called a *prosopon.* And they were determined to avoid this danger. Their method of doing this was to adopt in substance the theory of Cyril of Alexandria which is usually known as that of the 'hypostatic union'. Though the Chalcedonian Formula does not adopt these exact terms, it does include the words, 'the property of each Nature being preserved, and (both) concurring into one Prosopon and one Hypostasis'. By this it means (as Cyril meant) that the divine nature and the human nature combined in Christ to create a single separate individual entity in its own right (Cyril would have said at one period, and his Monophysite followers certainly declared, one incarnate *nature* in its own right). Their intention certainly was to safeguard the unity of the person of Jesus Christ as far as possible.

The Chalcedonian Formula is a comparatively short, and very much condensed, document, which has no opportunity of entering into the implications of what it says. But scholars are generally agreed that implied in the support for the 'hypostatic union' to be found in the Formula is the further assumption made by Cyril of Alexandria that the human nature of Jesus Christ in this union was 'anhypostatic' without the divine nature. The Formula does in fact give explicit approval to the Synodical Epistles of Cyril to Nestorius and to the Eastern bishops. To say that the human nature was 'anhypostatic' without the divine has sometimes been taken to mean that the human nature of Jesus was 'impersonal' without the Logos. Such a statement looks very like Apollinarianism, and it is no doubt significant that Cyril in his writings frequently quoted a work which he thought to be by Athanasius but which in fact was by Apollinarius. However, there is no doubt that Cyril knew what Apollinarianism was, and was very anxious to avoid the charge of succumbing to it, and on many occasions declared that Christ had a human mind. When we say that Cyril's view of the human nature of Christ was that it was 'impersonal', we need not commit ourselves (indeed we ought not to commit ourselves) to the conclusion that Cyril meant the word 'person' in our modern sense of the word. The Fathers always inclined to interpret the concept 'person' ontologically, and not, as we do, psychologically. By describing the human nature as 'anhypostatic' Cyril perhaps meant no more than that it lacked ontological ground, it lacked basis in reality, without the presence of the Logos. This is how the human nature of Christ was related to the divine in the Alexandrian view.

But by this interpretation of the doctrine of the 'anhypostatic' character of the human nature of Jesus Christ apart from the divine Word, the difficult questions are only put one stage further back. If the 'hypostasis', the grounding in reality, of the human nature of Christ was supplied by the Word, whence do we ordinary human being derive our reality? Do we have a kind of human, inferior, reality which his human nature lacked, or rather which in his human nature was suppressed in favour of the Word? Perhaps; but if so, how can it be said that Jesus was wholly human, if his human nature was not entirely like ours, indeed had a reality different from ours? The scent of Apollinarianism is never far from Alexandrian Christology. We may certainly credit Cyril of Alexandria with good intentions in his Christology (though not in his politics). But it cannot be said that he succeeded in producing a satisfactory account of the incarnation which reconciled the full divinity of Christ with his full humanity. He clearly had the intention of presenting the incarnate Christ as one person, not two. But, starting off with the concept of two elements, his attempts to relate them always failed to do full justice to the humanity of Christ.

A more elaborate defence of the 'one *hypostasis*' of the Council of Chalcedon can be made by appealing to the later development of this doctrine in both East and West. *Hypostasis* clearly meant to the Chalcedonian Fathers 'entity' or 'identity', with ontological rather than psychological implications. However the later development in the East (Constantinople II, 553, Constantinople III 680-1, condemning Monothelitism), and also the work of Leontius of Byzantium and later Maximus the Confessor, further refined the concept so that it approximated to our 'subject' (again without the psychological implications being much considered). In the West the definition of Boethius, (*persona est rationabilis naturae individua substantia*) and of Thomas Aquinas performed much the same function, again with no great attention to the psychological consequences. Consequently modern Orthodox and Roman defenders of the Chalcedonian Formula tend to say that it insisted that there was only one subject in Jesus Christ and that subject was the Logos. He was the subject of both natures. They are joined in this defence by E. L. Mascall and Karl Barth. This seems complicated and difficult to understand and in effect not to avoid Apollinarianism because as humans our human egos are our subject whereas apparently on this interpretation Christ did not have, or perhaps we should say was not, a human subject.

The Antiochene Christology, on the other hand, cannot be accused of not leaving full scope to Christ's humanity. Though Nestorianism, which was a product of this tradition of Christology, had been condemned at the Council of Ephesus in 431, and was expressly condemned by the Chalcedonian Formula itself, Antiochene Christology did leave its mark on that Formula. A few lines before the passage quoted above (p. 99), the Formula explicitly condemns Monophysitism, and in the passage itself it expressly attributes a human mind to Christ when it describes him as 'Perfect in Manhood; truly God and truly Man; the Self-same of a rational soul and body; consubstantial with the Father according to the Godhead, the Self-same consubstantial with us according to the Manhood; like us in all things, sin apart'. Apollinarius would not attribute a human 'rational soul' to Jesus, but only an 'animal soul', i.e. approximately what we mean by the nervous system. Undoubtedly the Antiochene tradition was determined to safeguard the full humanity of Jesus. But it does so at the cost of a juxtaposition of the divine and human natures which is intolerable when tested by the picture of Jesus given in the Gospels. We must admit that the discovery of the *Bazaar of Heracleides* has thrown a more favourable light on the views of Nestorius and shown that he was not a 'Nestorian' in the worst sense of the word. And

Nestorianism in its best sense has recently been defended as a viable christological option by Dr Norman Pittenger in an able and attractive book.[10] But the Antiochene Christology remains nevertheless a very weak Christology presenting a picture of a Christ who is constantly threatened with falling apart into a divine Word and a purely human man tenuously and uncertainly related. It is impossible to read Nestorius' *Bazaar of Heracleides* without being struck by the vagueness and looseness attaching to his concept of *prosopon*, which must by the nature of his whole scheme nevertheless be a key-concept, because it is the *prosopon* that unites the divine and human natures. This tradition of Christology fails to escape, no less than the Alexandrian tradition, the fatal consequences of envisaging the divine and the human elements in Jesus Christ as existing side by side, each observable independently of the other. The Chalcedonian Formula managed to express the good intentions of both the Alexandrian and the Antiochene traditions of theology, combining them in an admirably solid and logical statement. We must give it this credit, and recognize how much of value it consequently contains for us. But we must also recognize that it inherits the defects as well as the virtues of these two traditions. Not even Leo's doctrine of the *communicatio idiomatum* can save it.[11]

The 'Monophysite', i.e., non-Chalcedonian Cyrillian and Alexandrian, Christology, was certainly not heretical, was certainly as anxious to preserve the full humanity and full divinity of Christ and his unity as the Chalcedonians, and could even be said in a sense to have done so more successfully, because, in the first place, its champions were not committed to a Formula but instead possessed a tradition of doctrine and in the second place their slogan *mia physis tou theou logou sesarkōmenou* meant that the Logos was the subject but a divine subject incarnate, i.e., possessing a full humanity, indeed according to Severus of Antioch an individuated humanity, with a human mind and human will, the whole forming a single nature, that of the Logos incarnate. They insisted that the divinity was not confused with the humanity. They avoided thereby the difficulties created by Leo's account of the matter in his *Tome*, but they did not avoid the difficulties and complications involved in the Chalcedonian Definition. No ancient Christology did this. However, to admit this much means, of course, that the only danger avoided by the Chalcedonian Definition was that represented by Eutyches, and he constituted no serious danger at all. There can be no doubt that Dioscorus (whom the Chalcedonian Council never condemned for doctrinal error), would never have tolerated heretical Monophysitism. When later heretical Monophysitism did appear, the original Monophysite tradition, represented, e.g., by Severus of Antioch, gave it no welcome at all. This fact gravely reduces the ecumenical status and dogmatic importance of Chalcedon. It is evidently not a formula which alone could safeguard the truths which it was designed to safeguard. It is not necessary for all orthodox Christians to hold it, in fact the orthodox tradition had within it, quite apart from Chalcedon, the resources to safeguard those three doctrines which have already been described as the main concern of Chalcedon, that Jesus Christ was fully God, that he was fully man, and that he was one.

Another of the forces combining to make a 'two-natures' theory by far the most popular basis for Christology in the fourth and fifth centuries was the conviction of the theologians of the Antiochene and Western traditions that they must maintain intact the impassibility of God. This meant that the divine Word who combines with the human nature must not be thought to experience passion of any sort, for this would entail change and the possibility of corruption, and would be incompatible with divinity. And the Greeks interpreted the word 'passion' (*pathos*) in a very broad sense. A laugh would be an example of 'passion', and so would, of course, such sensations as sorrow or fear. If therefore the two elements of humanity and divinity in Jesus Christ were regarded as existing side by side, involving each other in some sense but, at least as far as influence of the human on the divine was concerned, not affecting each other, then it was thought that a genuine understanding of the incarnation might be arrived at without compromising the impassibility and immutability of God. Compromising passions and human experiences could be safely attributed to the human nature, to which the divine nature was joined but by which it was not modified. The Antiochene school of christology was particularly insistent upon the danger of teaching Christological doctrine that would compromise the impassibility of God. This partly accounts for their two-nature theory. They constantly accused the Alexandrian theologians of failing to guard against this danger. It is unfair to the Cyrillian and Eastern Orthodox tradition of Christology to say that it was restricted by the concept of impassibility. The slogan, begun by the Scythian monks, *c.* 515, 'One of the Trinity suffered in the flesh', was widely welcome in perfectly orthodox circles in the East, and is itself irreproachable, however little the Popes may have liked it. However, the Chalcedonian Formula does explicitly reject 'those who dare to say that the Godhead of the only-begotten is passible' and includes among its famous four negative adverbs the word 'unchangeable' (*atreptōs*).

To us today the divinity of Christ is only approachable and perceptible through his humanity. This is not to say that we must necessarily envisage his divinity as some aspect of his humanity raised to the nth, such as his moral ideals or his spiritual insight or his sanctity. But it means that we must first evaluate Jesus as a man, and through this (using, as Pannenberg has so clearly perceived, the resurrection as our sign and clue) see him as God. We cannot envisage the two elements as observable side by side independently of each other. It is quite inadequate to regard Christ's humanity as a mere tool for his divinity. His humanity at once veils and reveals his divinity. His divinity can only be perceived through his humanity, and only then by faith, not by demonstration. But his divinity *is* apprehensible through faith. We do not imagine it. Jesus is the self-communication of God, and therefore is God. He is wholly man and wholly God, but not in such a way that his divinity and his humanity can be perceived side by side, parallel, observable independently of each other. The analogy suggested by D. M. Baillie in his book *God Was In Christ* of divine grace and human free will, where all is of God and mysteriously because of this all is of man, is the best that has recently been produced. Basically it of course is based on the incarnation, so that we are using something that flows from the incarnation to understand the incarnation itself, and it is therefore scarcely a pure analogy. But it serves better than any other illustration.

Today the central problem presented by the incarnation is not ontological but psychological. It is the relation of the mind of Jesus to the mind of God. This was a problem largely ignored by the ancient Church. It is true that the doctrine of Apollinarius to the effect that Christ's mind or *ego* was divine while the rest of him was human brought up the subject of the psychology of the God-man. Here the ancient Church unhesitatingly decided that this was an inadequate account of the incarnation and that we must believe that Jesus had a fully human mind. Once again, the intentions and principles of the Fathers were sound. But their manner of envisaging how this doctrine must be applied to Jesus as he is pictured in the Gospels was very unsatisfactory. They in effect were convinced that Jesus was, as a man, omniscient, encouraged by some hints in the Fourth Gospel, but directly traversing strong evidence in the Synoptic Gospels and the Epistle to the Hebrews. The fact that they were sometimes driven to suggest that Jesus on occasion pretended not to possess a knowledge which in fact he did possess is a striking proof of their failure to deal with this subject adequately.

Christological thought since the advent of historical criticism has wrestled with this psychological question again and again. Basically the Fathers were not interested in psychology, but in ontology. But a number of different intellectual forces—and not least the Renaissance stress upon the individual as a subject, his feelings and experience—have combined to make modern man intensely interested in anything to do with psychology. Theologians of all traditions have therefore asked themselves again and again the question, How was the mind of Jesus related to the mind of God? (I assume here that 'social' doctrines of the Trinity which appear to hold that God has three minds are not to be reckoned with, and that God must be thought of as possessing only one mind.) Neither kenotic nor anti-kenotic Protestant theologians have made much progress here. That the knowledge of Jesus as a man was limited seems to be beyond dispute. It is impossible either to dismiss the subject, as did William Temple, or to adopt the neo-Apollinarianism of Brunner, or to maintain a point of view which in effect says that Jesus both knew and did not know at the same time. Nor is it satisfactory to say, with Mascall and Catholic theologians, that the divine mind supplied the human mind with 'suffused knowledge', as if knowledge were a kind of drug or liquid.

It seems to me that the best way of thinking about the incarnation, difficult, obscure, fragmentary and controversial though this may be—is to regard the incarnation as God's way of choosing to experience human conditions and human destiny, of seeing what it was like to be human. This was God, in the words of the poet Edwin Muir, 'riding against the Fall', making himself vulnerable, putting himself in the position of being subject to human vicissitude and of living by faith, not by omniscience. On this view God in as far as he communicates himself in Jesus Christ chooses not to know, chooses to be limited in knowledge. The psychological difficulty has recently been greatly lightened by a brilliant essay on the consciousness of Christ by Karl Rahner.[12] Among the useful points which he makes is the suggestion that not-knowing, nescience, is not necessarily a purely limiting condition indicative of weakness or inferiority. It has a positive role to play in freedom and can be constructive as well as restrictive. He also points out that knowledge is what he calls 'a multi-layered structure'. If we postulate that Jesus Christ from the earliest moment of his being a human had a knowledge of God of an unique sort, which some would describe as a knowledge of his own divinity (though some would not), this knowledge does not necessarily imply objectified, concrete, knowledge of propositions or facts. We all of us have all the time an undifferentiated awareness of ourselves as existing which cannot be resolved into such objectified, differentiated, knowledge. We might postulate in the mind of Jesus an awareness of God and of his 'being present to God' from his earliest moments, wherein God would not be encountered in his consciousness as an object. It would not include nor imply encyclopaedic knowledge of a propositional type; not all forms of knowledge are in all circumstances better than nescience. It is possible to envisage Jesus during his spiritual development gradually recognizing this awareness of God in the form of differentiated, objective, consciously held knowledge of God and of himself. And, it might be added, we could recognize this kind of epistemological history as appropriate to God's becoming incarnate as man without violating the limits of human nature.

The incarnation, then is God's method of subjecting himself to our destiny and limitations, a strategy or policy deliberately chosen by God to deal with the human situation, which admittedly implies that God is adding to himself some new experience, almost that he is learning something. But if we admit that God allows to man that incalculable and wholly new element in creation, genuine free-will, we have already implied the possibility of the emergence of something quite new. Much more serious is the dangerous possibility apparently opened up by this state of affairs that God, who seems to be taking a kind of risk, should fail, and thereby prove himself not God. If God commits himself in the incarnation, he commits himself and cannot draw back. He *cannot* cause the earth to open and swallow his opponents, he *cannot* come down from the cross (and not merely, as all the Fathers believed, he chose not to). To do so would be to abrogate his character, to reverse the way that he has chosen, to emancipate himself from the destiny which he has opted for, to prove an unfaithful God. He has chosen the way of weakness (a fact which the Fathers, blinded by their belief in God's impassibility, for the most part could not or would not recognize), and he cannot revert to the way of coercion. But what then is the difference between God and man in Jesus? Has God disappeared in this account of the incarnation?

God has not disappeared if we adopt this interpretation of the incarnation, though he is only to be seen through the man Jesus, and this for two reasons. First, because in the man Jesus of Nazareth we can and do see God. The complete self-abandonment, the entire dedication to what is known to be right and to a vocation from on high, the entire unselfishness manifested in Jesus Christ, all that Paul meant when he said that Christ emptied himself (Phil. 2.7), and did not please himself (Rom. 15.3), or gave himself up (Rom. 8.32; Gal. 2.20; cf. Rom. 4.25 and Eph. 5.2, 25), all this was accomplished within wholly human terms, without the benefit of divine foreknowledge or the security of divine infallibility, and yet is more than man could achieve. Before such immense generosity we can only acknowledge the act of God (Rom. 5.1–8). Secondly, God cannot fail and God will not fail. He is not in fact taking a risk in the incarnation. He is bound to succeed; he must win. Otherwise, he would not be God. But he has chosen that he shall succeed *only* by the pattern or strategy of crucifixion-resurrection, of life through death, of strength through weakness, and by no other. He has chosen that his victory shall be a victory costly to him. He cannot cease to be God. The resurrection must take place, and it is the resurrection which demonstrates God's victory, the divinity of Jesus Christ, the fact that God is God. But he has chosen to be God only through the last reach of self-afflicting divine generosity.

Have we then reduced ourselves to a situation where we in fact believe in two gods, a non-incarnate non-suffering and an incarnate suffering one? There have been periods in the history of Christian doctrine when Christians have believed teaching not unlike this. They have believed that Jesus by his death persuaded an angry Father to change his mind, to abate his wrath, and to forgive us. They have fled to Jesus to protect them from God the Father and even to Mary to intercede for them with a distant Jesus who will intercede with a yet more distant Father. But we must not take this path if we are to be faithful to the witness of the Bible and of Christian experience. Jesus is not a convenient half-way house between a God who cannot suffer and a man who suffers as we do. Jesus Christ is the self-communication of God, and if he endures suffering, then God is affected by suffering. We must remove the last remnants of Platonism from our Christian doctrine. Plato deeply distrusted suffering, emotion and subjectivity, and would not associate the divine with them. We must respect the philosophical tradition which flows from Plato and which had its last great representative in the ancient world in Plotinus. But we must recognize that the god of Plato is ultimately not the God of Christianity, however useful Christian theologians may at various times have found some of Plato's ideas. The purest well from which the tradition of Christian theology flows is the Judaism of the Old Testament. Here we have, not a Greek god, profoundly rational, restricted by impassibility, but a free, passionate God who is not at all compromised by contact with human beings and human destiny, who is to be found in the context of history and eschatology, of faith and worship. This God presents himself to us as one who has within his being resources for incarnation, who has in his nature the possibility of so scandalous, so drastic, so demanding a generosity as this.

This concept of God taking a risk, adding to his experience, seeing what it is like to be human, of a God who has a history, as outlined here, will certainly sound strange in the ears of those who are accustomed by traditional philosophy to the concept of God as outside time and beyond change. And it is only put forward here tentatively, as an example of *fides quaerens intellectum*, and of a faith looking for a philosophy. But it seems to be the best way of doing justice both to the full weight of the New Testament evidence, and especially to its eschatological quality, and to the fact, too often obscured in christological discussion, that the God of the New Testament is the same God as the God of the Old Testament. And it is consistent with the contemporary tendency (observable not least in the thought of Karl Barth) to conceive of God in dynamic terms, and terms of motion (not to say of process), rather than in static terms, or terms of subsistence.

Ancient Christology, though it acts as a series of lights to show the orthodox tradition, can only bring us a certain way. Perhaps it is not impossible to conceive of the incarnation according to the intentions of Chalcedon, and of orthodox Monophysitism, though not by following out the precise details of either model. We could say that the Word of God was united to a complete human individual, with a human will, human mind, and human ego, and that the Word entirely filled and controlled this human individual at every moment, using that individual's free and full response, so that his will was in saving effect the will of the Word and his mind the mind of the Word subject to human limitations. Here we shall open ourselves to a charge of Nestorianism and of reducing God's presence in the incarnation to a merely 'spiritual' and 'noetic' one. The point of the 'hypostatic union' was to ensure that God really was objective, ontologically and unquestionably present in the incarnation. But after all, what is a 'subject'? Is it ontological and objective? The type of 'Antiochene' union sketched above is not an hypostatic union. But suppose that we add to this 'Antiochene' model the further statement that this union represents God 'seeing what it was like to be human', making a move into human destiny and pledging himself into human history, etc. Does not this guarantee the reality of God's presence here, especially if we are prepared to say that in this union God suffered? We may adopt a solution approximating to the Antiochene, because we must preserve the full humanity of Jesus, but not because, like the Antiochenes, we wish to preserve the impassibility of God. Here again we perhaps achieve what Chalcedon intended without precisely following Chalcedon's path, because to admit the passibility of God in the incarnation is to contribute towards securing his authentic presence there.

In conclusion, Chalcedon was useful but not necessary; a statement of the existing tradition on the subject, but not the only possible one. It did not solve the problem which it was intended to solve. It contributed both to the clarification and to the obfuscation of the Christian understanding of the incarnation. It is a fine example of the truth that a dogma is not exhausted in the words that formulate it.

NOTES

1 See Melito, *Homily on the Passion* 8. p. 2, 16; Origen *de principiis* 1.2.1; *Comm. on John* 19.2; 32.16; *contra celsum* 3.28; 7.17. Tertullian approaches this concept with his doctrine of two 'substances' in Christ.

2 E.g., Hilary *de Trin.*, ix. 66, 67; other examples could be adduced from Athanasius.

3 I do not, of course, here attempt to follow out in any detail the development of the formula 'two *physeis* in one *hypostasis*', and the confusion resulting from the use of *hypostasis* for strictly Christological

ends, when the term had been used already for Trinitarian purposes. This subject can be studied in the magisterial work of A. Grillmeier, *Christ in Christian Tradition* (London 1965).

4 The translation is from T. H. Bindley, *The Ecumenical Documents of the Faith*, 4th edn. by F. W. Green (1950), pp. 234–5.

5 As has been admirably shown in R. V. Sellers, *The Council of Chalcedon* (London 1953).

6 Origen, *Comm. on Matthew*, Com. Ser. 100.

7 Hilary, *de Trin.* x. 23, 24.

8 Cassian, *Conferences* 5.6; 22.11.

9 *Agit enim utraque forma cum alterius communione quod proprium est; Verbo scilicet operante quod Verbi est, et carne exsequente quod carnis est. Unum horum coruscat miraculis, aliud succumbit iniuriis, etc.* (Leo, *Tome* V, 125–8, Bindley, op. cit., p. 170.)

10 *The Word Incarnate* (1959).

11 This is the doctrine that each nature in functioning according to its proper laws and scope associates with itself the characteristics of the other nature so that neither can be said to be operating alone. But this theory, though (once again) its intention is clearly sound, fails entirely to explain how this is or can be so and remains little more than a purely abstract concept.

12 *Theological Investigations*, vol. 5 (E.T., 1966), pp. 193–215.

6 *The Holy Spirit*

I

In discussing this subject it is useful to begin with a little healthy iconoclasm. Let me compress my iconoclasm into two sentences. There is no doctrine of the Holy Spirit in the Old Testament: the doctrine of the Holy Spirit as a third hypostasis (i.e., 'Person') within a Trinitarian God-head is inadequately supported in the New Testament. When I say that there is no doctrine of the Holy Spirit in the Old Testament, I do not mean that there is no mention of a holy spirit or a spirit of God in the Old Testament. There are of course plenty of such references. But they do not, all put together, amount to anything remotely approaching or even anticipating the Christian doctrine of *the* Holy Spirit. They are simply one of the ways in which the authors of the Old Testament refer to the activity of God, and not even a very common or significant way. They are comparable to references to 'the arm of the Lord' or 'the Word of the Lord', a vivid and characteristically concrete way of describing God's action. When the Bible tells us that the Spirit of the Lord brooded upon the waters at creation or that the Spirit of the Lord came upon Samson or Saul or activated Bezalel, or when those of us who follow lectionaries are led a bizarre dance round curiously ill-assorted snippets of the Old Testament at the season of Pentecost, all these references mean no more than that God produced the circumstances or inspired the people mentioned. Except in so far as they help us to understand that God is Spirit, i.e. free, unconditioned, not bounded by physical limitations, these texts contribute nothing towards the doctrine of the Holy Spirit and cannot seriously be described as foreshadowings of the Christian concept of God the Holy Spirit, not even as much as the Messianic texts are foreshadowings of the Christian concept of God the Son.

The figure of Wisdom in the Wisdom literature of the Old Testament will give us very little help towards the doctrine of the Holy Spirit, because, with the best will in the world, we cannot prevent this figure being wholly ambiguous. What does it prefigure, if anything? The Word? Or the Spirit? The early Fathers, who cannot be accused of backwardness in trying to find prefigurations in the Old Testament, were markedly confused on this point. The majority of them see the Word, the Son, the Logos, foreshadowed in the figure of Wisdom in this literature. The great key text of the Arian controversy, fought over as the dead body of Patroclus was fought over in Homer's *Iliad*, was Proverbs 8.22, which in the Septuagint translation ran 'The Lord created me the beginning of his ways', referring to Wisdom. Bitterly though both sides in this controversy differed on this text, everyone who dealt with it on both sides assumed that it referred to the Son, not the Spirit. A few Fathers see the Spirit in some of the other references to Wisdom in the Old Testament, but there is no sustained or elaborated tradition in this direction. The Fathers were ready to undertake the enterprise of finding evidence for a second divine being separate from God the Father in the Old Testament zealously enough. But even their stout hearts quailed before the task of finding evidence for a *third* divine being separate from God the Father there, and by their silence they quietly admit their failure at this point to live up to their exegetical principles. Where they failed we are not likely to succeed, especially as we are under no obligation to adopt their exegetical principles.

My second example of iconoclasm was to assert that the doctrine of the Holy Spirit as a separate hypostasis within a Trinitarian Godhead is inadequately supported in the New Testament. By this I mean that the usual method followed to discover evidence for this doctrine in the New Testament is a most unsatisfactory one. Evidence is produced that the Holy Spirit is in several texts spoken of as if he is a personal agent or even as if he were God himself, and this is usually regarded as a sufficient proof from the Scriptures of the divinity of the Holy Spirit. There are of course passages where the Holy Spirit is spoken of as a personal agent, notably in the 'Paraclete' sayings in the Fourth Gospel and in a few other passages, such as Acts 16.6, 'having been forbidden of the Holy Spirit to speak the word in Asia'. But in the first place we ought in justice to set against these the many passages in the New Testament where the Holy Spirit is spoken of in an impersonal way, not only in Acts but also in Paul, and we should note the manifest tendency of Paul to confuse or identify the Spirit with Christ (2 Cor. 3.17; Rom. 8.26, 34). In the second place even if these 'personal agent' passages were thought to outweigh the 'impersonal force' passages, this evidence by itself is not sufficient to prove that the Spirit is an hypostasis within the Godhead separate from the hypostasis of God the Father, wholly God but possessing an individual existence separate from that of the Father and the Son. Some of them, perhaps most of them, could, if no other evidence from the New Testament is called in, perfectly well be interpreted as meaning no more than what the Old Testament means by its references to the Spirit of God, simply the action of God himself, presumably God the Father. Far less can they reasonably be construed to witness to the separate existence of the Holy Spirit as a personality, i.e., as a 'person' in our modern sense of the word, within the Godhead, though a surprising number of modern writers have attempted this impossible task. As will become evident later in this book, not only do most modern theologians in my opinion draw conclusions about the Holy Spirit from the New Testament which the evidence alleged by them for it does not adequately support, but in my opinion they usually leave out entirely one of the most important pieces of evidence about the Holy Spirit to be found in the New Testament. It is not surprising if their accounts usually fail to carry conviction.

It is a well-known fact, and has been repeated in textbook after textbook ever since Harnack first proclaimed it, that the treatment of the Holy Spirit in the Fathers of the first three centuries is very inadequate. Many of them, such as Justin Martyr and Lactantius, seem to confuse the Spirit with the Word or to leave the Spirit a very subordinate or restricted place in the activity of the Trinity. They are by no means unanimous about the characteristic function of the Holy Spirit. Even when in the middle of the fourth century Christian writers begin to pay special attention to the Spirit the impression of confusion and uncertainty is not entirely removed. Athanasius in his *Letters on the Holy Spirit to Sarapion* provides by reference to Scripture quite a good description of the function of the Spirit in redemption, but does not come near a definition of it, and his account of the peculiar characteristic of the Spirit within the Trinity is not very satisfactory or clear. The most important work on the theology of the Holy Spirit done in the fourth century came, of course, from the pen of Basil of Caesarea. We can trace a developing and maturing movement of his thought upon this subject from his relatively early book *contra Eunomium*, through a short later work known as *de fide* up to his final *magnum opus*, written not long after the *de fide*, his *de Spiritu Sancto*.

In his *contra Eunomium* he betrays an uncertainty and hesitation in writing about the Spirit, and he appears to be aware of the frailty and insufficiency of the Scriptural evidence on the subject. In his *de Spiritu Sancto* hesitation has been replaced by confidence, both because he has by now properly integrated his doctrine into a philosophical background, and because he has discovered another source of doctrinal support for the theology of the Spirit—tradition.

The possibility of calling in tradition to supplement the inadequacy of Scripture on a subject under dispute had been realized nearly forty years earlier. The first person to make an appeal to it, Eusebius of Caesarea, writing against Marcellus of Ancyra about the year 340, had appealed to the baptismal formula to contradict the view of Marcellus that the Son only achieved hypostatic independence of God the Father at the incarnation. Some sixteen or seventeen years later, Athanasius makes the same appeal to the traditional baptismal formula in order to establish the co-eternity of the Spirit with the Father and the Son, and makes it more fully and confidently than had Eusebius. Basil's invocation of this evidence is much fuller and more elaborate than that of either of his predecessors in this argument. He appears to believe confidently in the preservation in the Church from the time of the apostles of a non-scriptural tradition both of ceremony and of doctrine which regulated not only such matters as the baptismal formula, the formula of consecration in the eucharist, and the manner of Christians turning to the east for prayer and crossing themselves, but also some important doctrinal themes, and in these he appears to include the divinity of the Holy Spirit. This treatise has consequently been the refuge and palladium of all theologians in subsequent ages who have been anxious to argue for tradition as a separate source of Christian truth from Scripture and one equal in authority and authenticity to Scripture. It is clearly no coincidence that the Holy Spirit should be the subject in connexion with which this appeal was apparently first made as a major theme handled carefully and after long deliberation by a great theologian. It is interesting to compare how Gregory of Nazianzus, Basil's great friend, handles this subject when shortly after Basil's death, and not long after the publication of the *de Spiritu Sancto*, which Gregory must have read, he writes his *Fifth Theological Oration*. After arguing that we are bound by the logical consequences of Scripture even though they are not stated in Scripture, he produces a very interesting theory of progressive revelation which extends even beyond Scripture. In the Old Testament God the Father is clearly revealed but God the Son only dimly. In the New Testament God the Son is clearly revealed but God the Holy Spirit only dimly. He refers to the argument from the baptismal formula but does not give it much prominence. He makes no explicit mention at all of non-scriptural tradition. He is quite as much aware as Basil of the insufficiency of Scripture on the subject of the Holy Spirit, but has found a different, and to my mind much more satisfactory, way of dealing with it.

II

Let us now return to the doctrine of the Holy Spirit in the New Testament. I have earlier said that most writers on this topic seemed to me to omit a vital element for understanding the subject. This is that the doctrine of the Holy Spirit in the New Testament is deeply eschatological. The Holy Spirit is the sign of the Last Time. Apparently in rabbinic thought of the first century before and the first after Christ the Holy Spirit was associated with the Age to Come. Eminent rabbis were declared to be 'worthy of the Holy Spirit', but not to possess the Holy Spirit; this gift would be given to them in the Age to Come (whether this was conceived as the Messianic Age or not). This accounts for the curious fact, which has given difficulty to several commentators, that whereas Jesus is recorded, in the Synoptic Gospels at least, as saying almost nothing about the Spirit, the book of Acts and the epistles of the New Testament are full of references to him. With the resurrection and the ascension the time of the Spirit came. John 7.39 indicates this explicitly. 'This he said concerning the Spirit which those who believed on him would receive; for the Spirit was not yet (given); because Jesus was not yet glorified.' But it is expressed in almost every line of the New Testament after the Fourth Gospel. In Paul the Spirit is a foretaste, first instalment of redemption (2 Cor. 5.1–5); Christians have the privilege now of knowing 'things which eye hath not seen nor ear heard', things which the rulers of this age do not know, because the Spirit, the Master of the new age, has revealed these things to them. The reason why Christians can be sure that they will receive new bodies at the resurrection is because they now have the Spirit, who is the link between the old time and redeemed time, between old creation and new creation

(1 Cor. 2.9, 10; 2 Cor. 5.5; Rom. 8.11, 23). To belong to the new creation is to walk after the Spirit (2 Cor. 5.17; Gal. 5.16–18, 28). The last Adam, the second Adam of the new age 'became a life-giving spirit' (1 Cor. 15.15–45). Joel's prophecy of the coming of the new age and last time is fulfilled in the pouring out of the Spirit (Acts 2.16–21; Rom. 5.5). Christians are partakers of the glory of the Last Time because they have the Spirit (1 Pet. 1.5; 4.14). Today is the 'end of these days', and one of the distinctive doctrines of the Community at the end, the Church, is that they are 'partakers of Holy Spirit, and have tasted ... the powers of the age to come' (Heb. 1.2; 6.5). The case is completed by the fourth Gospel's deliberate identification of the Parousia with the coming of the Spirit (John 14.16–18, 26; 15.26–27; 16.12–24).

This eschatological presentation of the Holy Spirit means that the Spirit in the New Testament is not a vague influence associated with Jesus Christ but the form in which, or in whom, God appears to reign over his people at the Last Time. The Spirit is God as the dynamic, the life-giving power of the Church, the unseen Lord, Master, Guide, and Inspirer of the Christian community, who gives instructions to apostles and disciples, sustains the faithful in persecutions and sometimes gives them glimpses of the future through Christian prophets or initiates them into mysteries through *glossolalia*. For the same reason the Spirit is peculiarly associated with prayer, with religious experience, with everything that has to do with man's response to God in the New Testament. There is scarcely a reference to prayer, to worship, to speaking with tongues, prophesying, singing hymns or psalms, making moral decisions or doing good works, in the New Testament which does not include, explicitly or implicitly, a reference to the Holy Spirit. Contrary to some Lutheran opinion, there *is* a doctrine of man's response to God in the New Testament. It is contained in the New Testament doctrine of the Holy Spirit. In the New Testament the Holy Spirit is God in whom man returns to God. It is only in God that we can understand God; it is only the Spirit who can give us the power to perceive that in the story of Jesus of Nazareth we are encountering, not a myth of late Jewish antiquity, not an unhappy tale of cruelty and failure, not a curious example of the capacity of men to deceive themselves, but the move and offer and demand and loving act of God himself (1 Cor. 1 and 2; Rom. 5.1–11). The Holy Spirit therefore is God-at-the-end-of-the-world, God reigning over his people at the last time, God creating and sustaining a community in whom mankind can be enlightened by faith and return to him in worship and love as the first fruits of a new creation, God the quickener and illuminator. The eschatological understanding of the Holy Spirit gives a depth and dimension and an unlimited significance to the subject which many recent treatments of it have lacked.

But the Spirit is not, of course, an isolated phenomenon. The Spirit is indissolubly connected with Jesus Christ. He is the Spirit of Christ, given within the framework of Christ's act and work, given as the climax and outcome and consummation of Christ's career, given so that we can understand the significance of Christ and so that his work can be applied to us. If space allowed, something could here be said about the parallel between Christ's relation to the Father and the Spirit's relation to Christ. As Christ is God as far as he can be apprehended under the conditions of human existence, so the Spirit is Christ as far as he can be apprehended under the conditions of existence in history. Much could here be said about the Spirit's relation to the Church and to sacraments. But let it suffice to expand only one point, the relation of the Holy Spirit to time. The Holy Spirit is God sovereign over time, God resolving the tension between the once-for-all-event and eternity. Christianity is an irretrievably historical religion; we cannot emancipate ourselves from the historical career of Jesus Christ. But it is not a purely historical religion, dedicated to the memory of a great historical personality. It combines in an unique way the details of unrepeatable events which took place nearly two thousand years ago and the present and continuing activity of God who is eternal and perennially contemporary. By its insistence upon the eschatological significance of Christ and of the Holy Spirit the New Testament indicates in its own way that the life and death and resurrection of Jesus Christ was the move of God himself into human affairs; it represented God pledging and committing himself into history and still remaining God. This is what the New Testament means by its account of God the Holy Spirit. This is what the fourth Evangelist intended when he represented Christ as saying that the Spirit would bring to mind what Jesus had said and would guide his disciples into all truth (John 16.7–14). The functions of the Holy Spirit which have been outlined here, seen in the light of the last time, given an eschatological significance as the signs and activity of God in the new age and the new creation, are the proper basis for the later doctrine of the divinity of the

Holy Spirit, and not the essentially futile search for evidence in the New Testament for the attribution of an *hypostasis* or a 'personality' to the Spirit.

III

With this eschatological dimension of the Spirit in mind, we can face more confidently some of the difficulties concerning the doctrine of the Spirit which we inspected earlier in this book. It is obvious why to expect to find the Spirit clearly mentioned in the Old Testament is futile. If the Spirit is an eschatological phenomenon, then he will not appear till the *eschaton.* If we seek for predictions or foreshadowings of him in the Old Testament, then we should look for them in eschatological passages, such as (perhaps) Isa. 44.1–5; Ezek. 37.1–14; 47.1–12; Joel 2.28–32. Otherwise the Old Testament can only help towards our understanding of the Holy Spirit in the same way as it helps towards our understanding of the incarnation. It pictures to us a God who is unconditioned, free, bound neither by physical nor metaphysical limitations, i.e., he is not restricted to one area or one Temple, neither is he impassible nor incapable of communicating with men.

We can also perceive the reason for one fact, a fact which does not perhaps strike theologians as odd but which does impress philosophers. We can give some answer to the question, Why should the Church have troubled to retain a doctrine of the Holy Spirit at all? The answer to this question is far from self-evident to those who have studied the history of early Christian doctrine. It manifestly is one of the questions which needs answering, which presents something of a problem. The Holy Spirit does not easily or naturally fit into any of the theological systems of the Christian writers of the first three centuries. Justin tends to confuse the Spirit with the Word. Irenaeus and Tertullian do rather better, but still cannot be said to have found a necessary and satisfactory place and function for the Spirit in their thought. Hippolytus and Novatian do no better, but rather worse. Origen of course, as an eminently sophisticated and able philosopher and theologian, made a much more impressive attempt to integrate the Spirit into his thought than any other Christian writer before him. But even he cannot possibly be said to have been completely successful. He subordinates the Spirit within the Trinity to a disastrous extent, and while we may say that the Word or Son is unequivocally necessary for his system, we could not confidently say that the Spirit was. Even with Athanasius we do not gain the impression that the position of the Spirit is the very heart of his thought, that in this point everything with him is at stake, as we do in the case of his advocacy of the divinity of the Son, but rather that he is defending a position which tradition logically demands that he shall defend. The Cappadocian fathers were the first to find a way of fully integrating the Spirit within their theological thought. It is remarkable that it took the Church three hundred years to achieve this position. In many ways it would have been much easier for the Church simply to drop the doctrine of the Holy Spirit, simply to preach a Binitarian God, unhampered and uncompromised by the necessity of including this awkward phenomenon, the Holy Spirit. It is surprising that the Church did not do this. The fact demands explanation.

The explanation, as I have suggested, lies in the eschatological nature of the Holy Spirit. It is not that as long as the expectation of an early Parousia lasted, so long must Christians have believed in a Holy Spirit. The expectation of an early Parousia did not last long, but the belief in the Holy Spirit was not pushed into the background as the belief in a Parousia was. It is more accurate to say that the Holy Spirit was realized eschatology (I should say *is* realized eschatology) and realized eschatology could not be reduced nor dismissed nor demoted. Perhaps it was transposed or demythologized. But it was not deprived of its dynamic and effect. Here the Church was not dealing merely with a nexus of ideas, but with a reality felt by all believing and worshipping Christians. Here it was dealing with a continuing manifestation of God in a new mode of being, and this phenomenon could not be dismissed nor depreciated nor reduced, however difficult it might be to fit into theological or philosophical systems.

Our examination of the eschatological aspect of the Holy Spirit will also explain why the Fathers of the Church found it so difficult to ground their doctrine of the Spirit adequately in Scripture. Basil of Caesarea and Gregory of Nazianzus were outstandingly able theologians, among the most intellectual men of their time, and they had the advantage of three hundred years of Christian tradition behind them, that is to say three hundred years of intellectual trial and error, of intellectual experience. When they betray the fact that they find it difficult to discover adequate scriptural support for their doctrine of the Holy Spirit, we must take notice of them. They were being exceptionally honest and perceptive. But if the Holy Spirit is God sovereign over time, God reconciling time and eternity, we should not expect to find full and satisfying witness of his activity in one collection of historical evidence, however crucial and indispensable that collection may be. We are ourselves involved in history and we cannot stand outside it. The Church is the sign of the activity of the Holy Spirit, the Church which is involved in history. It follows that we cannot understand the Holy Spirit simply from an account of the origins of the Church, even though we cannot understand the Holy Spirit without this account. We may describe the Holy Spirit as God continually bringing the Church into an encounter with the events of the career of Jesus Christ, the incarnation, the crucifixion, the resurrection and ascension. But even then we must take into account what happens in this encounter, what has happened and what may happen. There is therefore an incompleteness, an open-endedness about the Holy Spirit in Christian doctrine, and there ought to be. Basil of Caesarea tried to fill in this incompleteness by a spurious doctrine of secret tradition. Gregory of Nazianzus, more wisely, did not. He said that the doctrine of the Holy Spirit was one of the things which the disciples could not understand when Christ was with them but would understand later. He appealed in fact, as did Basil, to the experience of the Church, but not (as did Basil) to the experience of the Church as supplying formal concrete original doctrine or information.

This 'open-endedness' of the doctrine of the Holy Spirit, the measure of freedom from Scripture which it has, is a witness to the freedom of God himself. We cannot make theology about the Holy Spirit in quite the same way as we can make theology about Christ, because Christ is God as he has chosen to limit himself to an historical career whereas the Holy Spirit is God as he has chosen to manifest himself as also free and sovereign over even the history of salvation. Here again the eschatological aspect of the Holy Spirit makes itself felt. Eschatology puts all previous history under a question mark; history is obviously incomplete and we cannot yet know how it will end. So God as Holy Spirit puts all church history under a question mark, and consequently all church doctrine and institutions also. God chooses to retain his freedom in Holy Spirit. He has pledged and promised himself to us in Christ. Of that we can be sure. But he has not done so in such a way that we can confidently map out the future, either as a steadily increasing growth of the Church in an ever more powerful institution with an ever more elaborately articulated theology, or as a steady retreat of the Church to the catacombs and an indefinite existence upon the iron rations of Christianity. God retains his right to cause the explosions and discontinuities in Church history. We cannot tie him down to history any more than we can tie him down to sacraments, to Scripture or to philosophy. God is the Holy Spirit.

The consideration of the Holy Spirit which has been advanced so far in this chapter should bring us to understand why less attention has been paid to the Holy Spirit by writers and theologians through history than to almost any other major part of Christian doctrine. The doctrine of the Holy Spirit is peculiarly elusive and difficult. It is a doctrine in which we ourselves are involved more intimately than in any other. The Holy Spirit is God returning in love to his own outgoing in love manifested in Christ, and therefore it is a doctrine of God in ourselves, God in human experience; not God *as* human experience, but God in human experience, in the experience of the Church. We find it very difficult to analyse ourselves, impossible to stand completely outside ourselves and view ourselves with entire objectivity. Similarly we find it not only difficult to analyse and write theology about God as we experience him, as we subjectively grasp him, but also embarrassing. It is easy to fall into a miasma of subjective fancies. It is easy to objectivize our experience of God and stereotype it so as to impose it as a rule on other people. It is easy to fall into Pentecostal fanaticism; it is easy to freeze into hieratic institutionalism. This is why conducting theology about the Holy Spirit is particularly difficult. But at the same time as we are aware when we begin discoursing theologically about the Holy Spirit that we are in a field where self-deception is specially easy, either about our own experience or about the experience of the Church, we are also aware that we are here at the fountain of life as far as our transitory sublunary human affairs are concerned. We are dealing with the Lord and Giver of Life, he who assures us that the Church and all its components and accessories, however dreary and ineffective they may appear, are the chosen people of God, that the Bible, for all its human limitations, is the record of the Word of God, and that the sacraments, however meanly or uncomprehendingly administered, are the places where the Church encounters God. The difficulty of exploring this area of theology is great; the subject is obscure and not wholly comprehensible. But the reward and the satisfaction are great also, if as we probe the subject of God the Holy Spirit we are led by the Spirit to realize his power and activity.

IV

The relative lateness at which a serious consideration and definition of the divinity of the Holy Spirit was achieved accounts for the slowness of the theologians of the Church in defining the position of the Holy Spirit in the Trinity. We must here distinguish between the temporal mission and the eternal characteristic of the Third Person of the Trinity, even though these two cannot be completely separated and indeed must have a close relation to each other. We are concerned here with what the Holy Spirit is that the other two Persons of the Trinity are not, corresponding to the ingenerateness or paternity of the Father and the generateness or filiation of the Son. Athanasius, the first of the Fathers to attempt, in his *Letters to Sarapion*, a serious treatise on the Holy Spirit, does not help us much here. In one passage[1] he speaks of the relation of the Spirit within the Trinity as 'co-ordination' and unity, and adds that the Spirit is the image of the Son as the Son is the image of the Father. The nearest he comes after this to defining the position of the Spirit within the life of the Trinity is when he says that 'the same individual relationship which we recognize the Son to have towards the Father, this we shall find the Spirit to possess towards the Son'. Shapland points out that Athanasius defines the Spirit's position within the Godhead only in negatives; that he is not concerned with the mode of the Spirit's existence, but only with the question of whether he is created or uncreated; and that Athanasius had no separate term for the relation of the Spirit to the Father; he never uses the noun *ekporeusis*. We cannot avoid the impression that whereas Athanasius had quite a rich conception of the Spirit's function in the economy of redemption, as far as the Spirit's position in the Trinity is concerned he had very little to say.

The Cappadocian Fathers are, of course, much more sophisticated in their theology of the Holy Spirit, and dispose of

1 For the details of references on p. 127 readers are referred to *The Church Quarterly*, April 1971, pp. 270 ff.

more philosophical resources. Their account of the Spirit's activity in the strategy of redemption is brilliant and full, especially in Basil's *de Spiritu Sancto* and the *Fifth Theological Oration* of Gregory of Nazianzus. They are honest in their acknowledgement of the paucity of scriptural evidence. But on the subject of the position of the Spirit within the Trinity, they can find very little to add to Athanasius' small store of doctrine. More than this, they confess boldly that they can say nothing. Basil declares that the Spirit must be conceived as inseparable from the Son and the Father and as completing the Trinity, and as 'a living substance, lord of holiness'. But nothing can be known or said about the mode of his existence, except that he proceeds from the Father, and that he is third in rank, though not in nature, and (a reluctant confession) that he is third in order. Basil does in fact define the mode of the Spirit's procession, but in terms which amount to a non-definition:

> He has this distinguishing characteristic in his separate existence whereby he may be recognized, that he is recognized after the Son and with him and that he derives his existence from the Father.

Elsewhere he tells us that the Holy Spirit is neither generate, because this applies to the Son alone, nor ingenerate, because this applies to the Father alone, 'but we have learnt that the Spirit of truth proceeds from the Father, and we confess that he is from God uncreatedly'. Gregory of Nazianzus is little more illuminating. He speaks of the Holy Spirit going or coming forth from the Father; sometimes he uses the word *proodos*, and he warns against inquiring curiously into this movement forth; sometimes he speaks of the sending of the Spirit. Once he says, 'Do not fear the movement forth, for God has no necessity either not to put forth or to put in a similar way', i.e., the Spirit is not to be compared to any other emanation or projection from God. He can also use the term 'proceeding'; 'proceeding', he says, means neither ingenerateness nor generateness; the Spirit is God between begottenness and unbegottenness. Nobody can tell what 'proceeding' is; but then nobody can tell what the ingenerateness of the Father is, nor what the generateness of the Son. In another passage he says, 'The Holy Spirit is truly the Spirit, going forth from the Father but not filially nor begottenly but processionwise, if we must produce new-fangled names for the sake of lucidity'. How little this advances our understanding of the subject the reader can judge for himself. Similarly, Gregory of Nyssa can express the Holy Spirit's individual characteristic in wholly negative terms: it is, to be neither of those things which individually characterize the other two Persons, 'neither in an ingenerate nor in an only-begotten way, but just to be'. Hilary of Poitiers, on the other hand, had earlier described the individual characteristic as gift and possession, but was equally unable to express any peculiar mode of existence for the Spirit: 'When [St Paul]', he says, 'was recording that everything was created in Christ and through Christ, he thought this a good enough description of the Holy Spirit for him that he should declare him to be thy Spirit' (i.e. God the Father's).

The Greek Fathers echo the doctrine which we have already found in Athanasius that the Spirit is the image of the Son as the Son is the image of the Father; and the Greek Fathers of the fourth century do on the whole support the view that the Spirit proceeds from the Father *through* the Son, though without that doctrinaire intensity evinced by later writers on the subject, whereas as early as the time of Hilary of Poitiers theologians in the West tended to say that the Spirit proceeded from the Father and the Son.

For Augustine the word expressing the relation of the Holy Spirit to the other members of the Trinity is not 'spirit' (unlike Father and Son which do express relation) but 'gift' (references to John 15.26 and Rom. 8.9):

> When we say therefore 'the gift of the giver' and 'the giver of the gift', we do so relatively of each to the other. So there is a certain indescribable communion of the Holy Spirit with the Father and the Son and perhaps this is the reason why he is so called, because the same title is also suitable for the Father and the Son.

Father and Son can be called 'Spirit' and 'holy', but the Holy Spirit is so peculiarly, 'because he is described in the Gospel as sent by one and by the other'. This is why Augustine can speak of the Holy Spirit as 'bond of love' (*nexus amoris*). The Holy Spirit, he says elsewhere in the same work, is consubstantial because he unites the two other Persons of the Trinity; there can only be three because God is love and there must therefore be one to love and one to be loved and love itself. 'God is love' can be said of all three members of the Trinity, but of the Holy Spirit in a peculiar way. It is because God is love that the Holy Spirit can be called *donum*

Dei. The Holy Spirit is eternally the gift of God (*donum*), but not eternally given (*donatum*); he was only *given* for us.

Augustine is very explicit indeed on the subject of the *Filioque*: the Spirit is sent by the Father and the Son, 'For what is said generally of them is said particularly of him'. 'We cannot say', he writes, 'that the Holy Spirit does not proceed from the Son; and it is not for nothing that he is said to be Spirit of both Father and Son'. The proof-texts for this doctrine are John 15.26 and 14.26 (procession from the Father) and John 20.22 and Luke 6.19 (procession from the Son). Augustine realizes that this theory opens him to the charge of envisaging two sources or principles in the Trinity and attempts to guard against it:

> It must be confessed that the Father and the Son are the principle of the Holy Spirit, not two principles; but just as the Father and the Son are one God, and in relation to the creation one Creator and one Lord, so they are in relation to the Spirit one principle.

This is the basis for the Western doctrine of the *Filioque*. The West followed the mighty Augustine in this, as in so much else. The Councils of Lyons (1274) and of Florence (1438–9) are following Augustine when they declare that the Spirit proceeds from the Father and the Son 'as from (or of) one principle'. But it is clear that Augustine both in his doctrine of the individual characteristic of the Spirit and of the procession of the Spirit already represents a considerable divergence from the opinions on these subjects held in the Eastern Church.

V

Modern writers in the Eastern Orthodox tradition defend in a spirited manner the views on these subjects of the Greek Fathers, which became in course of time characteristically Eastern doctrine and were developed and championed by such great names as Pseudo-Dionysius, John Damascenus, and Gregory Palamas. To take first the point that was last touched on, recent Orthodox writers attack the Western *Filioque* clause as stoutly as their predecessors ever assailed it. Their reasons can be summarized briefly: this doctrine breaks the unity of the Trinity, infringing the absolute monarchy of the Father and substituting the concept of nature or essence for the triune unity of the Father's hypostasis which should be the uniting factor; on the assumption of the *Filioque* the Father and the Son join to form a common nature that produces the Spirit. The triune Monad divides thus into two Dyads, one the Father with the Son and the other the Father with the Son and the Spirit. Only the Father can generate, only the Father and the Son can breathe, the Spirit alone can neither generate nor breathe and he alone as an hypostasis has nothing in common with the other members of the Trinity. The fundamental mistake here is to assume that the relations are the basis of the hypostases, to assume in effect that nature is prior to Person, that Person is a kind of efflorescence of nature, whereas in fact the nature of each should be regarded as the content of their Persons. P. Eudokimou declares that in thinking about the Trinity all concepts of production, or even causality, in connection with the relations of the three Persons should be discarded. One must not envisage relations between the Father and one or other of the remaining Persons, but 'des relations de Celui qui se révèle et de ceux qui le révèlent'; each Person ought to be thought of simultaneously with the others. The relations of the Persons are not of production, but of correlation: 'L'Esprit n'est pas reduit à l'instrumental de l'Amour entre le Père et le Fils, mais il est celui qui actualise l'Amour où se complaisent les Trois'. This objection to the theory of the Spirit as the *nexus amoris*, which is also voiced elsewhere in Eudokimou's book, is very forcibly stated by other writers too. Lossky says that to make the Person of the Holy Spirit the bond of union between Father and Son is to regard it as incomprehensible. Here 'the relations intervene to establish the distinction of Persons'. The word 'love' does not describe the hypostatic character of the Holy Spirit (Lossky in fact believes that it is indescribable), even though the Holy Spirit enables us to participate in love in the Trinity. The fault lies in the wrong assumption that the relations of the Persons are the Persons, expressed in the well-known phrase of Thomas Aquinas, 'the Persons are the relations themselves'.

These writers insist upon one point especially concerning the Holy Spirit's position in the Trinity, a point which can be abundantly illustrated from the writings of Greek patristic and Eastern Orthodox authors. The Spirit is the image of the Son as the Son is the image of the Father: 'the Son makes known the Father, and the Holy Spirit bears witness to the Son', says Lossky; but he goes on to say, 'the Person of the Holy Spirit remains unmanifested—

having no image in another Person'. And Eudokimou says, 'Le Père est la source de la Verité, le Fils est le Principe de la révélation de la verité du Père, l'Esprit est le principle de sa manifestation dynamique et vivifiante, il est la Vie de la Verité, son Esprit'; and elsewhere, 'L'Esprit est la "Force du Verbe" qui repose sur le Fils de toute éternité et le manifeste et c'est pourquoi il est appelé "Image du Fils".' Lossky can say that the Father is the possessor of any attribute which God may have and which is manifested, the Son is the manifestation of the Father, and the Holy Spirit is he who manifests.

But Lossky goes much further than this. He distinguishes between the exterior aspect of God's self-manifestation, in which the Holy Spirit, sent by the Father and the Son, reveals the Son, and the interior aspect, in which the Holy Spirit proceeds from the Father without having the Son as origin. The first is the result of the operation of the will of the Trinity, the second is the result of the nature of the Trinity; the will never operates in the interior relations of the Persons. This is, of course, the distinction between the temporal and the eternal missions of the Spirit. Involved with this also is the distinction, traditional to Greek and Eastern Orthodox theology, which Lossky develops throughout his work and which can be found in the work of Ware and Eudokimou also, between God's essence, which is inaccessible to our knowledge, not merely incomprehensible but to us totally unknowable, and the energies, external to himself, whereby he makes himself known to us. 'The Trinity', Lossky says, 'dwells in us by means of that in itself which is communicable', i.e., God's energies or grace. It is obvious therefore that to people who think like this, it is impossible to know what is the mode of the hypostatic existence of the Holy Spirit. That which the Spirit is and the other Persons are not is indescribable and beyond knowledge.

VI

We may well agree with the Eastern Orthodox criticism of the doctrine of Augustine that the Holy Spirit is the *nexus amoris* which unites the Persons of the Trinity. As reproduced by the most recent of great expounders of Trinitarian doctrine, Karl Barth, it results in a concept of God as one mode of being God loving himself as another mode of being God, and being united in love of himself as yet a third mode of being God. This does not make sense and is indeed the *reductio ad absurdum* of Augustine's doctrine. It is impossible, too, to avoid in this doctrine a suspicion of reducing the Holy Spirit to something less than fully personal, something analogous to an abstraction or an emotion or an ecstasy. If it is replied that nothing is more personal than love, we may ask whether this means that the Holy Spirit is in some way more loving than the other Persons, or has some sort of monopoly of love. Behind this doctrine of the *nexus amoris* lies the suggestion that the characteristic of the Holy Spirit is 'gift', not giving or givenness, but 'gift'. This is ingenious, understandable, perhaps even praiseworthy, but it runs into unsurmountable difficulties, as the theologians of the Eastern Orthodox Church have seen. We have to ask why we should say that the Father gives the Holy Spirit to the Son any more than that we should say that he gives the Son to the Holy Spirit, or indeed that the Son gives the Holy Spirit to the Father. We are clearly here dealing with a factor in the temporal mission of the Holy Spirit which cannot be erected into an all-important corresponding characteristic in the internal life of the Trinity.

But Augustine at least realized that there was a question to be answered here. The answer of Eastern theology, which is to the effect that there is no answer, that we can know nothing about this subject, is most unsatisfactory, and to compare it with our ignorance of the meaning of ingenerateness and generateness in the case of the Father and the Son is disingenuous. 'Generateness' and 'ingenerateness' convey some meaning, some distinction from other concepts or things. When we have made all allowance for the limitation of the analogous, symbolic, and equivocal nature of language, these terms are still left with some meaning. But 'procession' leaves us with virtually none, except a vague sense of movement—the significance of which the Greek Fathers would, of course, emphatically deny. The extraordinary statement of Gregory of Nazianzus that the Spirit goes forth from the Father 'processionwise' shows the bankruptcy of this theology. What is the point of maintaining a doctrine of the Holy Spirit if we can say nothing at all about how his mode of hypostatic existence differs from those of the other two Persons of the Trinity, except that it differs? Augustine was making a serious effort to fill a blank which demands to be filled. Here we are surely justified in echoing his *ne taceretur*.

Again, the Eastern doctrine that the Holy Spirit is the image of the Son as the Son is the image of the Father, and that the image of the Holy Ghost is concealed from us, is a very curious one. It seems to result in turning the self-disclosure of God into a supreme example of *obscurum per obscurius*. It is no better to say that the Father is the possessor of the attributes of God, the Son is the manifestation, and the Holy Spirit he who manifests, or that the Father is he who is true, the Son is truth and the Spirit is the spirit of truth, or that the Father is the source of power, the Son the power, and the Spirit the spirit of power, nor even that the Father is he who reveals himself and the Son and Holy Spirit those who reveal. Why do we need two images, two revealers? Why should there not be an infinite series of images or revealers if there are to be more than one? This sort of language constantly skirts two dangers, one, at which we have already hinted, that revelation turns out in the end not to be revelation but obfuscation, and the other, that the Holy Spirit appears to be superfluous. This last is a very distinct impression left on the mind by the language of the two Gregories and of Lossky, and is a sign, whenever it occurs, that philosophy is outrunning the data of revelation.

Both these impressions are strongly reinforced when we look at the language of Lossky, echoing in part the doctrine of the Greek Fathers, about the distinction of essence and energies in the Godhead—but we should not even say *in* the Godhead, for these energies are described as external to the Godhead. We have apparently reached the extraordinary position of believing that Jesus Christ is divine because he is the self-communication of God and then, as soon as we arrive at that point, of being told that God cannot communicate himself. What is the point of all this elaborate apparatus of revelation, culminating in the doctrine of the Trinity? This apophatic tradition of theology has a very respectable pedigree, but its modern exponents do not seem to realize that it is constantly in danger of falling into Gnosticism and upsetting the balance between God's self-disclosure and God's incomprehensibility. As far as Pneumatology is concerned, Lossky's doctrine amounts to saying that the Holy Spirit in his eternal mission is different from the Holy Spirit in his temporal mission. The former, constituted by nature, has an origin from the Father through the Son; the second, controlled by will, has an origin from the Father and the Son. What authority have we for distinguishing the eternal mission of the Spirit in this way? Not Scripture, by definition. We can only reply, philosophy. Here we must join forces with Karl Barth and insist that our ideas concerning the internal relations of the Persons of the Trinity must be strictly controlled by the knowledge of God which we have through revelation. Though we may, indeed we must, use philosophy as an aid in articulating a proper Christian doctrine of God, we must not allow philosophy to intrude itself as an authority whereby we can correct the witness of Scripture.

VII

Much traditional thought about the position of the Holy Spirit in the Trinity seems to me to have been darkened by two defects. The first is the tendency to handle the witness of Scripture in a wooden and unrealistic way, to assume that we can find in the Bible ready-made Christian doctrine, prefabricated, already packaged, and fitted for being immediately adopted in unaltered form into theological treatises. This is very obvious in the case of the poor word 'proceeds' at John 15.26. Hugely more weight has been attached to this word than its significance justifies. If our Lord spoke the words of the sentence which includes this word, he was not officially stating Christian dogma, he was not speaking *urbi et orbi* in defining a matter of faith or morals to be accepted unquestioningly by the faithful as infallible truth. But it is wholly unlikely that we have here the *ipsissima verba* of Jesus at all. It is altogether probable that these words represent the comment or interpretation of the Fourth Evangelist. If we consider the text in this way, much of the heat can be taken out of the *Filioque* controversy. Perhaps a very rigid and literal interpretation of the words attributed to Jesus in the Fourth Gospel justify the retention of the *Filioque* clause; but then, that is not the way in which we should interpret the New Testament's witness to the Holy Spirit. We should consider the Spirit in the whole context of the New Testament, in Paul, in Luke, in the Synoptic Evangelists, in the author of Hebrews, and if we do so we shall realize that 'from the Father through the Son' is a more adequate way of representing the Spirit's temporal mission, *and therefore his eternal mission*, than the *Filioque* clause suggests. All God's activities and gifts in the New Testament come to us from the Father through the Son; the Spirit should be no exception. If the Spirit is God reigning in his people at the Last Time, God taking charge of history and sovereign over time, God in whom we experience

God, we apprehend him as such because of our recognition of what he has accomplished in Christ and through Christ. Our ideas of what the Spirit is in himself should as far as possible follow the same pattern.

The other defect is the failure to realize the dynamic and eschatological nature of the Holy Spirit. This is an indispensably important part of our understanding of the Spirit and must be in some way read back into the interior life of the Trinity. It is because of their inability to appreciate this that the Greek Fathers develop their very unsatisfactory doctrine of the Spirit as an image of an image, and it is because ancient philosophy did not appreciate this that we sometimes gain the impression that the Spirit is superfluous and an encumbrance in developing a Christian doctrine of God. The Fathers were trying to turn a dynamic conception of God into a static one. In many ways their enterprise was a necessary and admirable one; but at some points they removed a dynamic conception which was indispensable to the whole. We can very well conceive of God as in perpetual movement without necessarily committing ourselves to the proposition that he is a process in himself or that he is becoming. Indeed, readers of Karl Barth's work on the doctrine of the Trinity will constantly be impressed by his tendency to turn traditional static terms into new dynamic ones without ever transgressing the limits of orthodoxy. He describes the Trinity as 'God a second time', as the *repetitio aeterna in aeternitatem*; he prefers to speak in terms of movement among the Persons rather than of a communication of essence. We should therefore be able to conceive of God as movement, as eternally moving out from himself and returning to himself in love, and on this interpretation the characteristic of the Holy Spirit must be *response*, return in love. As the Father's mode of being God is ingenerateness and the Son's generateness, so the Spirit's is response and return. We need not leave the Spirit's mode of procession dark and unknown at this point. This conception can include and integrate all the functions and characteristics of the Spirit which have been traditionally observed, love gift, sanctification, illumination, life-giving. This can well correspond to Eudokimou's conception of the Holy Spirit as 'he who actualizes love', perhaps even to Lossky's thought of the Spirit as he who bears witness to the Son. This idea has been well expounded by Norman Pittenger in his book, *The Word Incarnate* (1959). He describes the members of the Trinity as 'God the Ultimate Source, God Self-Expressive both in himself and in creation, God responsive both in himself and through creation', or alternatively, as Unoriginate Source, eternally generated Self-Expression, and 'the equally eternal Response in and by which the Self-Expression is fulfilled in the "Amen" both in God himself and in creation, who is called "the Spirit"'.

It is indeed true that in a sense the Spirit is obscure, but not because he is the image of an image, himself without an image. This doctrine is a symptom of the dilution of the dynamic terms of witness to revelation in Scripture by the static terms of ancient Greek philosophy. The Holy Spirit is obscure, first because he is immediately concerned with our own intimate subjective apprehension of God, and we find it impossible to regard with complete objectivity a phenomenon which involves ourselves as subjects. But he is obscure much more because, as an eschatological force, his work is not yet completed. He is sovereign over history and cannot be completely understood by us because we are in history and because, unlike him, we cannot see the end of history, its completion, its consummation. It is not metaphysics that stand in the way of our knowing him, but our involvement in history. We are caught up in his movement which involves the whole human race and the whole of history, and cannot stand outside it. But we would not realize our limitation here did we not also believe that he is the Illuminator by living in whose life we do in truth perceive that God is approaching us, speaking to us, accosting us in Jesus Christ.

7 *The Grace and the Wrath of God*

I

In Anglican congregations today the word 'grace' is not always as familiar as it should be, but 'grace' is one of those words 'borne in the bosom of revealed religion'. It is a word which caused revolutions in Europe in the sixteenth century, and in the past it has always been held in honour and reverence in the central tradition of Reformed Catholicism (which is what Anglicanism essentially is). St Paul once summed up Christianity in three words: a three-word summary of Christianity might vary considerably according to who made the summary; it might be 'Love, Joy, Peace', or 'the Crown, the Church, the Bible', or 'Jesus, Mary, Church'; but Paul's three words were 'Jesus, Spirit, Gospel' (2 Cor. 11.4). If Paul had wanted to sum up Christianity in one word, that word would have been 'grace'. Grace does not mean a kind of spiritual liquid or electric current supplied to us through sacraments. Gerard Manley Hopkins once preached a sermon in which he compared the Church to a cow with seven udders, the udders being the seven sacraments. This was one of the less happy flights of fancy of that great poet. Grace means the free, unmerited, unexpected love of God, and all the benefits, delights, and comforts which flow from it. It means that while we were sinners and enemies we have been treated as sons and heirs.

I do not think that within Anglicanism today a proper appreciation exists of the sheer gratuitousness of grace. This is partly because we are so much exposed to ingenious rationalizations of sin. We are tempted to persuade ourselves that sin is neurosis or some form of psychological compulsion which we can be excused from resisting because it is subconscious. I knew a student who regularly failed to return books to his university library and thereby deprived others of the opportunity of reading them, but who excused himself on the ground that 'he had a thing about' library books. We have many of us met the similar case of the parish priest who is quite content to say that he never answers letters. He would be ashamed to say that he never stamps letters or never pays his debts, but he does not mind in other matters taking refuge in a comforting theory of psychological compulsion. Another force which weakens our sense of sin today is the widespread notion that it is intolerant to pass moral judgements on anybody. I remember being amazed as a member of the Senate of a university at the bland readiness with which the university official responsible for informing the Senate about punishments inflicted on students for various offences would assure us on each occasion that 'We are not passing moral judgements, but only enforcing the rules of the University'. In other words, if you enforce any discipline at all in a university, you cannot help making moral judgements, but you must on no account say that this is what you are doing. 'Who shall cast the first stone?'—as Cain remarked after the murder of Abel.

But in order to understand grace, we must realize that we are sinners, people who are constantly capable of giving way to irrational impulses to do what we know to be wrong, to plunge into a course of action which in our heart of hearts we know to be an illusion and a snare. Moral evil is at once powerful and illusory. When the Fathers, from Origen to Augustine, insist that evil is non-being, they have more sense on their side than appears at first sight. Moral evil, the deliberate choice by the human will of that which is less than the highest good (to adopt Augustine's account of it), is something that has an immense force and causes every moment appalling and wide-ranging consequences. But it cannot be thought to have a permanent grounding in reality. When we do wrong, we first have to persuade ourselves, or half-persuade ourselves, that we are doing right. A large part of wrong-doing is illusion, an illusory judgement about the facts of the case. And when we repent of our sin, part of our repentance is a realization that we have been the victims, the willing and guilty victims, of an illusion. One of Screwtape's clients, in C. S. Lewis' famous book, remarked to Screwtape when he finally reached hell, 'I now realize that I have spent my whole life doing neither what I ought nor what I wanted'. The gratification expected before the sinful act proves illusory. If we are to face the existence of sin honestly, we must realize that we are constantly liable to be caught by this illusion. We are not consistently rational creatures. We are not well-balanced personalities, wending our even way through life, pipe in mouth, smile on face, untroubled by moral failures, undisturbed by serious pangs of conscience, like some impossibly hearty parson in an advertisement. We would like to think that we are, and we would like to induce others to think that we are, but in our heart of hearts we know that we are not. We are frightened, unbelieving, lustful, selfish, jealous, vain, and niggardly. Can anyone disown these charges? We profess to believe in God, but we insult and offend him every day. And yet God loves us and justifies us. God loves this unlovely complex of selfishness which is I—and you. He has sent his Son to die for us. He has called us adopted sons in his Son. This is grace, wholly undeserved, embarrassingly free. Blaise Pascal said that mankind is divided into two classes: sinners who think themselves righteous and saints who know that they are sinners.

Another reason why we do not properly appreciate the gratuitousness of grace is because today we have largely forgotten the sovereignty of God. In England we live in a society where the greatest virtue of all—nearly the only virtue—is tolerance. We tolerate those who disagree with us on political and economic and social matters; it is the great virtue of the Englishman; foreigners admire him greatly for it, and with justice. We tolerate those who disagree with us in matters of morality. Who are we to judge? We must not adopt an attitude of 'I-am-holier-than-thou'. To understand everything is to forgive everything—as Herod said after the Massacre of the Innocents. The logical outcome of such an attitude is the Moors Murders, as some observers realized with startled horror at the time of the discovery of these murders. We tolerate the noisy vulgarity of public entertainers reaching us from our neighbour's transistor set in public places and vehicles. We tolerate the callow, self-assured impudence of the young, the grasping greed of trades unions, who always assure us hypocritically that they have no alternative but to make the demands which they put forward; we tolerate the unscrupulous violence of criminals. And consequently we unreflectingly assume that God is tolerant. He is a sort of universal uncle, a cosmic Santa Claus, a divine Welfare State who gives unlimited benefits and never exacts taxes. 'Dieu pardonnera, c'est son métier.'

But if we are to be true to the Bible the very last quality which we can attribute to God is tolerance. The Old Testament expressly calls him a jealous God, the New Testament repeats the vivid phrase of the Old applied to him, 'a consuming fire'. Fire is not a tolerant element. God is not a tolerant person. The God of the New Testament is still the same sovereign, demanding, imperious

God of the Old Testament, the God who in Isaiah is described as smashing civilizations, leading rulers away spoiled, loosing the loins of kings and making fools of statesmen and priests, the God who claims exclusive authority, who says, 'I am God and there is none other', the Lord of nature, the Lord of history, the Lord of man. Now, either God is still this sort of God or he does not exist at all. He cannot be a God with limited powers, with limited rights on us, whose demands are partial and restricted, a constitutionalist sort of God. We cannot plead against him a cosmic Bill of Rights or Magna Carta. We cannot think of him as a God who is in charge of the universe but is gravely hampered by strikes. It is part of the definition of God that he is not limited, and that he has unlimited rights over us. We have no ground upon which we can stand when we approach him; we are like condemned criminals, waiting for reprieve or death. We must not regard God from the point of view of liberal democracy, much though we may be tempted to do so.

Yet this sovereign and demanding and authoritative God has chosen to approach us in the form of suffering love. Shakespeare, who is not famous for his piety, had a true appreciation of the situation, when he caused one of his characters in *Measure for Measure* to say:

> And he who most advantage might have took
> Found out the remedy.

God still makes imperative and authoritative demands on us. He is no more tolerant in the New Testament than he is in the Old. He still faces us relentlessly with a choice of infinite importance. We still have no grounds for believing that we can be left unaffected if we reject him, that we can remain neutral, return the answer 'Don't know', or 'No comment'. But the form that his demand now takes is that of his Son Jesus Christ hanging upon a cross. This unexpected, extraordinary, embarrassingly touching initiative of love taken by God is grace. But we cannot understand the gratuitousness of the grace till we understand the sovereignty of the God who offers it. As Karl Barth put it in the most famous version of his *Commentary on Romans*, 'God does not need us; indeed, if he were not God, he would be ashamed of us'.

But if we are to think of Christianity primarily in the form of grace, we must give up trying to find it or to present it in other forms. We must, for instance, give up thinking of religion as law.

We are much tempted to do this, partly out of an understandable reaction to the lawlessness and all-tolerant amorality of the society in which we live. It is in many ways easiest to think of religion as a number of commands laid on us by God, and any form of Christianity can turn its religion into law. The Evangelical can think of religion as a series of negative commands, of prohibitions: don't drink, don't smoke, don't dance, don't go to the pictures. Once, many years ago, I met a family in a country town in the North of Ireland who told me with pride that they would not dream of cleaning their shoes on Sundays, but who never took the trouble to worship God in church on that day. This was a perfect modern example of Pharisaism. But the Roman Catholic or the Anglo-Catholic can just as easily think of his religion as obedience to the law of the Church, and indeed before the Second Vatican Council the Roman Catholic religion did often look to outsiders as if it had been irretrievably bound up with a basically legalistic interpretation of Christianity. Any Christian at any time can easily slip into a state of mind in which he regards his religion as a series of duties or burdens or responsibilities, or even as a number of principles. We become convinced that we must steadily continue maintaining these burdens or duties or principles, and we imagine that this is how we please God. It was once my privilege, by the kindness of the Dean of Durham, to read some of the unpublished letters of the late Bishop Hensley Henson. The impression I gained from these, one which can also be gained from his published letters, was that Hensley Henson conceived of Christianity primarily in terms of duty. This accounts for the curious sadness which pervades almost all his writings and utterances.

But to think of Christianity as law or as duty is the contradiction of a religion of grace. Grace says, 'You cannot bear the burden: Christ has borne it for you. You cannot undertake the responsibility; Christ has undertaken for you. Rejoice that God has removed your burden and made you free, that you can think of your religious activities as gratitude, not as duty, as worship and service, not as law.' The same argument applies to idealism. The popular thought of this country is still soaked in idealism; we cram idealism down the throats of defenceless schoolchildren; we deplore the fact that there is so little idealism left; we give the impression on all sides that Christianity is equivalent to idealism. I once deeply shocked the headmaster of a secondary school by telling him that I did not believe in idealism; he almost regarded me as an atheist. But in fact Christianity is grace, and idealism is grace turned on its head. Idealism says, 'Strive earnestly to be gentle and pure and just and loving, and you will in the end be conformed to Christ. Hitch your wagon to a star, aim at the highest ideals, and you will become Christ-like.' Christianity, in the Pauline version at least, says just the opposite; 'You have been given Christ, and with Christ everything. You have died in Christ, you have become sons of God, you are now in heavenly places, your life is hid with Christ in God. Now live up to all this.' God has acted first, while we were sinners. Idealism is a well-intentioned nineteenth-century version of Christianity which still believes in the nineteenth-century theory of progress and virtually ignores the existence of sin.

Grace, then, is free, and if we understand it and accept it and respond to it, grace makes us free. But grace is not cheap. God gives us freely everything that we should desire and that we cannot achieve of ourselves, without considering our merits or demerits, even though he knows that we do not deserve his gift. But his gift is also his demand. All God's gifts are double-edged, dangerous mercies which can turn to judgement if we refuse them. God is a dynamic and demanding God, and when he gives he gives with royal and generous freedom. He gives himself, and he suffers in his giving. But just because he is God, his gifts are embarrassing, compromising, and demanding. To accept his love involves an active and intensely serious calling which we cannot let alone and which will not let us alone.

This is the clue to the centuries-old controversy concerning justification by faith. It is not true to say, with extreme Lutherans, that God calls us justified and righteous by a kindly legal fiction, that righteousness is imputed to us which is no more than external and forensic. In former days British Railways used to issue to its passengers dog-tickets when they wanted to carry bicycles with them in the train, and for all I know they still do so. One might say that British Railways imputed to the bicycle for the purposes of the journey a forensic and external caninity. But of course if anyone whistled to the bicycle and expected it to come running out of the guard's van and leaping up on its owner, or put a dish of food in front of it and urged it to eat it up, he would be acting absurdly. Similarly, on this theory of purely forensic imputed righteousness it would be quite wrong to say that justified men and women were righteous. This extreme view is no more consistent with the full and proper Christian doctrine of grace than is the view at the other extreme—that which some Catholic theologians have taught and which is supported by some aspects of Augustine's doctrine of grace—the view that God by justifying us infuses goodness into us, so that we can put our hands on our hearts and say, 'Now I know that I am good.' This theory breaks upon the rock of St Paul's letters, and not least the letter to the Galatians (and especially 2.14–21). God's justifying grace constitutes a dynamic calling which, if we respond to it, will lead us further, into sanctification, but never into such sanctification as we can call *ours*, or if we are to call it ours it is always ours because we are in Christ and not because of our achievement or moral success. If we do not respond to this dynamic calling, it will ruin us.

This grand act of making us freemen instead of slaves and sons instead of enemies is not a simple volcanic moment, after which we can relax and bask in its glow for the rest of our lives. It is the mighty initiating move of God towards us, a move of pure, undeserved, inexplicable love, but it is only the beginning of continual activity of God in our lives. We can never be rid of God, we can never run away from him, we can never rest content with possessing his gifts. If we do, they dissolve in our grasp, the talent laid away in a napkin turns to judgement, not reward. Grace does not make us independent of God; this was the great truth which Augustine perceived, and perceived almost alone among the theologians of the Church since St Paul up to his day. God's love consists of a continuously active calling and demand. It is rather like the call of Garibaldi to his followers at a critical moment of the Italian Risorgimento. When he wanted Italians to follow him as soldiers he did not offer them good pensions, comfortable billets, education and training schools, increased pay and married quarters. 'All I can offer you', he said, 'is wounds and weariness and danger.' Yet they responded to his call. So it is indeed the love of God that calls us, but it calls us to a strict and strenuous life.

We must be clear about this, because there is a tendency today to offer Christianity as cheap grace, an expression we have already met, coined by Dietrich Bonhoeffer in his book *The Cost of Discipleship*. This is a tendency to represent Christianity as offering an easy solution to all our problems, to represent God as giving everything and demanding nothing, whereas in fact he gives everything and demands everything. 'Come to church,' says cheap grace, 'and we will make everything easy for you. We will simplify the language, relax the rules, water down the dogma, lower the moral demands, shorten the services. All you have to do is to come. It is easy, it is simple, it involves no trouble, no effort, no suffering. It is as quick as our detergents, as soothing as our cigarettes, as painless as our contraceptives, as narcotic as our television.' But we have no right to treat Christianity as if it were a prefabricated, cellulose-covered, glossy modern product, to be sold with the same slick fraudulent salesmanship as cigarettes, petrol, soap, chocolates, underwear, beer, television sets, and cars. We have no right to speak of God's love without mentioning God's demand, to publicize the crown without the cross. Christianity does demand self-discipline, self-denial, self-examination. The motive for all these is gratitude for God's extraordinary love. But they are nonetheless a necessary part of our response to that love. We have no right even to assure our converts or our fellow-Christians that Christianity will necessarily be spiritually comforting. The experiences of Jeremiah and of Søren Kierkegaard, of St John of the Cross and even, if we have examined with any care the Second Letter to the Corinthians, of St Paul, should make us pause before we advance that claim. It is dangerous to judge our religion by our religious experience. The last illusion of the Evangelical is justification, not by masses, pilgrimages, almsgiving, and indulgences, but by his religious experience; it is the subtlest form of justification by works. All that we can promise to anybody who is contemplating the acceptance of Christianity is reality, reality exchanged for illusion, for godlessness is illusion. But there is something abidingly satisfactory in finding reality. We are attracted at the depth of our being by truth which makes a moral demand upon us.

Ultimately the motive for our being Christians and behaving as Christians—that is to say enduring a good deal of heart-searching and discouragement and difficulty over prayers and disgust with ourselves and consultation with others—is the attractiveness of God. Our motive is not that we are convinced of the advantages of obeying God's law, nor of the necessity of sticking grimly to our duty, nor that we are dazzled by bright ideals, nor that we find in Christianity a ready-made and painless solution to all our psychological and moral problems. Ultimately the motive of our being Christian is that we cannot resist the love of God, a love which is not merely a declaration nor a message nor an appeal, but a mighty act of self-giving, undeserved, unexpected, unasked and embarrassingly generous. Some years ago a film was made of the life of St

Vincent de Paul, and in the course of it the saint was represented as finding an infant abandoned on a snowy winter's day outside the orphanage which he was running in Paris in the first half of the seventeenth century. He took up the bundle in his arms and brought it into a room where was sitting a committee of wealthy, upper-class women of Paris who used to help him in his work. 'What are we to do with this child?' he asked them. One of the women suggested that perhaps God meant it to die as a punishment for the sin of its mother. This put the saint in a rage. 'Madam,' he said, 'when God wants dying done for sin he sends his own Son to do it.' This is grace, mysterious, inexplicable, but touching and overwhelming. It is worth devoting the whole of our lives to a response to this grace.

II

The other side of God's love is God's wrath. The wrath of God is a subject which does not detain the attention of modern Christians much, but it greatly preoccupied our forefathers. If you read some of the works of William Law, the non-juring Anglican divine and mystic (1686–1761) you will find him struggling with the subject of God's wrath. In his day the difficulty was *not* to believe in God's wrath. Law found it intensely uncongenial to his spirit and judgement to imagine that God could be angry, but he found it a most difficult task to explain away the biblical references to the wrath of God and he made no great success of his attempts to do so. Calvinists who were dominant in the theological world of eighteenth-century England, could easily accept the idea that God was angry. Even Charles Wesley, who was no conventional Calvinist, could write

'Captain, God of our salvation
Thou who hast the winepress trod,
Borne th'Almighty's indignation,
Quenched the fiercest wrath of God'.

This acceptance of the validity of language about the wrath of God was still prevalent in the Irish Evangelical circles in which a certain Miss Humphreys, better known by her married name of Mrs Alexander, was brought up in the early decades of the nineteenth century. When she came to write a children's hymn about the atonement she included the line, 'He died that we might be forgiven', and no doubt intended by this that Christ's death propitiated the wrath of the Father and so enabled or indeed induced him to forgive us. The leaning towards the Tractarian movement which she certainly had later in her life would hardly have altered this inherited doctrine.

Today such language sounds to us strange and horrible. Today we view the wrath of God much as the Victorians viewed the subject of sex. They talked freely from their pulpits about wrath but preserved a strict silence in public on the subject of sex. We speak freely about sex from the pulpit, but follow a hush-hush policy about wrath. Most congregations in England, if they use the Canticle *Venite* (the 95th Psalm) omit the last few verses just because of the awkward allusion to God's wrath which occurs in them. Very few, if any, parishes any longer use the old Commination Service appointed in the 1662 Prayer Book for use on Ash Wednesday, because it contains so much embarrassing material about God's wrath. Only the Gospel Halls mention the subject frequently and freely, and they completely misunderstand it, as this essay will make evident.

In the first place, it must be conceded openly that both Old and New Testaments mention the wrath of God, and that even if we confine ourselves to the New Testament we cannot excise mention of God's wrath from its pages without being untrue to its witness nor ignore the passages where the idea occurs without being dishonest in our handling of the text. Let us look at some of the places which seem to justify the Calvinists, Charles Wesley, and Mrs Alexander:

Romans 5.8, 9: God commends his own love.... Much more, then, being justified in his blood shall we be saved from the wrath.

Revelation 14.19, 20: the angel puts the vintage of the earth into the great winepress of the wrath of God and 'the winepress was trodden outside the city' (i.e., at Calvary).

Romans 1.17, 18: a righteousness of God is revealed in the Gospel; the wrath of God is revealed from heaven. Are not both righteousness and wrath revealed in Christ?

2 Corinthians 5.21: For our sake he made him to be sin who knew no sin, so that in him we might become the righteousness of God.

Galatians 3.13: Christ redeemed us from the curse of the law, having become a curse for us, as it it written....

It looks in fact as if a good case can be made for the view that Christ bears God's wrath for us, makes himself, though innocent, the object of God's wrath. Calvin, Charles Wesley, and Mrs Alexander were, at least, not talking nonsense.

What, then, are we to make of this embarrassing subject? It is impossible and irresponsible to ignore it. Are we to accept the explanation which the Gospel Halls give? This explanation says that God's love is limited by his wrath or his justice or his ethical demands. Much though God would like to forgive us freely, he cannot, for these demands must be met. Christ, by dying, was able to meet the demands of God's wrath or justice, and in consequence God was able to forgive us. But this is a horrible caricature of the biblical doctrine. God is not subject to fits of schizophrenia during which two contrary impulses conflict in him, one to love and one to be angry. This is what is gravely wrong with the 1662 Commination Service, which gives a fine catena of passages concerning God's love of us and follows this by a long list of passages about God's anger with us, but makes no serious attempt to relate the two lists to each other. It is profoundly unsatisfactory to say that God's justice or wrath limits his love. God's righteousness is not the same as God's justice, and much damage has been done in the course of Christian doctrine in the West because the accepted Latin translation of the Greek word for righteousness, *dikaiosyne*, was *iustitia.* The New Testament is not interested in God's justice. God's righteousness means that God is in the right and when he asserts or manifests his righteousness it means that he demonstrates that he is in charge of the situation, not that his action conforms to acceptable ethical norms. We limit God's sovereignty if we envisage him as complying, even complying reluctantly, with the demands of justice, or of law. To envisage him doing so would be to surrender to the old Greek belief that beyond and behind the gods there operates Themis, a more ultimate and powerful principle of justice. When the Old Testament contrasts or balances God's love with God's justice (as it sometimes does), it puts the case the other way round: God's love breaks through and goes beyond God's justice. 'If thou, Lord, wilt be extreme to mark what is done amiss, O Lord, who may abide it? for there is mercy with thee ...' (Psalm 130, BCP version). The highest expression of this conviction occurs in the eleventh chapter of the prophet Hosea, where the prophet declares that Israel has treated God with vile and unprovoked ingratitude and infidelity, and that she deserves complete rejection and destruction, but that God will not go to that length because his love for Israel is stronger than human love. The Bible, in short, gives no satisfactory grounds for the altogether too human view of God's wrath limiting his love.

Even more revolting is the idea that Christ persuaded the Father to be kind to us. This represents a dangerous separation between the Father and the Son. Out of this distortion flows much bad theology and worse piety which pushes the Father into the background as the God of justice and occupies the foreground with a forgiving Christ who modifies the sternness of the Father. One further stage of disintegration is reached when the Blessed Virgin Mary occupies the foreground as the intercessor with and sweetener of a Christ who has become remote and stern in his turn. Christ does not have to persuade the Father to forgive. He is the expression of the Father's forgiveness. The atonement is not the prelude to our forgiveness but the enactment and focus of it. God does not merely *say* that we are forgiven. In his Son he acts forgiveness. Vincent Taylor established this some time ago in his fine series of studies of the atonement in the New Testament. But forgiveness is a hard and costly business, both for the forgiver and the forgiven. God does not merely say, 'Forget it, chums', to men and then forget all about their sin. Nothing could be more superficial than Faber's silly line,

> Come to the God who forgives and forgets.

Forgiveness is a deep and tragic experience, both in relations between men and men and in those between men and God. This is one of the main themes of Tolstoy's tremendous novel *War and Peace*. But we cannot speak, as we must, of *agapé*, of God's undeserved, unexpected initiating love poured out in Christ upon sinners, while they are yet sinners, we cannot speak of the gratuitousness of grace, and at the same time pretend that God had to be persuaded by Christ's death to forgive us.

We can find a more satisfactory answer to our dilemma if we first ask the question, 'Was God angry with Jesus?' We can quite confidently Answer 'No' to this question. There is not the slightest suggestion of this in the New Testament. We can think of many expressions at once which rule this out, 'Son of his love', 'I and the Father are one', 'Glorify thou me', 'Nevertheless, not my will be done but thine'. Could God possibly commend his love to us. (Rom. 5.8) by being angry with his Son? God's wrath, whatever it may mean, cannot possibly mean his personal anger with Jesus. Then why with anyone? Can we conceive of God being angry with sinners and commending his own love to sinners at the same time? This is a quite irrational idea. Did Jesus perhaps himself endure innocently but voluntarily God's anger against us, as Sidney Carton endured, innocently but voluntarily, the anger of the French people against their aristocrats? This idea is nothing less than disgusting. We all have the experience of venting our anger unjustly on others. A husband and wife quarrel, and they take it out on the children. A man loses a lot of money gambling, and he vents his disappointment and rage on his wife. James Joyce's short story 'Counterparts' in *Dubliners* is a superb account of a man visiting his rage at his own failure and humiliation on his little son. But we cannot possibly believe that God behaves in that way. When we vent our anger upon those who have deserved it we know in our heart of hearts that it is wrong for us to do so. We know that it is even more odiously wrong when we vent it upon those whom we know not to deserve it. We cannot possibly attribute such a state of mind to God. This type of theology tends inevitably to make the Son appear morally better and more attractive than the Father. It is a despicable theology, and Evangelicals should be ashamed to profess it.

In fact the New Testament, in contrast to the Old, never declares in so many words that God is angry with anyone. When it speaks of God's wrath, it does so in a carefully indirect way. It speaks of 'the wrath', as if it were a force somehow separate from God, of wrath 'coming upon' people, of God 'bringing his wrath to bear' upon certain people, of condemnation, of sin, of curse, of law. The distinct impression is left on the reader that the New Testament writers find it embarrassing to say directly that God is angry with anyone, and deliberately refrain from using such language.[1] The truth is that on the subject of the relation of God's wrath to God's love the New Testament is confused and incoherent, as it is on a number of other subjects (such as the form of the ministry or the relation of faith to baptism). We are left with a full and strong doctrine of God's initiating, gratuitous, redemptive love, and some references to God's wrath which fall short of saying that he is angry, and we must make the best of this material. Making the best of the material of the New (and where relevant the Old) Testament in the light of the tradition, the life and the experience of the Church is in effect the process of making Christian doctrine.

I suggest that the following account does most justice to the state of the evidence and to all the aspects of our knowledge of God. What the New Testament means by the wrath of God is the result of our disobedience to God. It is an indirect and impersonal relationship to God, in contrast to the relationship of grace, which is direct and personal. It is the situation of those who are alienated from God. God is never angry with anyone, but people can become involved in 'the wrath'. If men will not have grace then they must have law. If they will not have love, then they must have wrath, just because God is God. Wrath is the obverse of love, to use numismatic terms, the other side of the coin. Wrath is what happens when you reject God's love. We cannot remain unaffected by God's love. It must either redeem us or ruin us. We can afford to reject all other demands upon us, the claims and expectations of our parents, our sweethearts, our employers, even of the State. But we cannot afford to reject God's claims and advances, because God is God, really sovereign and really Master. 'I am the Lord, and there is no other, besides me there is no God' (Isa. 45.5); 'Who has directed the Spirit of the Lord ... To whom then will you liken God?' (Isa. 40.13 and 18). Rejection of God's advances to us must involve us in disaster, because we are quarrelling with the ground of our being. To offend God is to displace ourselves in the universe:

> All things betray thee, who betrayest me.

But this does not mean that God is angry. We have no experience of good anger, pure anger, as we have of pure and good love. We cannot attribute such a passion to God. We all know what anger is like, we know it too well. The ancients justly called anger a brief madness. The idea of an incensed, provoked, wrathful, or indignant deity demanding propitiation is a repulsive one and should be banished finally from the Christian religion, however it may figure in other religions. It has driven some sensitive souls, such as the poet Cowper, into madness. It is true indeed that God punishes. Even if we did not have plenty of support for this conviction in the Bible, we should know this from our own experience. God punishes all the time those who deserve punishment, whether they know it or not, for nobody can push God out of his life by the simple device of forgetting him. But God's punishment is not retributory; it is reformatory and remedial and deterrent. He does not punish in anger. God is never angry with anyone. We should exorcize from our thinking this nightmare of an angry God. The total and vigorous rejection of the concept of God's anger is not the product of nineteenth-century Liberalism, with its shallow doctrine of progress and its underestimation of sin. The rejection was first advanced in the Christian Church seventeen hundred years ago by those two great scholars, Clement of Alexandria and Origen. They were intoxicated by no deceptive and ephemeral worldly prosperity into a false theological optimism, they lived in days when the Roman Empire appeared to be sliding into final collapse, and as members of a Church which was constantly liable to persecution by the State. But on this subject they exemplified at its best the sweet and perceptive gentleness and reasonableness which is one characteristic of their thought. They were quite certain that, whatever the Bible might appear to say, God is never angry with anyone. He would not be God if he were. We, living in our post-Liberal and in some ways regressive twentieth century, must acknowledge the truth of their conviction.

When therefore we read that Christ bears God's wrath, it means that he bears the consequences of our alienation from God, and nothing else. He bears, innocent and obedient, the consequences of sin and disobedience. The consequences are horrible because the offence is not merely a matter of anti-social behaviour but because the sin is against God. Christ becomes sin, he becomes a curse, he endures condemnation in the flesh (Rom. 8.1–4). He stands where we stand, without being compelled to do so. He is innocent, and therefore God cannot possibly be angry with him, even if God could ever be angry with anyone. But God can and does allow him to bear the consequences of our sin, alienation and guilt. The austere and terrible passion-narrative in St Mark's Gospel seems designed to bring out this point. It is totally unsentimental; it is relieved by no cheerful or hopeful note. The Messiah does not comfort a fellow-sufferer nor declare confidently that he has conquered; he dies in dereliction and darkness. Mark seems to envisage this as the final horror, the final alienation of men from God, before the final salvation.

But one more important point must be added before we finish with the subject of God's wrath. In the action of the Son the Father acts. As has already been suggested, we must not wrongly separate the activities of the Persons of the Trinity. What we witness on the cross is not the suffering simply of a man nor of a semi-divine being undertaken to expiate sin against the High God. This is not a repetition of the experience of Jephtha's daughter nor of Iphigenia, who in legend were innocently sacrificed in order to remove divine displeasure. Nor is it an historical enactment of the legend of Prometheus, who suffered divine wrath because he had benefited mankind and who knew that he was morally greater than the god who tormented him. The High God is here involved in the suffering 'In all their affliction he was afflicted, and the angel of his presence saved them' (Isa. 63.9). It is as if a man had left his children alone in a house, warning them not to play with matches or with fire; but they were disobedient, played with fire and set the house on fire; he returned, and saved them from death in the burning house at the cost of seriously injuring himself. Sin has been committed against the High God, and in his compassion the High God himself takes the consequences. God himself provides the sacrifice and, in the words of the American theologian Bushnell, the sacrifice 'makes cost' for him.

It is impossible to rationalize the Christian doctrine of the atonement, however long and profitably we may reflect about it. It rests upon a kind of axiomatic intuition deeply fixed in the minds of most men and in the assumptions of most cultures that wrongdoing must be compensated for by some sort of a rightdoing and that this concerns God. We may eventually arrive at a state of society in which the community does formally forgive and forget all crime, in which the victims of murder and rape and violence and fraud, or their relatives, are, as far as possible, compensated by monetary payments, but the perpetrators of these crimes are never punished, because society has ceased to want to punish, or has lost its nerve sufficiently to be incapable of having the confidence to punish. In that case, the desire for atonement will have disappeared from the human mind and all sin will have been relegated to the category of disease. But I very much doubt if this ever will happen, or ever could happen. Men and women will always retain, and will rightly retain, a sense of outrage at wrongdoing. That is why men and women will continue to call upon God to atone, and why the Christian intuition (which again cannot be given a completely rational explanation) that voluntarily accepted suffering on the part of innocent people is the only means of atoning for serious evil will always remain valid. And the worst crimes and sins will always be those which no compensation can put right, where no human means can give any satisfaction. When the Jews were erecting a monument at Belsen, one of the worst of the Nazi concentration camps where hundreds of thousands of Jews were ruthlessly murdered during the Second World War, they did not inscribe on it any of those conventional sentiments which we are used to see adorning our memorials to those who died during the war, 'They died that we might live', or 'To our glorious dead', or some such inscription. They simply placed on the memorial a verse from the book of Job (16.18):

> O earth, cover not my blood
> And let my cry find no resting place.

God alone can atone, because only God can bear the cost of atonement.

NOTE

1 The discerning reader will perceive that I here accept the thesis put forward in Professor A. T. Hanson's book *The Wrath of the Lamb* (1957).

8 *The Church: Its Authority and Ministry*

I

It may appear an altogether obvious question to ask how we define the Church. Is not the Church palpably, before us in all its visibility? Are not its archdeacons, its Sunday schools, and its harvest thanksgivings among us? Do we not all know it in the very con-concreteness and particularity of churchwardens, rural deanery returns, sick visits and missionary societies? The Church surely is the institution which we now serve as it always has been in some form or other from the beginning. But this line of argument is too facile and too easily overturned to stand. In the first place, we are asking, not how does the Church look, or how has it always looked, but what defines the Church? What makes the Church to be the Church? And we cannot take archdeacons or churchwardens or rural deanery returns to be the essential marks of the church, to be that without which the Church would be no Church. In the second place, purely institutional survival is not necessarily a proof that a Church is the true Church. We can point to many examples of Churches which have survived very little changed for centuries, in some cases for over a thousand years, whose institutional continuity is impressive and unimpeachable, but whose life and doctrine show features which should make us pause long before we decide that they are true Churches just because they have survived. The ancient Church of Ethiopia is such a one. And thirdly, if we appeal to the continuous survival of institutions within our Church as proofs that it must be a true Church, or the true Church, then we must be very sure that the institutions which we pick out as significant really have existed continuously since the beginning of the Church. And this is not an easy thing to do.

Are we, for instance, to take the existence of the threefold Christian ministry, and in particular the episcopate, as the institution or feature *par excellence* which ensures that our Church is the Church or a true Church? Certainly this threefold ministry goes back to a very early period of the Church's existence, but not to the very beginning. We cannot trace the existence of a threefold ministry of bishops, priests, and deacons recognized as the solely authoritative pattern of ministry further back than the second century. We cannot find monarchical bishops as a feature of the ministry earlier than the last decade of the first century, and I should think their existence as early as that very improbable. Indeed, in the period of the primitive Church, the period mirrored in the letters of St Paul and less clearly in the early chapters of Acts, we cannot find any permanent fixed official form of Christian ministry at all. There is no satisfactory evidence whatever in the New Testament that the apostles appointed successors to themselves as officers of the Christian Church. If the doctrine of apostolic succession means that bishops—or other ministers—are successors in an unbroken line of single officials appointed in succession from the apostles' time onwards, then this doctrine must be pronounced false. It is not merely that there was a body or committee of officials called elders or presbyters in the earliest period who later devolved their powers on to a single bishop. It is that there is no evidence for the Church in the primitive period having been governed universally and uniformly by presbyters, nor by any person whom we can recognize as a permanent official minister.

Are we then to discover with what permanent features Jesus Christ endowed the church when he founded it and regard these as the criterion of what constitutes the Church? We have already seen that this is an unsatisfactory method of procedure when we apply it to the apostles. The Twelve are the most obvious feature of the Church in those passages in the gospels where Christ is represented as founding the Church, and yet the Twelve were not to be permament. In their chief function, that of bearing witness to the words and deeds of Jesus, and to the resurrection, they had no successors and by the nature of the case they could have no successors. They did indeed wield authority in the Church, and we shall be considering that point later. But we cannot identify any officials to whom the apostles uniformly and deliberately handed on their authority.

An even greater objection to the project of finding the original plan of Christ's Church when he founded it is that the earliest documents of the Christian faith, though they speak constantly about the Church, do not seem to be the least interested in the fact —if it is a fact—that Christ in the days of his flesh founded the Church as an institution. I refer, of course, to the letters of St Paul.

They are decidedly earlier than any Gospel, and give us a picture of the primitive Church which we can only supplement fragmentarily from the Gospels and uncertainly from the Book of Acts. St Paul does not think of the Church as an institution founded by Christ during his earthly ministry, as Ignatius Loyola founded the Society of Jesus and William Booth founded the Salvation Army. Paul speaks of the Church exclusively in terms of the community of the faithful bound together as Christ's Body by faith, by baptism, and in the Holy Spirit. In other words, Paul thinks of the Church as springing out of the resurrection and does not appear to be interested in it as an institution founded by Christ during the days of his flesh. This suggests that to look for institutions built into the Church according to some blueprint developed by Jesus Christ during his years of preaching and healing in Galilee and in Jerusalem, and to take these as the means of defining the Church, may be a wild-goose chase. In other words, we do not find a simple picture of the Church in Scripture. Most people when they speak of 'the simple scriptural gospel' or the 'simple scriptural teaching about the atonement' or 'the simple scriptural facts about Christ' are talking nonsense. The Scriptures are not simple and the picture which they give of the Church, if we examine it critically, as we must, is of a development. The earliest, primitive Church does not rest upon institutions which we can easily recognize as existing in the Church of our own day. It is not therefore possible to define the Church by appeal to institutions.

By what then are we to define the Church? I believe that there can be only one answer. The Church must be defined by the Word of God. The New Testament doctrine of the Word of God is not one that has received much attention in recent Anglican theology, though our Prayer Book is full of this doctrine and though the Reformers made this the main point of their programme of reform. The doctrine of the Word of God dominates the New Testament from the Book of Acts onward. Continuity in the Church according to the account in Acts is provided, not by a carefully preserved order of ministers succeeding each other, but by the Word of God, by the Spirit who guides the Church and perhaps also by the tradition of the words and deeds of Jesus handed on in the Church. The all-engrossing subject of the early chapters of this book is not apostolic succession nor the primacy of Peter but the *kerygma*, the preaching. It may be that Luke does not give us an exact transcript of what the apostles preached. It may be that the *kerygma* was somewhat more diverse and less uniform than Acts represents it to be, or even than C. H. Dodd assumed it to be in his classic books upon the subject. But there can be no doubt that the preaching of the Word greatly occupied the mind and the activity of the primitive Church. When we move from the pages of Acts to the epistles of the New Testament which follow this book, we find no less an emphasis upon the Word. It is the Word by which we are saved, the Word of God or the Word of the Cross or the Word of truth or the Word of the Lord or the Word of hearing or the Word that is living and active and sharper than any two-edged sword or the engrafted Word or the Word of God that is living and abiding or the Word of Life. The Word was something that was there from the beginning; without the Word there would have been no Church. It is by this Word of God that we must define the Church. This is a point upon which both Roman Catholic and Reformed theologians can agree.

But when we say that the Church is to be defined by the Word of God, we must be careful to know what we mean by that phrase, 'the Word of God'. We are here open to a Protestant misinterpretation or misunderstanding. To take the position that the Church is defined by the Word of God is not to assume that any or every assembly of people who allege that they have heard the Word or that the Word is preached among them can rightly be called the Church. It is not to surrender to the doctrine of the Gospel Halls which see the Church in terms of a number of isolated pietist groups created by their concentration on Scripture and Scripture alone. Far less is it to define the Church in terms of religious experience. This last fate, which is the destiny of almost all groups who attempt to define themselves by Scripture alone or who interpret the concept of the Word in a narrow and subjective way, has befallen a very large part of the religious life of Protestant denominations in Ireland. Under the pretext of subjecting everything to the Word of God the devotees of this type of religion in effect subordinate every feature of the life of their sect to religious experience—sacraments, ministry, worship, preaching, and study. And the religious experience to which they sacrifice everything is of a peculiarly intense but also peculiarly narrow, unsophisticated, and often uncharitable type. 'I am not a Protestant,' Karl Barth once wrote, 'if by Protestantism is meant the hideous and mistaken notion that men are justified by their secret knowledge of God.' We are not justified by our religious experience; this delusion is the last and most subtle form of the doctrine of justification by works, and it is still very widespread in the North of Ireland. To say that the Church is defined by the Word of God is not to say that the Church is defined by my, or your, or anybody's experience of the Word of God.

In fact the New Testament is remarkably reticent on the subject of religious experience. In the single place in all his works where St Paul refers to his conversion on the Damascus road, it is most instructive to see in what terms he speaks of it. We would expect him to say something like, 'When I had that overwhelming experience', or 'When I found Christ', or 'When I experienced God's saving power', or even simply, 'When I was converted'. Nothing of the sort! What Paul says is 'When it pleased him who had separated me from my mother's womb and called me through his grace to reveal his Son in me' (Gal. 1.15). Could any statement of a conversion more rigorously exclude the element of religious experience? This attitude is characteristic of the New Testament. There is no word or words for 'religious experience' in it from cover to cover. Paul does once refer to very intense and exalted religious experiences which he had, at 2 Cor. 12.1–7. But he does so in studiously restrained language, largely referring to himself in the third person, and he produces the subject only to dismiss it as an unworthy argument which he will not use. He prefers to speak of his weakness. The truth is that though what we call religious experience is an inescapable part of all genuine Christianity, the New Testament is not very much interested in it. It is far more concerned with what God does to man, what a writer in the *TWNT* has called 'the holy God's handling of sinful man', than with what it feels like for man to experience God. We therefore must not think of the concept of the Word of God primarily in terms of religious experience nor allow it to be drowned in a dreary subjectivity.

The New Testament concept of the Word of God implies the activity of God in Christ. It means the presence and power of God at the Last Time. It is an eschatological concept, like all the leading concepts of the New Testament. God has brought in the Last Age through his great act or move or drama which has been expressed in the career of his Son Jesus Christ, and above all in his death and resurrection. The case is not merely that Jesus Christ has brought the Word or declared the message that contains the Word or taught the leading points about the Word. He *is* the

Word: he is God's last Act. He has not only given us holiness and redemption, he has been made for us wisdom from God, righteousness and holiness and redemption (1 Cor. 1.30). The Word of God therefore is God active in this new state of affairs, this new dispensation or covenant, this new Last Time. It is therefore of course God active in Christ. We must not interpret the word 'Word' in exclusively wordy terms. This, as Tillich used to point out, is one of the besetting sins of Protestantism. If you go to the island of Iona and look round the beautifully preserved Abbey buildings there you will see some religious cartoons by an artist called R. O. Hodgall. One of them represents a preacher in a pulpit, clad in a black Geneva gown and holding out his hand in an arresting and dramatic gesture. Clearly he imagines himself a second John Knox or John Calvin. But out of his mouth there comes an obfuscating cloud consisting of the word 'words' written over and over again. His preaching, for all his histrionic gesture and self-esteem, consists of nothing but words, words, words. This is a danger which all Reformed churches in Ireland face. We dissolve our religion into words, comforting words, fine-sounding words, words full of sound and fury, and we think that we are being good Protestants. We exalt the sacred mystery of Mattins at the expense of the mystery of the Eucharist; we refuse to have Christian symbolism in our churches but we cover their walls with texts from the Bible—more words, and in an archaic and obsolete translation. Our religion is constantly in danger of melting into words, words, words, and nothing but words.

But the Word of God in the New Testament is not just words. Paul knew very well the contrast between *logos* and *ergon* or between *logos* and *dynamis*. It means the activity of God, and it can be conveyed in a sacrament or a political or social situation or an apparently casual happening, like the Ethiopian eunuch meeting Philip on the road from Jerusalem to Gaza. It does not mean that God is a talkative God, though sometimes from the loquaciousness of his ministers you might think so. It does not simply mean that God speaks to men. It means that he confronts them, faces them with an all-important decision, forces them to choose. When the Word of God meets men it meets them in such a way that God remains Lord and master. Here the inheritance of the Old Testament's knowledge of God becomes effective. That is why the Word of God, if it is to be accepted and received, can only be accepted and received in faith. Otherwise God would not remain master.

The whole Bible defines God as one who only can be known through faith. In the encounter between God and man Jacob does not win his wrestling-match. Man cannot so know God as to master him, as a scientist masters a thesis or a lawyer a brief. The form of knowledge of God offered to man in the Bible is faith. And faith—as the New Testament makes clear in several passages—also means obedience.

The final characteristic which we must detect in the doctrine of the Word of God is that it forces men to be self-critical. The Epistle to the Hebrews describes it as 'sharper than any two-edged sword and divisive even to the point of separating soul and body, joints and marrow' (4.12). This is a function of the Word of God to which those sects which use this phrase with such indiscriminate loudness seem to be totally blind, for they are completely and deplorably unwilling to criticize themselves and, one fears, incapable and unfit to do so. But the Word of God in the New Testament compels men to criticize themselves, to investigate their hearts, to subject themselves to the searching, perhaps even searing, light of the Word. This means that Christianity always carries within itself the possibility of criticizing itself, and this has been most important for its development in history. No age has been so blind, no generation so complacent, no era so sunk in satisfied self-approving stagnation and conservatism that it has not been succeeded by one of criticism, of reform, of correction. It has never been possible completely to stifle criticism in the Church; not even the papacy succeeded in doing that. Within the very heart of Christianity is a dynamic principle of self-criticism, and this is part of the nature of the Word of God.

The Church, then, is to be defined by this Word of God. The Word gathers together the Church, and this is what makes the Church to be the Church, not possession of apostolic succession, nor of Petrine primacy, nor even of a 'scriptural ministry', nor even of a foundation by Jesus Christ in the days of his flesh. By this thesis we define the Church by means of something which must have been there from the beginning, unless Christianity simply is not Christianity, something which must always have been at the very heart of Christianity. In effect this is to define the Church by Christ, and not, as has sometimes been done, to define Christ by the Church. Where Christ is, there is the Church; and if we can detect or observe Christ anywhere, even in the most unlikely places, there the Church must somehow be. 'The visible Church of Christ is a congregation of faithful men, in which the pure Word of God is preached' (Article 19). It is the Word that determines and calls the Church.

But before we finish our consideration of the answer to the question with which this chapter started, and before we become intoxicated with the freedom which this definition of the Church apparently gives us, we must sober ourselves by a glance at what this Church which is called by the Word is actually like in the pages of the New Testament. It consists of a closely-knit company of men and women, so intimately united to Christ that Paul can call it the Body of Christ. What this may imply we shall consider later. For the moment it is enough to note that one consequence of being the Body of Christ is that all Christians are members of each other, that according to the Second Epistle to the Corinthians they share a common experience; when one church is persecuted all are persecuted; where one rejoices all rejoice; in each church all are apparently responsible for the conduct of each. We can look at Luke's picture of the early chapters of Acts and can be confident of the accuracy of his narrative about the common meals, the common prayer, the common life and fellowship of the early Christians, even pushed to the point for a time of a common sharing of goods. This is exactly how one would expect the Church described in Romans, ch. 12, in 1 Corinthians, ch. 10–12 and in Ephesians ch. 4, to behave. We must also note that this primitive Church is conscious of possessing authority and does not hesitate to exercise it. Paul does claim far-reaching authority in the churches which he has founded, even though he exercises that authority with gentleness and tact. He expects the Corinthian church to assert their own authority by excommunicating, at least temporarily, a member who has had improper relations with his step-mother. The primitive Church in Acts takes decisions, performs administrative acts, sends commissioners on various tasks, plans missionary strategy, and debates about Christian ethics. Above all, the primitive Church takes on itself to forgive sins. We may not regard the words of Matthew 18.15 and 17 about how to deal with a recalcitrant brother as a transcript of the actual words of Christ, but they are an interesting picture of how the early Church sometimes resolved questions of discipline. This tightly-knit community, very conscious of its unity and its separateness from the world, claiming authority which it is not afraid to exercise, is the Church gathered together by the Word. It is not the picture of happy spontaneous charismatic chaos which some famous German scholars of sixty or seventy years ago painted for us. It is not the jealous little guilt-laden pietistic community of the sects. The primitive Church is astonishingly confident of itself, amazingly free of institutions, and full of enormous potential.

II

It would be as well at this stage to give some sort of definition of the word 'institution' in the theological context in which I shall now be using it. By 'institution' I mean any permanent or long-lasting feature or structure in the life of the Church, and any organization or office or practice established as a regular part of the functioning of the Church. Obviously some institutions in the Church are more lasting and more essential to the Church's function than others. The General Synod of the Church of Ireland is an old respectable institution, but not one that has always been there; it has only existed for a little over one hundred years. Rural deaneries are an established feature of the Church and could well be called an institution, but they are no more than medieval in origin. We could imagine the Church of Ireland existing and functioning at some point in the future without either rural deaneries or general synods, and, however desirable these institutions now may appear to us, we could not say that the Church would be no Church without them. The Book of Common Prayer is an old and venerable institution in the Church. In my opinion, and in the opinion of most churchmen, it is a highly desirable one with which I would be very unwilling indeed to dispense, but I could not say without qualification that the Church would not be a Church without it. The institution of episcopal government brings us on to most debatable ground. It is of almost immemorial antiquity and is so highly valued in our tradition that we might go as far as saying that for us it is *articulum cadentis aut stantis ecclesiae*. When we ask further about the ministry as a whole and about sacraments considered as institutions we clearly have reached a nodal point in the discussion.

Perhaps we should first ask whether the Church itself should be regarded as an institution. At first sight it looks obvious that the Church is an institution. It strikes us as a very institutional thing, and people even contrast the institutional Church with some other, perhaps an invisible one. But we should pause before we decide that the Church is by nature an institution. It would be safer to describe it as a society which has institutions as part of its life, though we have yet to decide which institutions, if any, are necessary to its life. But if we define the Church as the company of those who are called by responding to the Word of God into a society we are thinking of it in basically uninstitutional terms, and though we may find some features in its life which are clearly institutional we should not without further consideration call the Church an institution.

We should indeed note that many people have defined the Church in terms which in effect make it an institution. If we were to identify the Church with the *Civitas Dei*, for instance, we would have to think of it in a primarily institutional way. There are still some who think of the Church as identical with the Kingdom of God, who regard the Church as a state within the state, called and destined to dominate society. This was the concept of the Church which prevailed in the Middle Ages, and the greatest crisis which the Middle Ages had to face was caused by the failure of the Church to make itself credible as a super-state, as an international state interpenetrating and controlling all states. But the failure of the medieval Church alone should not convince us of the mistake of identifying the Church with the Kingdom of God. The witness of the New Testament does not allow this identification. The Kingdom of God was a phrase constantly upon the lips of Jesus, whereas it is very doubtful if he ever spoke of the Church (*ecclesia*). The Kingdom of God meant the kingly rule of God and the people who accepted that rule and so became God's people. It was an eschatological kingdom whose exact connection with Jesus, who proclaimed it, is difficult to determine. It is wholly likely that in the thought of Jesus his death was to be in some way decisive for the Kingdom. In the New Testament after the Synoptic Gospels the concept of the Kingdom of God has been pushed into the background. Instead of the Kingdom and its prophet Jesus we find the Church and its Master and Lord Jesus. But we have no right facilely to identify the two concepts. The Kingdom is a new order, a new dispensation from God which creates a people. The Church is that people united with their Messiah, the Son of God, in the interim period between the inauguration of the Kingdom and its consummation. We have no right to say that the government of the Church is the government of the Kingdom, the Church's ministry its civil service, the laws of the Church its laws, and so on. This is to anticipate eschatology, to regard eschatology as already fully realized, to do away with the 'Not yet', with what has been called the 'relativism', of the New Testament, to attempt to walk by sight not by faith, to turn the servant and pilgrim Church into the triumphalist and imperialist Church. As I have already suggested, the history of the Middle Ages in both the Western and the Eastern Church should warn us against the disaster inevitably involved in making such an identification.

More recently many people have been ready to see the Church as the extension of the incarnation, and the fact that Paul describes the Church as the Body of Christ has made this view plausible. Let us see therefore whether we can agree that the Church is the extension of the incarnation. In the first place, I do not like the implied suggestion that the incarnation needs extending. The incarnation is not, according to orthodox Christian doctrine, a closed episode in history. There have been theologians, such as Origen in the third century, who held that the human nature of Jesus disappeared completely at the resurrection or the ascension, was entirely swallowed up in his divine nature. But the central tradition of Catholic orthodoxy has always held that the human nature of Jesus Christ still exists, even though it must in some way have become spiritualized. If he is not still in some sense human he could not act still as our mediator. Further, his spiritualized human nature has always been supposed to give us some clue to the ultimate destiny of our own natures. If this then is so, we cannot speak of the incarnation being extended. It is here already wherever Christ is present. Behind this concept of 'the extension of the incarnation' may lie an unexamined assumption that Christ is absent, or at any rate that he is only present on special occasions such as the celebration of the eucharist. This idea is reminiscent of the dreadful line in J. M. Neale's hymn.

> And still the holy Church is here
> Although her Lord is gone.

The Church is here regarded as the substitute for an absent Christ; the apostolic succession of bishops is presumed to form a kind of telephone wire with him. Nowadays fortunately this view has only to be stated to be rejected.

Anyway, the expression 'Body of Christ' applied to the Church does not necessarily imply that the Church is the extension of the incarnation. This expression and the passages in St Paul associated with it have formed the subject of much study and discussion during the last thirty years or so. The best known and indeed classic treatments of it have been those of the Belgian Roman Catholic priest Emil Mersch in *The Mystical Body of Christ*, of the Anglican monk Lionel Thornton in *The Common Life in the Body of Christ*, and of the Ulster-born Presbyterian theologian Ernest Best in *One Body in Christ*. It is possible to argue as, in different ways, both Mersch and Thornton do, that by the expression 'the Body of Christ' Paul meant to identify Christ with the Church in the most literal and realistic way. Where the Church spoke and acted there Christ spoke and acted, because Christ is the Church. During its triumphalist and imperialist phase before the Second Vatican Council this doctrine suited the Roman Catholic Church well, as can be seen from Pope Pius XII's Encyclical *Mystici Corporis*. But the work of Ernest Best should prevent us from unreflectingly adopting this interpretation of Paul's great phrase. He points out that, important though this description of the Church is in Paul's thought, it is not the only image which he applies to the Church. He also calls it a temple in which Christ lives, a people led by Christ through the wilderness, a body of which Christ is the head, and so on; no other image which he uses for the Church implies actual identity between Christ and the Church. Further, it is quite clear from other passages both in Paul and in the rest of the Epistles of the New Testament that Christ judges the Church, purifies the Church and rules the Church, all of which functions are incompatible with the concept of Christ actually *being* the Church. It is therefore better to conclude that Paul's doctrine of the Church as the Body of Christ is intended to convey the closest conceivable union of the Church with Christ short of actual identification. After nearly two thousand years of Christian history we ought by now to have learnt the lesson that it is disastrous to take the imagery of the Bible literally. The subject of the nature of biblical imagery and symbolism is a crucial one for our understanding of belief in God in the twentieth century, and we must not by an unreflecting literalism deprive ourselves in advance of possible options.

Generally speaking, history should teach us how unwise it is to identify the Church or any office or institution within the Church directly and without qualification with the voice or the activity of God, to say that when so-and-so speaks, or under such-and-such circumstances, we can be infallibly sure that God is speaking directly to us, whether this deified organ be the Pope, the Bible, or

—most dangerous deification of all—the religious experience of the individual believer. This is the sign of a craving for unmediated, direct, knowledge of God which the insufficiently regenerate human heart is always liable to entertain and which can only end in one form or other of idolatry.

We reject the view therefore that the Church is an institution in the sense that it is the extension of the incarnation, a kind of substitute-institution for Christ himself. But might it not be an institution in the sense that a sacrament is an institution? It has become quite fashionable recently to call the Church a sacrament, to say that the Church is the sacrament of Christ in the world. If the Church is a sacrament, then it well might be an institution.

But it will not do to call the Church a sacrament. If we do, we shall do an injustice either to the Church or to the nature of a sacrament. A sacrament is essentially a thing, an object, something material, physical, used by God for holy purposes, such as water or bread or wine or the action of human hands in blessing. But the Church is composed of human beings, and what makes the Church in its human aspect is the wills and intentions, the faith and the love, of these human beings. These cannot be equated with bread and wine and water and so on used in sacramental action by God. Of course our intentions and our faith and our love have to be expressed through our bodies, but that does not make our bodies sacramental. Our bodies are instruments, the outer expression of our inner selves, and the Church may well be the instrument of Christ, but that does not mean that it is the sacrament of Christ. To call it so would be to give way to a false objectivization, one might almost call it a reification, of the Church. Here perhaps we come to the heart of the matter. Though we can identify some people as belonging to the Church and some as not, the Church as a whole, the Church in God's design, the Church as God's gift, is not an object. It is a mystery. Therefore it cannot be an institution.

God gives us the Church, as God gives us Christ. We do not create the Church, we receive it. It is not an institution founded by Jesus Christ according to carefully laid plans during his earthly ministry. It is a society of men and women called together by the Word both in the days of his flesh and after the resurrection when he comes in the Holy Spirit. In both modes there is a givenness about his appearance; he is the gracious gift of God. There is a givenness consequently about his people who are inseparable from his existence here on earth. Grace is not an institution. The incarnate Word of God is not an institution. In as far as it lives by grace in union with the Word of God the Church is not an institution.

But the Church does not consist wholly of disembodied spirits existing independently of a physical universe. 'The visible Church of Christ is a congregation of faithful men, in which the pure Word of God is preached': so far we have reached already. But Article 19 continues, 'and the Sacraments be duly ministered according to Christ's ordinance in all those things that of necessity are requisite to the same'. From the very beginning of the Church's existence there have been at least two sacraments, baptism and the eucharist. I will not here discuss either the question of precisely how far Christ can be said to have instituted these sacraments nor the subject of how many sacraments there are. Both these questions are strictly irrelevant to my argument, which is satisfied if it is granted that at least baptism and eucharist were there at the very beginning of the life of the Christian Church. It is impossible not to call these institutions. They are permanent and prominent features of the life of the Church. They remind us that the Church lives in the world of touch and sight and hearing, that God—according to the good Jewish tradition—has no difficulty and no objection to coming into contact with gross, material, physical things, with the stuff of which this world is made. Does this undoubted fact that it has sacramental institutions and that materials sacramentally used appear in the very centre of its life commit the Church to institutions, restrict it within an institutional framework? Have these original institutions doomed the Church from the outset to institutional ossification, inevitably stifled and restricted its life?

To answer these questions we must first consider the nature of a sacrament. Sacraments are not holds established on God. They are not taps or pipes leading from God to us to whose apertures we can apply our mouths and suck grace. They are not machinery for exploiting God, handles for turning on God. In all his relationships to men God is master. The gift given in sacraments can only be received through faith; our practice of infant baptism strains the meaning of sacraments to the utmost; the concept of vicarious faith which is later taken over by personal faith is, I suppose, just tolerable within the context of a Christian family, but our consciences ought to be a good deal more troubled by it than they appear to be. We should as a Church be reconsidering our practice of infant baptism in the light of the doctrine of the Word of God. Sacraments are controlled by the Word, are the means of the Word expressing himself. They are not strait waistcoats placed upon the Word nor abandoned river-courses through which no water now flows. They do not exclude the vital element of existential decision which man's encounter with God must contain. They are not fossilized obsolete rites which the march of history has long left behind. They are made contemporary by the Word of God.

On the other hand, sacraments are, as I have already suggested, reminders that we are of the earth, earthy, and that God likes us that way. They are a most appropriate method for God to use who has endured all the messy particularity and concreteness of an incarnation. They are a standing contradiction of the Greek tendency to dissolve Christianity into ideas, the Protestant tendency to reduce it to words, and the sectarian tendency to remove it to some refined sphere of spirituality, of inward experience. We do not justify ourselves by our own wonderful religious experiences; meeting Christ is not an encounter confined solely to our own minds and souls. We are forced to meet Christ in community and to meet him as coming to us from outside ourselves, apart from our own subjectivity, though not completely divorced from it. We must be initiated into him in baptism; we must continually renew our union with him in the eucharist. Sacraments are not only reminders of grace, they are also the means and the pledges of grace, as the Thirty-nine Articles and the Catechism unequivocally teach. Sacraments are indeed basic original institutions in the life of the Church, but they are not institutions that choke or restrict its life. On the contrary, they are institutions of such a nature that through the Word of God they give life. They are the places where, the circumstances under which God chooses and covenants to meet man, God is spirit; he is free, unconditioned. We have no right to doubt that he is free in his decision to give life to the Church through sacraments.

All sacraments are institutions, though not all institutions are sacraments. We can therefore take what is true of sacraments and apply it analogously to other sorts of institutions. There is nothing whatever wrong with institutions as such. The Church started with three institutions only, baptism, eucharist, and the Scriptures of the Old Testament. It has no fixed ministry, no creed, no New Testament. The period of the primitive Church was one of eschatological and charismatic spontaneity, though, as we shall see when we come to consider authority, not one of formless chaos. But gradually many more permanent institutions began to be formed. By the year A.D. 96 we can discern a permanent official ministry and by the middle of the next century monarchical episcopacy. Not long after, a very rudimentary creed appears, the nucleus of the New Testament has been formed, an agreed structure has been worked out for the eucharistic service, though it will be three centuries before the first liturgy proper follows. Later the ministry becomes much more elaborate, each local church becomes quite a complex institution, and dogma begins to form. The Church, in short, has become thoroughly institutionalized.

Not only was there nothing in principle wrong with this development, but it was an unavoidable and perfectly natural and healthy one. All societies must form institutions or perish. Institutions are devices whereby societies protect themselves against change and vicissitude, against 'the wrecking siege of battering time'. Once the Church has accepted, as it had to accept, what Charles Williams in his book *The Descent of the Dove* calls 'the reconciliation with time', once it had emerged from the first fine careless rapture of eschatological expectation, it was inevitable that it should form institutions. This was part of its recognition that it was a society living in time, with a past (which it tended to idealize into a Golden Age) and a future which could not be described only in terms of eschatological imagery. Some scholars, notably Germans at the end of the nineteenth and the beginning of the twentieth century, have thought of this development as a sort of Fall, a wicked lapse from charismatic purity into institutional pollution. But this is a romantic and unrealistic estimate of the situation. Institutions were inevitable if the Church was to survive. If the Church had formed no institutions such as we have been considering it would not be alive today.

But, just as sacraments are not means of manipulating God, so institutions are not that which creates the Church. As sacraments are vehicles for the Word, for the life of God in Christ, and improperly understood or wrongly used do not convey the saving Word or life, so institutions in the life of the Church are only of use and of advantage as far as they serve the purposes of the Word of God and do not obstruct it, obscure it, or distort it. No institution in the Church is worth preserving simply for its own sake, out of an antiquarian or conservative or sentimental motive, but simply as far as it furthers the progress of the Word, and when an institution is a block to the Word it must be reformed or even abolished. Institutions are good servants but bad masters. I am not advocating a wholesale abolition of institutions in the Church. Some, such as sacraments, ministry, and Bible, are obviously indispensable. Others are wholesome and right if properly used. If we regard the Church as the mystery of the people of God called together by the Word we shall probably decide that the Church must have institutions, but we shall be obliged to see that the institutions are at the disposal of the Church and not vice versa.

III

There can be no doubt that the Church possessed and exercised authority from the earliest moment of its existence. Jesus is represented in the Gospels as giving authority of various kinds both to the Twelve and to a large and vaguer group of the Seventy. In his parting charge to the Eleven in St Matthew's Gospel, Jesus, given all authority in heaven and earth, gives his apostles authority to evangelize everywhere. Similar authority is promised to the Eleven in the last few words of St Luke's Gospel and the beginning of Acts, and this promise is fulfilled at the descent of the Holy Spirit at Pentecost. In the twentieth chapter of St John's Gospel Jesus breathes upon the Eleven and specifically gives them authority to forgive sins.

It is only by reading into the text a later state of affairs that we can see these incidents as a commissioning of the ministry. It is much more likely that they were seen and intended by the evangelists, and understood by the evangelists' first readers, as a commissioning of the Church. Had these accounts been intended to tell us about the ministry, then we should expect to find some evidence in the New Testament that the Eleven appointed successors to carry on the ministry. But there is no evidence whatever that the Eleven did this. At the beginning the Eleven apostles of course are the Church. They are the great initiators of the Word, and as they broadcast the Word so the Church grows. On more than one occasion (1 Cor. 12.28: Eph. 4.11) we find in the New Testament a list of different functions in the Church, starting with the term 'apostles' placed first. That this is not an account of a hierarchy, like 'first archbishops, then bishops ...' is shown by what follows the mention of apostles: 'first apostles, second prophets, third teachers, then powers, then gifts of healing etc' (1 Cor. 12.28);

'some apostles, some prophets, some evangelists, some shepherds and teachers' (Eph. 4.11). These are not lists of officials, but of functions, and the apostles come first, not because they are highest in rank of the ministers (there are no ranks), but because they are the first chronologically. They inaugurate the Church wherever it is planted. That is why Paul claims what authority he does over his churches. He planted them as their apostle. Elsewhere he describes this process both as begetting (1 Cor. 4.14.15; Philemon 10), and as bringing forth in labour (Gal. 4.19). The apostles therefore are first the only Church there is and later the initiators of the Church in different places.

It is the whole Church therefore which at the beginning possesses authority. When Paul is making suggestions or giving directions to those churches which are under his authority he seems to expect them to act as a community in exercising authority. It is as a community that they are to discipline the man who has misbehaved with his step-mother (1 Cor. 5.1–13), or those who will not take notice of Paul's words (2 Thess. 3.11–14). The little vignette of the treatment of a sinning brother given us in Matt. 18.15–17 leaves the same impression. Many incidents in the Book of Acts reveal how decisions were made by a kind of common council of the local church. By this means 'the brethren' or 'the disciples' or similar groups choose the Seven (6.4), rescue Paul on more than one occasion (9.25–30), determine to send relief to Judaea (11.29–30), despatch Barnabas and Saul on a missionary journey (13.1–3), send them to a conference about circumcision at Jerusalem (15.1–2), and so on. O. Linton, in his valuable book *Das Problem der Urkirche*, written about forty years ago, pointed to this remarkable phenomenon of what might be called collective decision in the primitive Church. This was not a matter of counting of heads after the manner of modern liberal democracy. It was more like a committee of the Society of Friends which will take no decision till all are agreed. But it suggests that in the earliest period of the Church's existence authority apparently resided in the local church as a community rather than in any officials or ministers.

But the authority certainly was there. It could be expressed in a number of ways. One of the most important was the forgiveness of sins. Even to quite a late period, as late as the fourth century, it was understood in the Church that the forgiveness of sins was a communal matter, involving the whole local church. This is one reason why auricular confession was so comparatively late in developing; the penitent had to confess his sins to the whole local church, even though by the second half of the second century it was the bishops who decided whether he should be forgiven and how far. But originally no doubt it was the community that decided about forgiveness, and about excommunication. Similarly the whole Church had the authority to communicate the gospel. There were people who had gifts in that direction, apostles, evangelists, teachers, prophets; but if they evangelized they evangelized as the representatives of the whole Church. When difficult decisions arose as to whether the Good News should be imparted to Gentiles the whole Church was involved in deciding the issue. The picture which the Epistles of the New Testament give at first sight seems to be a Church where charismatic chaos and formless spontaneity prevailed. The sessions for worship as reflected in the first Epistle to the Corinthians, for instance, suggest that people prophesied, spoke in tongues, or interpreted almost at will and that the celebration of Holy Communion could take on the appearance of a noisy and disorderly picnic. But a closer look at the picture makes it clear that the primitive Church was conscious of possessing authority and was responsible about exercising it even though it had its own way of discharging that responsibility. Disorderly brothers and sisters were disciplined. The preaching of Christ crucified was not dissolved into a thousand different subjective interpretations. The traditions were maintained intact, such as the story of the Lord's actions at the Last Supper and the list of the resurrection appearances (1 Cor. 11.2, 17–34; 15.1–11; 2 Thess. 2.15; 3.6).

This authority the Church has possessed ever since and still possesses. In its later development the Christian community in each place gradually handed over its authority to a permanent official ministry and eventually to the ministry *par excellence*, that of bishops, and, if we are to pursue the story far enough, in the Western Church to the Pope. But for a long time some vestiges of the communal exercise of authority were retained: bishops could not be chosen except with the consent of the local *plebs*. Cyprian was accustomed to summoning laymen as well as clergy to his local councils. Even at its most oppressive the Church has acknowledged that the *sensus fidelium* is an indispensable element in deciding dogma and that General Councils can only be admitted to have the binding force of ecumenical councils if they are recognized by both laity and clergy, in fact by the general verdict of the whole Church, of later ages. I do not see any point in regretting the disappearance of the primitive way of exercising authority, the charismatic waiting upon the Spirit to produce a communal unanimity. As the development of a permanent ministry, of a New Testament, of a creed, and of dogma, was inevitable and wholesome, so was the placing of the Church's authority in the hands of the Church's ministers. It would be as romantic and unrealistic to attempt to reproduce the pattern of authority in the primitive Church as to attempt to reproduce the charismatic informality of its worship. History moves. Men change. Development is right and proper. We cannot put back the hands of the clock of history. Those Christian communities which at the Reformation attempted to reproduce faithfully the pattern of authority in the primitive Church have not been strikingly successful in their experiment. Some of them, such as the Congregationalists in England, have been compelled by circumstances to modify the primitive purity of their structure.

But our definition of the Church, our concept of the place and function of institutions, and our examination of authority in the primitive Church should convince us of one conclusion to which theologians of many different traditions are now tending to move: all ministry is representative. No minister is so set over the Church that the Church consists in him. The authority of the Church does not exist solely in the clergy who have derived it by direct succession from Christ's or the apostles' institution independently of the rest of the Church. This theory ought to be banished for ever from the counsels of the Church and the minds of theologians. The ministers of the Church do indeed possess authority; they should not function if they do not think so. But they have authority as representatives of the whole Church, as those who have been given authority by the whole Church when they were ordained, or rather by Christ acting in and through the whole Church. Just as we have learned in recent years that the liturgy is the act of the whole congregation, so we have learned that the authority of the Church's ministers is the authority of the Church. Their ministry is representative and not substitutionary, expressive, not vicarious; they enable the Church to act, they do not act instead of the Church.

We are attending a service of Holy Communion. The priest comes and blesses the bread and wine in Christ's name. We communicate, believing that thereby we are united with Christ's very life. But Christ initiated this sacrament nearly two thousand years ago. How do we know that this man has the right to bless the elements in this way? How do we know that the sacrament is valid? That these are not just empty gestures like children playing at church, as my children sometimes do? Can any persons celebrate this sacrament in any form according to their whim and be confident that God will obligingly co-operate? If the Free Presbyterians pretend to celebrate this sacrament (I do not know whether or not they do) do they, unordained and unauthorized, self-promoted and self-appointed, enjoy the same blessing as we? It is a question worth asking.

Christianity is something handed on. In one aspect Christianity is all tradition. It has to be handed on from generation to generation, from father to son, or it perishes. The Bible has to be handed on, to be translated, printed, circulated, explained, and taught anew every new generation. The faith has to be handed on and the sacraments. The life of the Church must be handed on, the piety of the individual believer and the worship of the Church. We do not create Christianity anew every fifty years, starting from the Bible alone. This would be, in the strictest sense of the words, an impossible task, and the result of such an enterprise would not be recognizable as Christianity. We inherit a vast sum of unacknowledged tradition which we do not change and which we unreflectingly accept and pass on. Christianity is a movement in history. It has continuity from which we can never escape and from which we should not want to escape. The continuity of Christianity is part of the guarantee of its greatness and the authority of the Church could not survive without the continuity of the Church. It is the continuity of the Church which makes sure that when a man is given authority in the Church he genuinely possesses that authority. This continuity can be expressed in a number of different ways. It can be a purely institutional continuity without any necessary relation to the continuity of the Word of God. There have been plenty of examples of this in the course of Christian history. In these cases the formal authority of the Church has allowed itself to become divorced from the authority of the Word. But a Christian body which concentrates exclusively upon the Word of God without any concern for institutional continuity, continuity of ministry, government, and sacraments, has to justify its authority; and this is not at all an easy thing to do. Protestants tend to be very conscious of the danger of stifling the free Word of God under man-made ordinances and institutions. But they must meet the disturbing question about authority. If they think that they had authority from the Word of God at the Reformation, then must they not allow the claims of all who appealed or who today appeal to the Word of God in making drastic alterations in the structure of the Church? From where do they derive greater authority than the others? Anglicans will answer, from antiquity, from the tradition of the first five centuries. This is a kind of appeal to continuity. This is in fact an appeal to an authority which is not simply that of the Word of God. I entirely agree that this is a proper and necessary appeal, but we must face the awkward question of why we should not allow the much stronger appeal to the authority of continuity which the Roman Catholic and Eastern Orthodox churches make. They appear to be able to outbid us here.

I believe that we must make some such answer as this: Properly and rightly the authority of the Word of God should be fully and effectively expressed in the structure of the empirical Church, in its ministry and sacraments and its institutions. But a situation may arise wherein the structure of the empirical Church fails dangerously to express the authority of the Word of God. We may reasonably conclude that such a point was reached in the sixteenth century. The very fact that that century witnessed not only a Reformation but also a Counter-Reformation that was not a mere undoing of the Reformation but an antitypal Reformation, a reaction under the pressure of the Reformation to the evils that caused the Reformation, proves this. It became necessary to break the continuity of the Church's structure in order to re-establish the authority of the Word of God. The result was a partial loss of authority by all Christian denominations in the West. A dislocation took place between the authority of the Word of God and the continuity of the Church's life and structure. All were losers, though perhaps the loss was not as great as the loss would have been had the Reformation never taken place. The loss of unity and the loss of continuity were involved with each other. This was not a splitting off of heretical bodies. It was a loss of continuity and unity within the Church itself, a loss which reproduced a similar earlier loss when the Eastern and Western Churches drifted apart. The authority of the Word of God was no longer reflected in the Church's structure, in its unity and continuity, or was reflected only dimly and brokenly.

We can now see why the search for the restoration of the Church's unity, which has now been in process for nearly a hundred years, is a search for the restoration of something vital in the life of the Church. It is a search for the renewal of the Church's authority and thereby for the renewal of the authority of the Word of God. It is a search which cannot be satisfied with a merely federal recognition of different denominations by each other in a kind of friendly competition in an open market, such as is apparently taking place in South America today. There must be a *communicatio in sacris*, inter-communion, though one can imagine such inter-communion as existing between very diverse and variegated Christian bodies. Otherwise the authority of the Church is impaired. Until Christians come together, we cannot be sure that we are dealing with the genuine article. We may well be sure that our orders have conferred upon us the authority of Christ, but we should honestly admit that it is an impaired authority, and this applies to Roman Catholic clergy as well as to others.

We have arrived at a point of our argument where we can also see that the Church must be a visible Church. An invisible Church lacks authority. Of course we must admit that the vast majority of the members of the Church are invisible, for they are in heaven. And we must also admit that only God knows whose destiny among all those now alive on earth it will be to reach heaven and be finally saved. If we try to argue that the only real Church is the number of those whom God, and God alone, knows to be destined to be saved, we deprive the Church of continuity and of authority. It becomes impossible to say in what sense an invisible church of this kind has authority or could forgive sins or celebrate sacraments. But the Church in the New Testament quite manifestly does all these things. Therefore the Church as God wills it to exist on earth must be a visible Church. This is a very fitting dispensation by a God who has chosen to disclose himself to us by the incarnation of his Son.

And finally we perceive that the Church must be a permanent and not an occasional Church. There is for some people a great attraction in the kind of Church described by Karl Barth, a Church which only exists when and where the pure Word of God is preached and the sacraments are *duly* administered, but otherwise and on other occasions the Church does not exist at all. There is more than a hint of this in the nineteenth of the Thirty-nine Articles, derived from the strong Calvinist strain that runs through these Articles. But this will not do. If the Church only appears where these conditions are fulfilled and otherwise or in other places ceases to exist at all, it cannot have any continuity. Its continuity is the continuity of the Cheshire Cat in *Alice in Wonderland*. We can have no confidence that the occasionally appearing Church has the authority of Christ because nothing has been handed on, or rather because what has been handed on is regarded as nothing. Strictly speaking, of course, the Cheshire Cat theory of the Church is nonsense. It is impossible for a Church which consists of men and women of flesh and blood to disappear and reappear. The Bible has to be there, and Christian doctrine, piety and practice. None of these can exist if they have not been handed on in a continuous tradition from the beginning. God is a good deal less doctrinaire than his theologians. He is prepared to put up with a very sorry Church and allow it some authority and some effectiveness in the expectation of persuading it to reform itself, as his Son was prepared to put up with some very sorry disciples, who misunderstood him and deserted him, in the expectation of their becoming the apostles of the whole world.

IV

Among the institutions and ministries of the Church one of those which causes most confusion and uncertainty today is the priesthood. This chapter on the Church will end with a consideration of this much debated subject.

The New Testament firmly rules out a Christian priesthood on the model of the Old Testament priesthood. The revolution in historical scholarship which is sometimes called 'historical criticism' has made the business of deciding what the New Testament allows and what it does not allow a complex and confusing task. It is no simple matter to determine how the Bible can be a norm of faith (see above, chapter 2). But on this point the evidence is quite clear. The Epistle to the Hebrews takes as one of the main points of its argument that the sacrifices offered according to the Jewish law are no longer necessary or significant. They have been superseded by a final sacrifice, made by Jesus Christ the Son of God. Even if one were to play down the significance of this Epistle and push its witness into the background (as Raymond E. Browne does in his recent little book *Priest and Bishop*), it would still be impossible to ignore the evidence of St Paul's letters. For St Paul, the Jewish law has been finally rendered insignificant and optional for Christians by the voluntary sacrifice of Jesus Christ, the Son of God. Paul's attitude to the law is complex, at times ambivalent, even perhaps dialectical, but this is quite clear: Christ allowed the law to wreak its full force, to exact its full penalty, on himself though he was personally innocent. He thereby instituted a new state of affairs, a new agreement or relationship or covenant between God and man. The old covenant, expressed in a sacrificial cult, was thereby for ever abandoned and rendered meaningless. Sacrifice was an universal phenomenon in the religion of the world of antiquity, pagan or Jewish. It was accepted as part of the ordinary furniture of the religious scene and few ever bothered to ask exactly what it meant. Explanations by modern scholars of the exact meaning attached to sacrifice by the ancient Jews have been as varied as they have been inconclusive. But certainly for Paul there was no place left, once Jesus Christ had been accepted as Lord, for an imitation or prolongation or adaptation or Christianization of the Jewish sacrificial system or of the Jewish priesthood. He would have called any attempt to produce such a thing 'building up those things which I tore down' (Gal. 2.8). Christians have died to the law; to return to a sacrificing priesthood in any form would be to nullify the grace of God (Gal. 2.19–21). He uses sacrificial language of his own ministry in one place (Rom. 15.16, *leitourgōn, hierourgounta, prosphora*); but here it is clear that this is metaphorical language used of his planting the gospel and of the fruit of this work evident in converts. This cannot be stretched to mean that he regards himself as in any except a metaphorical or poetical sense comparable to the Jewish priests who were at the time he was writing ministering a sacrificial cult. Obviously Paul had no intention, once he had weaned his converts away from reliance on the Jewish law with its sacrificial system, to substitute for this a system which included Christian priests in a Christian sacrificial cult.

Two hundred and fifty years after Paul's day, however, the Church was using language which made precisely this assumption. Its chief ministers, the bishops, were regarded as priests on the model of the ancient Jewish priesthood presiding over a sacrificial cult, the eucharist, which was comparable with the ancient Jewish sacrificial cult. The tendency to view not only bishops but the other major orders in this light increased during the fourth century. It was fed by two other streams: the practice of using terms taken from pagan cults, and especially from the mystery religions (which now offered less and less competition and rivalry to Christianity) to describe the ministry and the eucharist, and the necessity of 'fencing the altar', that is, preventing the enormous inrush of pagans into the Church consequent upon the Roman Imperial Government's recognition of it and patronage of it from diluting its standards and vulgarizing its sacraments. The result was that by the year 400 a strongly sacerdotal view of the Christian ministry was firmly established in both East and West, a view which saw bishops (and to a lesser extent presbyters) as the priests of a Christian cultus, comparable to the old Jewish priests of the Temple at Jerusalem, one of whose main functions was to offer the body and blood of Christ to God in the eucharist. They alone were qualified, empowered (one almost says insulated or inoculated) to do this, with all the privileges and advantages of belonging to an exclusive sacerdotal caste which this position conferred. This was the view of the ministry which prevailed during the Middle Ages. It was further developed only by the later tendency to regard the presbyter, as priest, as a basic and important order, whereas episcopacy was thought of as a kind of extension or intensification of priesthood. This view is still the official view of the Roman Catholic Church, though it is being strongly criticized within the fold of that Church (see J. J. Hughes, *Absolutely Null and Utterly Void* and *Stewards of the Lord*). When Pope Leo XIII in his Bull *Apostolicae Curae* of 1896 declared that Anglican orders were invalid, his main argument was that these orders were not designed to ordain a sacrificing priesthood but indeed were deliberately designed to create a non-sacrificing priesthood.

It is interesting to trace the origins of this idea of a sacrificing priesthood. The subject deserves more intensive study than recent scholarship has devoted to it. Perhaps the best explanation is that the Church found itself exposed to two different temptations at the same time, the temptations to exploit the law-books of the Old Testament and the temptation to claim the social *cachet* that possession of a priesthood gave. Once the Church had emancipated itself from a wholly Jewish *milieu*, it began to find the law-books of the Old Testament an increasing liability and embarrassment. The best efforts of allegorization could do little to make large tracts of the books of Exodus, Numbers, Leviticus, and Deuteronomy even faintly relevant to the Christian Church. But if the many ordinances and regulations in these books concerning the Jewish cultic ministry could be regarded as applying, *mutatis mutandis*, to Christian ministers, then much of their contents could be seen to be relevant to the Christian dispensation. The great third-century exponent of Christian priesthood, Cyprian bishop of Carthage, uses the law-books of the Old Testament with complete and uncritical confidence to supply a character and status to the bishops of his Church. They are sacrificing high priests or priests; their persons are sacrosanct; none but they may approach the altar; to oppose them is to incur the wrath of God, and so on. The temptation to turn the Christian bishop into a Christian version of the Jewish high priest was very strong; Cyprian had had no time between being converted and being chosen as bishop of Carthage to acquire a theological training which was more than rudimentary and his talents lay more in the direction of ecclesiastical leadership and administration than in that of critical theology. He yielded to the temptation enthusiastically. His example, enforced by the weight which his martyrdom conferred, was very influential in the West.

In another direction, Christians may have found themselves at a disadvantage in the society in which they lived because they could not claim that their cult had 'high priests'. They were not always under persecution; they could not completely isolate themselves from the society of the Greco-Roman world in which they lived. They must often have cultivated good relations with pagans, and they must often have been asked, 'What are the officials of your cult called?' They could only answer, 'Inspectors' (*episkopoi*, bishops). This was a pale, uninteresting word, for, as with us, an inspector could be anything. He could be an inspector of education, of drains, or of police. But the pagans could boast that they had priests, or even high priests. Many cities, like ancient Ephesus and Alexandria, had a city high priest (*archiereus*), whose business was to co-ordinate the city's cults. A high priest would usually be an important person locally; the title commanded great respect. The suggestion that Christians could legitimately call their bishops high priests (*archiereis*), when it was first mooted, must have fallen on fruitful ground.

But it must be made clear that this development of a Christian priesthood was not a natural, logical, and healthy development. It ultimately contradicted the work of Christ which was supposed to end all sacrificial cults. Nor was it a development which can be traced *in nuce* in the primitive period so that its later history was only an unfolding of what had always been implicit. It was not the answer to a question which was insistently confronting the Church. We can, as we survey the scanty evidence which exists, see no inevitability about its formation, nor raw material for it in the New

Testament, and no sure sign of its existence before the turn of the second and third centuries. There is a mysterious statement in the Didache (13.3), 'You must grant the firstfruits to the prophets, because they are your high priests' (*archiereis*), but this refers to prophets, not to presbyters nor to bishops. The First Epistle of Clement does indeed draw an elaborate analogy between the distinction maintained in the Old Testament between high priest, priest, and levite (Chapters 40–4), in a context in which the author is stressing the necessity for the Christian community to respect its presbyters, and this has led many people to conclude that the author of 1 Clement saw the presbyters as corresponding to the priests of the old cult. But this conclusion must be seen, not only as unlikely, but as positively inadmissible, because in another part of his work the author tells us what precisely is his Old Testament proof-text for the Christian ministry. This text is Isaiah 60.17, 'I will set up their bishops in righteousness and their deacons in faith'. This is a curious version of the Septuagint rendering which here considerably diverges from the Hebrew text (and is found also in Irenaeus). But it makes the point quite clear that 'Clement' envisaged only two orders of ministry—presbyter-bishops and deacons—and that he did not think of these as foreshadowed in the ministers of the ancient Jewish cult, but as predicted in a prophetic passage. It is easy, anyway, to establish from other passages in his work that he only knew these two orders of ministry. Both these phenomena, the existence of two orders only and the search for certification of Christian institutions in prophetic passages of the Old Testament, are highly characteristic of early second-century Christianity. Apart from these dubious and far from convincing pieces of evidence, there is no sign at all that the Church thought of its ministry in terms of priesthood until we reach Tertullian at the very end of the second century.

Two other points must be dealt with before we leave the subject of the ministry in the early Church. There certainly is a doctrine of 'the priesthood of all believers' to be found in the New Testament. It is one way of expressing the doctrine of the Church as the organ through which Christ is made known to the world. It is taken up in a few places in Irenaeus and quite often by Tertullian. But it could never have been so interpreted as to mean that each or any individual Christian was in his own right constituted a sacrificing priest of a cult corresponding to the ancient Jewish sacrificial cult. As there were no Christian priests known or thought of for the first century and a half after the Resurrection, so it would not have occurred to anybody to regard an individual Christian layman as a priest. The priesthood of the Christian people is something which exists communally and could be said to be expressed and even exercised by each individual Christian as he communicates the gospel to a world which does not know it; it is a priesthood like that which Paul mentions at Romans 15.16. But it must be obvious that this is something very different from the sacerdotal sacrificing priesthood which maintained the round of sacrifice and cult in the old Jewish Temple, and just as different from the later concept of the Christian bishop and presbyter as sacrificing priests constituting a hierarchic caste.

The other point is the connection of the presbyters with the celebration of the eucharist. There is no doubt that in 1 Clement one of the main functions of the presbyters is to celebrate the eucharist, or, as the author of the Epistle puts it, to 'offer the gifts' (*prospherein ta dōra*). There is no clear evidence of this function being attached to the office before the time at which the work was written (usually reckoned as A.D. 96), and it seems reasonable to assume that this function was performed by the presbyters in most churches at and after the time of the writing of 1 Clement until the rise of the monarchical bishop later in the century. Further, from a very early period (as early as the composition of the Didache which may tentatively be dated about 100), it was the custom of Christians to describe the eucharist as a sacrifice (*thysia*). From this evidence some modern writers have been ready to infer that already in the second century the Church regarded its presbyters as people who offer the sacrifice of the Eucharist, and therefore implicitly or potentially as priests somewhat after the Old Testament model. But this chain of argument is unsound. If we examine the eucharistic language of the writers of the first two centuries we shall find that though the presbyters may indeed offer the gifts, i.e., the bread and the wine, this is not the sacrifice. The sacrifice is the sacrifice of praise and thanksgiving. Writer after writer, not only in the second century but in the third and even the fourth, emphasize that Christians offer no material sacrifice, as the pagans do, but a 'pure offering' (citing over and over again the same text, Malachi 1.11), and that this pure offering is themselves, their hearts, and intentions, and the praises and thanksgiving which they make to God for what he has done for them in Christ. It is not until Cyprian in the middle of the third century that the idea appears that the celebrant at the eucharist is offering the body and blood of Christ, and even then Cyprian is for some time a pioneer in this uncritically formulated and highly dubious doctrine. The presbyter (or the monarchical bishop when he appears) offers the bread and the wine to be consecrated by God's Word so that the people may receive the sacrament of the body and blood of Christ. He represents the people as they offer to God in this rite themselves and their praises and thanksgiving as a sacrifice to God. This is as far as the Church of the second century goes. If this is the traditional 'Catholic doctrine of priesthood', then there can be no objection to it. But of course it is not. The action of the presbyter or bishop here is not that of a sacrificing cultic priest. A cult there is, but a cult *after* the sacrifice, in the meaning attached to sacrifice in the ancient world, and the 'sacrifice of praise and thanksgiving' is not a sacrifice at all as the ancient world, Jewish and pagan, understood sacrifice. The Christian writers of the first three centuries for the most part fully realized this, and went out of their way to emphasize how the Christians in this respect differed both from Jews and pagans.

At the Reformation the Anglican communion retained the orders of bishop and priest or presbyter, taking great care to preserve the succession of ordination from the medieval Church. But it deliberately dissociated these orders from any intention of maintaining or instituting a sacrificing priesthood in the medieval sense. The actions taken by the Reforming Churches were often crude and brutal. They were often based on insufficient knowledge of antiquity, an inadequate understanding of the Bible, and an imperfect acquaintance with early liturgies. They often resulted in cruelty and confusion and failed dismally to achieve the bright goals for which they were intended. But in this particular point the Anglican Reformers achieved a simplification and an effectiveness with which it is difficult to find fault. This was partly because they did not try to achieve too much. They inherited the orders of bishop and of priest. In accordance with what they regarded, not without justice, as the demands of Scripture, they wanted, not to remodel the whole ministry *de novo* (as the Church of Scotland attempted to do, with very dubious success), but to reform, adjust, the inherited orders. In consequence they deliberately stated, in the Preface to the Ordinal, that they wished to perpetuate the three orders of bishop, priest, and deacon as they found them mentioned in Scripture and as they were maintained in the early Church. But they removed anything which might suggest that they intended to institute a sacrificing priesthood in the traditional, medieval sense. They drastically pruned the rite and ceremonies of the existing, late medieval, ordinals, concentrating upon the ceremony of laying-on of hands with prayer in the case of all three orders. They defined the bishop as the main minister of word and sacrament, the chief shepherd, through whom authority in the Church flowed. They set out priests as subordinate to the bishop and receiving their authority from him, but also as ministers of word and sacrament, as shepherds, watchmen, and stewards of the Lord. It is impossible to cast doubt upon the validity of orders conferred in these terms without casting doubt on the validity of all orders conferred in the early Church, and so, of course, on all orders, Roman Catholic, Orthodox, and Anglican.

But does this kind of ordination leave any content in the concept of priesthood? Is there any point in perpetuating the title of priest under these circumstances? The Anglican priest is a non-sacrificing priest whose function is not defined in terms of a cult, or at least not in terms of the Eucharist. But he is a priest nevertheless, in as far as his function corresponds to that which is common to all priests: he represents man to God and God to man. In a sense, he stands between God and man. He does not do so by being the exclusively empowered controller of sacramental grace, by belonging to a sacerdotal caste which alone can manipulate access to God or to salvation. But by his very function as shepherd, watchman, messenger, and steward he does inevitably represent man to God and God to man. He is the site of a two-way traffic. He lives among his people to bring them to God, to speak to God for them, to lead them in worship, to represent them to God. But he also represents God to them. He preaches to them and teaches them. He comforts and encourages them. He sometimes rebukes them. The Anglican priest may be unwilling to recognize or to acknowledge that he is exercising a priestly ministry, but in effect he is clearly doing so. His people regard him as representing God to them, not as monopolizing God but certainly as being the representative of God among them. If they are embarrassed at his presence—and they sometimes are—this is because the thought of God embarrasses them.

The famous 'parson's freehold' which the priest of the Church of England usually possesses has a certain theological significance. He is not financially dependent upon his flock. He is not economically vulnerable to their displeasure. In the Church of England he is usually not appointed by them. In other parts of the Anglican communion the priest, while he does not possess the rock-like security against dismissal which his brother in England possesses, is usually not directly dependent upon his flock for his stipend and is usually not appointed by them alone; the diocese and the bishop, and through him the whole Church, have an important share in his appointment. These apparently trivial and practical arrangements are a kind of sign of his priesthood. This type of priesthood can, of course, result, as it sometimes does in England, in the priest becoming estranged or remote from his people, finding himself divided from them by a class or professional barrier. It can also result, and too often in Ireland does result, in the priest so sinking his interests and ideas in those of his people that he is afraid to act independently of them. Irish Anglicanism suffers from a kind of unconscious (and sometimes conscious) tyranny of the laity. The priest is afraid to do anything that will upset his flock or disturb them. The result is an atmosphere of timid conservatism in which the proclamation of the gospel and its proper expression in worship suffer. Word and worship are stifled; cautious legalism becomes the prevailing atmosphere in the parish and in the church. But a true understanding of priesthood, which is open to all Anglican clergy, should correct either of these unbalanced expressions of a priest's ministry. The true ideal of priesthood is neither that the priest should issue directions to a submissive flock nor that he should devote himself singleheartedly to keeping them happy. The Word of God must reach them through him, and in the process of speaking the Word of God to them as best he can he may have to disagree with them, to risk being unpopular with them. He cannot completely sink his identity into theirs. He is not, as sometimes in Ireland he appears to want to be, a tribal chaplain. He is a priest, and the knowledge that he has the authority of a priest should support him both when he is tempted to lose contact with the interests and troubles and hopes of his flock and when he is tempted to allow a desire for popularity to cloud his judgement and compromise his integrity.

Has the Anglican priest, then, no particular connection with the eucharist? It is true that the bishop and the priest (to whom he delegates this responsibility) alone are permitted to celebrate this sacrament; but this does not necessarily imply any closer or more theologically significant connection between the office and the function. In order to answer this question, something further must be said about the nature of this sacrament. The sacrifice of Christ has been made once and for all; it cannot be repeated. But this does not mean that the eucharist is a bare memorial, a simple act of remembrance, a reminder to ourselves concerning his atonement, as people today still hold memorial services in which they remind themselves of the execution of King Charles I or the charge of the Light Brigade during the battle of Balaclava. In the sacrament of the eucharist the sacrifice of Christ is *applied* to us, to use an old-fashioned but serviceable word much used by the early Anglican divines. Here we are continually brought into the redemptive act of Christ; here we are sucked into the drama of his self-giving by the wind of the Holy Spirit. The Holy Spirit is God sovereign over time, and sacraments are the occasions when by his activity what was done once for all in history as an apparently closed incident becomes alive, effective, and open to and for us. The eucharist therefore is not a static rite in which we either mentally recall what happened on Calvary or visually contemplate a Saviour present in a consecrated wafer elevated for us. It is a dynamic act or episode or drama in which we are involved in what Christ did for us and, because of the operation of the Holy Spirit, still does for us. We here return again to the justifying act of God, renew our union in Christ, receive his life into our lives, and offer ourselves anew to God in, and solely because of, his self-offering. Here the Church, renews in its union with Christ, becomes again the Church, offers itself again to God in Christ, and resumes its work of praise and gratitude in response to God's endless goodness to it. But neither the Church nor the priest offers Christ nor Christ's sacrifice. We do not need to offer him nor his sacrifice. We receive him and the fruits of his sacrifice and in response we offer ourselves and our thanksgiving. The idea that we have to offer Christ before we can receive blessing from God tends towards the error, which constantly threatened both Catholics and Reformed during the sixteenth and seventeenth centuries, of separating the Son from the Father, of representing the Son as more merciful and kindly than the Father. We plead Christ's sacrifice in as far as nothing that we do as Christians is done without his mediation nor independently of his life; the Body has no life without the Head. But we do not need to remind God of what Christ has done, because God has done it in Christ. The overwhelming weight of the witness of the New Testament is in favour of the view that *agapé*, not *erōs*, is the prevailing tone of Christianity. It is God who takes the initiative, not man. God loved us while we were yet sinners. Love consists in this, not that we loved God but that he loved us. And his love did not content itself with sending reassuring messages to us. He did not briefly visit us and then pass on, like a powerful American President descending fleetingly from a vast aeroplane at Dublin airport, driving swiftly to some point where he can salute some remote and hypothetical Irish ancestor, and then being whisked off into space again in his aeroplane. God came to live among us himself in the Person of his Son, in amazing self-emptying anonymity. It would be insulting to imagine that a God who could do this needs to be reminded of what he has done. We do not offer Christ's sacrifice nor offer Christ's body and blood, sacramentally or really, bloodily or unbloodily. They are all God's gifts to us. We accept them, we are brought into the act and drama which they convey to us, and in return and response we give ourselves and our gratitude. It is quite wrong to say that there is no New Testament doctrine of man's response to God. Neither Barthianism nor Lutheranism should frighten us away from recognizing that there is a perfectly good doctrine of man's response to God in the Christian tradition. This is part of the New Testament doctrine of the Holy Spirit. But the response is the response of adoration, self-giving, and gratitude in union with Christ, not the response of offering Christ's sacrifice nor Christ's self.

This is why the Anglican priest is not a sacrificing priest, though he is a priest who leads people into union with Christ's sacrifice. As their representative he calls upon God, confidently, in faith, to renew their union with Christ. He blesses bread and wine in Christ's name, in memory of 'the night when he was betrayed'. And as he does so, and as he and his people receive the consecrated bread and wine, they are again involved with, brought into, quickened in, Christ's self-giving. What Christ has done is again applied to them. In response they offer to God themselves, their praise and their gratitude. But though the priest in this rite is not offering Christ on behalf of the living and the dead, and though any attempt to calculate the effect of intercession at this service must be discouraged, the priest's part in the service is an excellent parable and expression of his whole life and function as a priest. Here he represents man to God and also God to man. Here he blesses the elements in Christ's name. Here he presents his people (and himself with them) to God, confidently trusting in what Christ has done.

The whole liturgy is the act of the people who take part, and the priest represents them there. But is also the act of God, and it is through the priest that God acts. Here, it could be said, his priesthood takes on its deepest meaning.

9 *The Last Things*

As Advent approaches each year, every honest man who has been appointed to preach the Word of God at that season should feel a sense of keen embarrassment. The man who finds it a simple and straightforward matter to preach about the Second Coming of Christ is either a genius or a fool. Consider the difficult alternatives which we are offered. Do we simply trot out the view that our Lord *may* return any minute, though so far nearly two thousand years have passed without this event taking place, and endeavour to work our hearers into a state of eschatological expectancy? Do we do this once a year, and once a year after a few weeks return to the humdrum assumption governing all the rest of our year that this possible event need not trouble us very much? This surely is the most dishonest of all ways of dealing with eschatology. Do we attempt to take the eschatological imagery of the New Testament literally, do we ask our congregations to begin learning to play the harp, to abandon their driving of Fords in favour of horse-drawn chariots, or to prepare for the big take-off mentioned in 1 Thessalonians 4.17 by achieving a little temporary levitation? Or do we abandon the whole attempt to cope with eschatology and make Advent simply a proleptic anticipation of Christmas? We would be honest at least if we did this, and told our congregations that we were doing so.

If we are to be true to the witness of the New Testament, there are two points concerning the Last Things which must be made clear. The first is that for the witness of the New Testament eschatology is in some sense *realized* eschatology, and it pervades and conditions the whole book. To the authors of the first three Gospels, to Paul, to the author of Hebrews and to the writer of the first Epistle of Peter, the coming of Jesus Christ has precipitated the world into the Last Age which in an unfinished, not completely realized, but actual, sense, is here now. R. H. Fuller's phrase 'inaugurated eschatology' is a useful one to express this. In naming these writers we have listed, with two important exceptions, the most significant authors in the New Testament. For these writers the gospel almost *is* the Last Time; the greatest proof of this is that the Holy Spirit, an entirely eschatological figure, is regarded as present now, not merely promised, though there are many other proofs. It is no coincidence that the phrase 'Second Coming' does not actually appear in the New Testament. The First Coming is so eschatological that the Second Coming cannot be more than a consummation, rather than an introduction, of eschatology. And the second necessary point to note about the eschatology of the New Testament is that the earliest authors certainly do expect a Second Coming to take place within a very short time. Paul and Mark cannot be set aside here. The eschatological expectation of the earliest period of the Christian Church looked forward to a Return of Christ in a very short time, and this event did not take place. No amount of smooth explaining away can disguise this obdurate fact.

Even within the limits of the New Testament itself we can trace a development in the course of eschatological expectation; we can observe a fading of the immediacy of the primitive eschatological hope. It may be that Mark reveals a state of affairs in which the resurrection appearances of Jesus are thought to be identical with, or at least to precede very closely, his Last Appearance at the End of Time. But certainly Matthew cannot be suspected of such a thought. He marks a stage beyond Mark in the cooling of eschatological expectation, though not a very long one. It has now, after the work of Conzelmann and his school, been pretty well agreed by the world of New Testament scholarship that the work of Luke, the Third Gospel and Acts, exhibits the intention of guiding the Church in a period when it had become evident that the Second Coming was postponed, if not indefinitely, then at any rate to a remoter date than had first been envisaged, and enabling Christians to endure and to live in faith in this new state of affairs. Those documents of the New Testament which we must place late in its time-span, such as the Fourth Gospel, the Pastoral and the Catholic Epistles, reveal unmistakably that an immediate Parousia has been abandoned as a datum of faith and eschatological expectation has moved towards the background. The third chapter of 2 Peter—one of the latest documents of the New Testament—puts this beyond yea or nay.

But to abandon the expectation of an immediate Return was not to abandon an eschatological framework for Christian thought, nor to jettison all at once the conviction that Christians were living in the Last Time, in the Last Crisis. All Christian literature up to the middle of the second century is inspired with this conviction, and beneath the remains which we have in our hands we can dimly discern the faint fragments of a large store of now lost Christian-Jewish apocalyptic literature. It is with Justin Martyr, and only with him, that a new and significant stage in Christian thought can be seen emerging. I cannot believe that Justin, judging by his surviving works, could have had the intelligence to originate it; he just happens to be one of the first surviving examples. What is happening is that Christology is replacing eschatology as the Church's main intellectual and spiritual preoccupation. Christian thought and piety will henceforward be concerned mainly with elaborating a theology of the relationship of Jesus Christ to God, by the aid of Greek philosophy, and not with the expectation of the Second Coming of Christ. It was a great, though a gradual, change, involving all parts of the Church's life. It was an entirely unavoidable one, because the Church had now moved out of a mainly Jewish into a mainly Greek milieu, and the people to whom it was addressing its gospel found no sense in a Jewish eschatological frame of reference. The great influence for accomplishing this change was St John's Gospel and the other Johannine literature. The Fourth Gospel must have been written about 100 but the evidence is clear enough that it was not widely received in the Church till 160 or 170; it was indeed Irenaeus who perceived that if this was a Gnostic Gospel, as it was suspected to be, it was a Gnostic Gospel to end Gnostic Gospels; he provided it with evidence for its apostolic authorship sufficient for the ancient world but in our eyes much too good to be true and launched it as the fourth and greatest Gospel. It was the prime instrument for converting eschatology into Christology. The immense genius and profound insight of its author achieved this vital task. By the power of Johannine tradition the Church discovered that its Lord was more important than his Second Coming and that he must be allowed to burst the bounds of Jewish thought.

The development of the Church's doctrinal tradition went its way; the dogmas of the Trinity and the incarnation were achieved. But what, meanwhile, happened to the doctrine of the Last Things? Well, first, it became the doctrine of the Last Things, i.e., a final article in the Creed, a series of mythical events expected at the end of time, and no longer the key to the whole gospel and the very air that Christians breathed. Eschatology became completely futurist and it was finally schematized into a Second Coming, a resurrection of the dead, and a Last Judgement. That this is a schematization and nothing more is evident to anybody who reads the very varied and scarcely consistent passages of apocalyptic imagery in the New Testament and follows this up by reading the Fathers from the Apologists through Tertullian and Hippolytus to Origen who finally with extraordinary daring entirely abolishes eschatology. One interesting impulse to which eschatology gave rise in its surviving futurist form was the calculation of the ages of history. This resulted in some bad and some surprisingly good chronological researches by people such as Julius Africanus, Eusebius, Victorinus of Pettau, and Augustine. Another function which eschatology performed in the course of the next few centuries was to secure the theologians of the Church from falling a prey to the cyclic theory of history, to the myth of the Eternal Return. Whether this myth is Greek or Eastern I do not know; it certainly appears in Plato and in other later Greek philosophers, and it undoubtedly works to deprive history of meaning; in its hands history becomes an endless recurrence. If one realizes how deeply many of the Fathers of the Church, such as Origen, the Cappadocian Fathers, and Augustine, were steeped in the philosophical ideas of their own day, it will be a matter of marvel that they did not succumb to the temptation of adopting this well-known theory into their thought. But in fact none of them did, not even Origen, though he has been accused of doing so, and though he goes further in the perilous path of undervaluing history than any other Christian theologian in the ancient world. No doubt one of the forces making against this tendency was the commitment of the whole Bible, Old Testament as well as New, to *Heilsgeschichte*, to regarding history as *par excellence* the place where God is to be seen working. And the existence of Christian eschatology, which regarded history as a meaningful process leading up to a final event or events, which is perhaps a kind of apotheosis of *Heilsgeschichte*, must have helped to protect the theologians of the Church against this weakness.

Perhaps most important of all was the fact that the existence of the eschatological clauses at the end of the creed ensured that nobody could imagine that the end had come yet, that there was no temptation to identify the Church as it was in its pilgrimage on earth with the true City of God, the Church reigning triumphant in heaven. In other words, the survival of eschatology was an assurance that what has been called the 'relativism' of the New Testament was not lost, that the 'not yet' of the New Testament was remembered. Now we walk by faith, not sight; now we enjoy salvation only proleptically, provisionally. Now our beliefs and our utterances are subject to the final revelation of the Son of God, not beyond criticism, beyond alteration. Now we see in a glass darkly and have no right to claim an absolute unalterable authority for what we see and say. What is to endure from this age of faith to the final age of sight is love, not dogmas, not church institutions, not canon law, not ecclesiastical offices. Eschatology is a very wholesome guarantee for the chastened humility of faith, and the Fathers of the first four centuries at least realized this very well. It is doubtful whether the Church of the later periods of the Middle Ages did, at any rate in the West. One might pass the judgement on the Church after the age of St Bernard of Clairvaux that it had forgotten its eschatology, it allowed itself by its very success to imagine that it could build and was building the City of God here upon earth, and took upon itself presumptuously the authority of that City, and suffered in consequence.

We should perhaps notice that a kind of realized eschatology has always tended to burst out riotously at periods of tension or strife in the Church as if the Holy Spirit were making explosions in order to move on the stagnant current of the Church's life. This phenomenon occurred at the collapse of the Western Roman Empire in the fifth century, in the period of strife over the Franciscan Order in the thirteenth and fourteenth centuries, and during the enormous upheaval of the Reformation in the sixteenth century.

Finally, I must make some brief suggestions as to how we are to approach the subject of eschatology today. It ought not to be necessary to say that the policy of taking eschatological imagery literally is hopeless. Even if we could make a consistent scheme out of the diverse imagery of Mark, chapter 13, of the epistles to the Thessalonians, of 1 Corinthians, of Matthew's gospel, of Luke's, and of the Revelation of St John—which it is impossible to do—it would be a futile exercise. On the next life, and on the sequence of events that will terminate history, the New Testament has no consistent doctrine, though it does have indispensable witness to give. That is why, for instance, some churchpeople become confused about whether we should pray for the dead. The New Testament gives no clear guidance here. It is only by leaving out important pieces of evidence and forgetting important facts that anybody can squeeze out of the New Testament a consistent doctrine on this subject. As I have said elsewhere, if Catholics have tended to take too little out of the Bible, Protestants have tended to take too much out of it.

But this does not mean at all that eschatology is useless to us. In recent years two leading German theologians, Moltmann and Pannenberg, have returned in a hopeful and fruitful way to a reaffirmation of Christian eschatology. They have reminded us that the Christian faith represents God as opening to us a new age of revelation and of hope which began, indeed, at the resurrection, but which is of its nature essentially uncompleted, forward-looking, *in via*, pointing onward to a significant consummation and climax to history, and have called upon Christian thinkers to join hands with these other movements of thought in the contemporary world which assign a movement and a meaning to history.

Again, the Church still needs the warning 'not yet' which Christian eschatology gives us. We still need to remember that all our Christian activities and beliefs, everything which we inherit in our religion except Christ himself and the love that his Holy Spirit produces in our hearts, are provisional. No dogmas, however ancient and august, no law, backed with however great an ecclesiastical authority, no bishop, no pope, yes even no Bible, can give us more than knowledge by faith, guidance and authority subject to the great revelation at the Last Day, words which may be corrected by the Last Word, doctrines which may at the end be shown to fall short of the fulness of truth. This does not mean that we must not now have firm faith and deep conviction. We must, but they must be held in a spirit of humility which the pilgrim condition of the Church in this age forces upon us. This is particularly important for a Church which, like the Church of Ireland, has an almost obsessive concern for its own life and institutions and for a person, like myself, who has a deep concern for and involvement with the Ecumenical Movement.

But most of all, as we consider the role of eschatology in the Church's thought today, can we not—must we not—think of the Christian gospel as somehow permanently eschatological? I do not mean, of course, that we are to revert to the futile business of imagining that the Parousia will take place within the next few weeks or months or years. A quite superficial acquaintance with Christian history should dispose of that form of neurosis. I mean that the Holy Spirit in presenting us with the gospel presents us in some sense with an *eschaton.* This is the last claim, the last thing that can happen to us, because the most important. After this, history becomes significant only as a consummation of the gospel; no more important thing could happen to us after it, not even death. Existentially the gospel of God's loving offer of himself in Christ brings us into the Last Age; our perspectives in a sense become eschatological, though not calculably so. A more than purely historical finality infuses the living centre of Christian faith, a finality from which it can never be entirely divorced. Christian eschatology has always been a difficult subject for historians and philosophers. It is present to plague us in the sects on the fringe of Christianity. It introduces a bizarre and grotesque element which theologians—especially Liberal theologians—have often, from Origen to Rashdall, attempted to remove altogether. But it is an indispensable ingredient in the Christian faith. It introduces a dimension which the pious believer and the theologian alike will neglect only at their peril.

Index of Biblical References

(On the left hand side of the column the biblical reference, on the right the page of this book.)

Index of Names and Subjects